Haneke on Haneke

Haneke on Haneke

Michel Cieutat
and Philippe Rouyer

Sticking Place Books
New York

Contents

In memory of Jean-Marie Boehm
Michel Cieutat

For my son Melvil
Philippe Rouyer

Introduction to the new edition

Five years after the release of this book, we met Michael Haneke once again, with just as much pleasure, in Paris and then in Vienna. In agreement with Manuel Carcassonne, who succeeded the late Jean-Marc Roberts at the helm of Éditions Stock, it seemed to us that the time had come to continue our interviews in order to publish an updated edition.

Since 2012, Haneke has directed another opera by Mozart, *Così fan tutte*, which we applauded at the Théâtre de la Monnaie in Brussels in June 2013, and spent more than two years unsuccessfully trying to bring his film *Flashmob* to fruition before giving up on it to focus on *Happy End*, which screened in the official competition at the Cannes Film Festival in May 2017.

To say that Haneke once again stirred up controversy in Cannes with this film is no understatement. After the international triumphs of *The White Ribbon* and *Amour*, some festivalgoers were puzzled by Haneke's return to a style he has embraced since the beginning, a fragmented, ensemble-driven approach to storytelling. The fact that the multitude of characters is confined to a single family no doubt threw some viewers off, though that's precisely what gives the film its strength and originality. Similarly, setting the story in Calais, which had sparked much speculation when the project was first announced, disappointed those hoping for a film about migrants. But how could Haneke have gone against his usual approach to portray a world he doesn't know from the inside? How could he, so late in his career, suddenly switch to making a full-blown message film? Migrants do appear in the film, of course, but they occupy exactly the place the characters give them in their own lives: the margins. They are there, clearly, but go unseen, as the characters remain blinded by their own petty problems and sufferings.

Happy End is no moral sermon. It's a clear-eyed though never hopeless portrait of bourgeois unease in our Western societies. "We are sad, alone and solitary," Haneke seems to be saying, as he reveals how, even under the same roof and bound by blood, communication falters and feelings struggle to be shared. Toward the end is an extraordinary scene between Jean-Louis Trintignant's character and his granddaughter, as he tries to forge a meaningful connection. But long before that moment the film quietly lays down its clues through a subtle, watchful mise-en-scène that echoes from one scene to the next, leaving it to the viewer to piece things together. Like all of Haneke's work, *Happy End* poses its questions without ever pretending to answer them.

He offers no more definitive answers in the long conversation that follows—recorded in February and June of 2017—than he does in his films. True to his principles, and to the spirit of our past exchanges, Haneke refuses to reduce to words what he has already expressed through images and sound. But what he does offer, with generosity, is a glimpse behind the scenes of his creative process. From the early days of staging *Così fan tutte* to some of the hidden mechanics of *Happy End*, he helps us see how his art has evolved. We might be tempted to call it a kind of late maturity. But this book is not here to prove that. It is up to the viewer to form their own judgment—hopefully guided, in part, by these new conversations—about the complex, at times unsettling, but always invigorating work of one of the great filmmakers of our time.

Michel Cieutat and Philippe Rouyer
June 2017

Introduction

Eleven feature films, with internationally renowned actors such as Juliette Binoche, Isabelle Huppert, Daniel Auteuil, Jean-Louis Trintignant, Ulrich Mühe and Naomi Watts. A multitude of international awards and honours, including two Palme d'Or awards at Cannes, one in 2009 for *The White Ribbon*, the other in 2012 for *Amour.* Yet this interview book, originally published in French in 2012, was the first in that language to be devoted to the work of Austrian director Michael Haneke.

Haneke's cinema is too radical to win over everyone. But it was precisely his rejection of sentimentality and his taste for abruptness that captivated us from the very start, beginning with *The Seventh Continent*, his first feature, which screened at Cannes in 1989. In charting the slow, relentless collapse of an ordinary family, he chose to confine the story to three days, each a year apart. That formal restraint laid the groundwork for all that would follow: characters unable to voice their emotions, a near-obsessive focus on everyday objects, a fascination with still and moving images, the power of ellipsis and off-screen space, and an unusually keen ear for sound. Not to banish emotion, but to distill it to hold it back and channel it through a kind of austere, sidelong grace.

At the heart of Haneke's cinema lies a paradox: the pursuit of truth—of people, of situations—through the deliberate artifice of recreated images and sounds. It's a tension he embraces from the first moment of writing, always working alone, always seeking a new form to match each story. *Benny's Video* (1992), his second feature, turns this very question—how to represent violence—into its subject. Two years later, *71 Fragments of a Chronology of Chance* shatters the flow of reality into pieces, each shard catching a different angle of the world. You could trace this formal restlessness through his entire body of work, from *Code Unknown* (2000), which interweaves lives to expose the limits of any utopian solidarity, to *Caché* (2005), which wears the mask of a thriller only to reveal a deeper, inescapable guilt. Even when Haneke revisits his own past, he refuses repetition as comfort. His American version of *Funny Games* (1997) remains the only remake in cinema history to replicate the original shot for shot, with different actors but the same camera angles, the same choreography.

Haneke's singular gift lies in the way he weaves his own obsessions into genres as familiar as the crime film, the ensemble drama, even classical tragedy—giving his work a style instantly recognisable. Whether it's the small German village of *The White Ribbon*, the contemporary Vienna of *The Piano Teacher*, or the imagined America of the *Funny Games* remake, the same gaze falls across them all: that of a concerned artist who sees art as the only way to come to terms with reality.

The imagined weight of his Austrian roots—along with a half-true tale of a thwarted calling as a pastor, his reputation for severity on set, and the austere silhouette he cuts—has been enough to paint Haneke as a moralist. Yet it wasn't religion that drew him in as a young man, but philosophy, in the hopeful belief that it might offer answers to his existential questions. He soon realised, however, that literature, theatre and film offered a more fitting path for his search. From his earliest works to *Amour*—his most recent film, which confronts the unbearable question of how to respond to the suffering of someone you love—Haneke's cinema digs into the places where life hurts. It unsettles, provokes, and urges the viewer to question their certainties.

But one has to know how to read his films, how to catch the nuances and ambiguities of the real world they reflect. The parents in *Benny's Video*, who cover up the murder committed by their son, or the TV host in *Caché*, unable to face his own shameful past—these are not villains. Their actions speak of panic, sometimes cowardice, but they're never condemned by a direction that carefully avoids showing what the "right" course of action would have been. And so we find ourselves wondering: would we have done any better in their place? This confrontation with films that act as mirrors is anything but comfortable or reassuring. Haneke's work never lets us believe things will turn out fine in the end. On the contrary, it insists that things won't get better, so we might better learn to live with that truth. Of course, anyone is free to prefer the soft contours of the Disney universe, though they carry little weight against the hard edges of reality, as suggested by the absurd Mickey Mouse masks swept away by Don Giovanni's death dive in Haneke's 2006 staging of Mozart's opera in Paris.

Philippe Rouyer, Michel Cieutat and Michael Haneke.

Those Mickey Mouse masks, worn by cleaning staff trying to celebrate in their workplace—a tower in La Défense—capture Haneke's singular sense of humour. A pitch-black humour that runs through all his films, highlighting the gap that will always exist between reality and its representation. One thinks, of course, of the vile jokes cracked by the two young killers in *Funny Games*. Gratuitous provocation? On the contrary, their jokes directly implicate the viewer and heighten the horror of the scenes through a dissonance that becomes unbearable. Haneke instructed the actors playing the victimised family to perform their scenes like a tragedy, while telling the murderers to play it as a comedy. Touches of humour surface in the mother-daughter clashes and sadomasochistic spirals of *The Piano Teacher*, as well as in some of the darker twists of *The White Ribbon*. Even Haneke's early television films embraced this paradox, slipping moments of dark comedy into the heart of the drama.

Haneke's ten television films (rarely screened outside Austria and, due to rights issues, mostly unavailable on DVD, with the exception of *The Castle*), remain largely unknown to audiences here. Shot mostly before his theatrical feature debut, they are essential to understanding the full scope of his work. From *Und was kommt danach?*, his first attempt in 1974, which already strives to distance itself from its theatrical roots, to *Lemminge*, an ambitious two-part fresco and his first original screenplay in 1979, all the way to *The Castle*, his Kafka adaptation from 1996, which was both his final television work and the first time he directed Ulrich Mühe and Susanne Lothar as a couple, are far more than just sketches for future masterpieces. Even though half of these telefilms are literary adaptations intended primarily as tributes to their source texts, they are filled with formal invention and narrative experimentation. From the very beginning, Haneke approached each production as a new challenge to be met head-on. Including these films in this volume felt self-evident. To grasp the full arc of the artist's vision, nothing could be overlooked: the formative years, his early passion for music, his radio work, the time in theatre, the television period, and the flowering of his cinematic voice, with an operatic detour along the way.

We had met with Haneke several times for interviews published in *Positif*, but it was after a particularly stimulating reunion around the release of *The White Ribbon* that the idea of turning our conversations into a book took root. Always precise and compelling in what he says, Haneke is one of those rare directors whose films reflect the way he speaks. Encouraged by our publisher, Jean-Marc Roberts, who granted us complete freedom on the condition that we start from scratch and not reuse any previously published interviews, we recorded nearly fifty hours of conversation over the course of almost two years, between Paris and Vienna. We worked in several-day blocks, with four- to five-hour sessions each afternoon, uninterrupted, before ending the day at the dinner table, most often in the company of Susie, Haneke's wife: his first reader, first viewer, a recurring on-screen extra, and an essential help when it comes to designing his sets.

Haneke, showing remarkable generosity throughout the project, agreed to speak with us in French. He insisted on rereading every single page, revising and refining tirelessly, not to censor, but always to clarify. More than the interviews themselves, it was this meticulous process of revision that gave us the clearest insight into Haneke at work: his energy, impatience, and unwavering drive in the service of perfection. And yet, through it all, the warmth of our exchanges, the spark of his thought, and his sharp humour remained intact. The result, we hope, is a portrait that brings us as close as possible to both the man and the artist.

Following the historical model of the famous *Hitchcock/Truffaut*, we structured the interviews chronologically, during the conversations themselves and in their transcription, with the exception of the later television films, grouped together for practicality, and the two versions of *Funny Games*. Haneke didn't shy away from a single question, refusing only—resolutely, and how could it have been otherwise?—to interpret his own films. So no, this book won't reveal who committed the crimes in *The White Ribbon*, nor what the two children whisper to each other in the final shot of *Caché*. But that hardly matters. What's essential lies elsewhere: in the musical architecture of his narratives, in the rigour of his direction of actors, and in the meticulous construction of a mise-en-scène that reflects his view of the world. If reading these pages helps deepen understanding of, and affection for, Haneke's cinema, then our goal will have been fulfilled.

Michel Cieutat and Philippe Rouyer
May 2012

One

Growing up in the countryside — My discovery of music — First memories of cinema — Becoming a pastor — Angry at everything — Philosophy student — Beginnings in radio and newspapers — The youngest script editor in Germany — 1968 and terrorism — Bergman, Bresson and auteur cinema — My favourite films

You have often stated that biographical details don't shed light on an artist's body of work.

Yes, because by showing that the questions raised by a film are linked to the director's biography, we limit our scope. It's the same with books. I always want to confront the work directly, without looking elsewhere for explanations. That's why I refuse to answer questions of a biographical nature. Nothing annoys me more than hearing: "What kind of person is this Haneke to make such dark films?" I find that all quite silly and have no interest in engaging in that kind of false debate.

Regardless, we do have some questions about your childhood.

Everyone will be disappointed because I didn't have a unhappy childhood. I'm a very normal person. That might be hard to believe, but it's true.

Your father was an actor and director, and your mother was an actress. You have been forever immersed inside an artistic milieu. That must have influenced you.

Not really, because I wasn't raised by my parents. I grew up with my mother's sister in the country, on a large estate. That was in Wiener Neustadt, a small town fifty kilometres south of Vienna, where I set the action of my film *Lemminge*.

Your aunt was interested in music. Weren't you influenced in any way by that musical atmosphere?

Not really. But I could have been, since there was a musician in the family. At the end of the war, my father, who was German, went straight home and never came back to Austria. My mother then remarried a Jewish composer, Alexander Steinbrecher, who, after fleeing to England from Nazism, had become the musical director of the Burgtheatre.

You're a great music lover.

But that's not because of my family. Rather, it was my encounter with music itself that ignited my passion. When I was a child, my aunt wanted me to learn the piano, as was the tradition in those days for the son of a middle-class family. At first I hated it and wanted to give it up. It must be said that when I played, my aunt was always at my side, chanting, "*Falsch!* Wrong!" But one day— I remember it vividly, it was All Saints' Day, I must have been about 10 years old—the entire family had gone to the cemetery. I didn't wanted to go with them. I heard some music on the radio that I thought was extraordinary. At the end, they announced that it was Handel's *Messiah*. It was a revelation for me, because up until then, I had only been interested in catchy pop songs. I started listening to classical music and a little later—I must have been 13—I saw the very kitsch film *Mozart*, starring Oskar Werner, who was brilliant in the title role. When I got home from the cinema, I gathered up my savings and went out to buy the scores of all Mozart's sonatas, and started working like crazy, non-stop. My passion for music dates back to that time. Of course, I dreamed of becoming a pianist. Fortunately, my father-in-law listened to me a lot. He composed sorts of *singspiele*, basically comic opera, as well as *lieder*. He had great success in Austria with several pieces that are barely remembered today. He was a very cultured man who had been something of a child prodigy at the piano. When I started writing short, very naïve compositions—at one point, I even started composing a mass—he told me that it was all very nice, but that I should stop thinking about becoming a composer.

Did your first desire to create come from music?

Yes. Then, as an adolescent, I turned to poetry, like many teenagers in that era.

Beatrix von Degenschild and her son Michael.

Do you remember your sources of inspiration? Did you read a lot?

I've always read a lot because, back then, there was no television.

What kind of teenager were you? Were you happy living close to nature?

Our family estate was in the countryside, but we also had a house in town, in Wiener Neustadt itself, and that's where I grew up because that's where the schools were. As a teenager, I felt very frustrated in the countryside because there was nothing to do. But at the same time, I was never bored. I always read and listened to music. Like everyone in my generation, I had neither a computer nor a television, but we did a lot together, like playing ping-pong and chess.

Did you play any sports?

Yes. Since I was quite thin, my parents asked our doctor what could help me develop. He recommended fencing, which I really enjoyed. I practised it until I was 16 or 17, and wasn't too bad.

Did you compete?

Yes, and I enjoyed it, but after a while, I didn't have any time. The other sport I started very early with was skiing, every winter in Bad Gastein. You could say it was standard for the Austrian bourgeoisie, but I was good at it and even won a municipal competition once. Even today, I love skiing. My wife and I regularly go skiing in Zürs in the Arlberg.

Did you have many friends in Wiener Neustadt? Did you go out a lot?

I don't have many memories from when I was very young, but as soon as I started high school, around 10 or 11, I was part of a group of boys. Back then, schools weren't co-educational. It was only with dance classes, around the age of 17, that boys and girls were encouraged to interact. That said, my family owned a property a few kilometres from Wiener Neustadt, right on a lake, where I spent all my summers. There, with the neighbours' children—who all came from the local bourgeoisie—we formed a close-knit group, boys and girls together.

As a child, you also went to Denmark. On what occasion?

That was a sad episode for me, which I mentioned in my essay on Robert Bresson's *Au hasard Balthazar*.* It was right after the war; I was 5 or 6 years old. My aunt and mother thought that because I was so thin it would be good for me to participate in a programme organised by the victorious countries to help children from the defeated nations. They believed that Denmark, with its abundant butter production, would be beneficial for their frail little boy, but they hadn't considered what it would mean for a 5-year-old—who had never left home—to be sent to live with a foreign family he knew nothing about. It was a real shock for me, so much so that when I returned home after three months, I didn't speak to anyone for several weeks.

And what did you do there?

Nothing. The people there tried to speak a little German with me, to explain things, but I was completely lost. I remember there was a swing with a metal bar in front to hold onto which I broke a tooth on. The only lasting memory I have from that stay is of a long, narrow cinema with doors opening directly onto the street, where I saw a film about Africa. After the screening, I suddenly found myself outside in the rain and couldn't understand how I had gotten back from Africa to Denmark so quickly.

What was your relationship with cinema in your youth?

My first experience was terrifying. My grandmother and I went to see *Hamlet*, directed by and starring Laurence Olivier, and I was so scared that I started crying loudly. We had to leave so as not to disturb the other viewers. But, of course, I don't know if I have a real memory of this or if my grandmother told me about it later. After that, I saw a lot of films, but not art-house things because we didn't have any repertory cinemas. I'm talking about popular German films.

Crime films?

More like *Schlagerfilme*, which were a kind of German musical comedy, and also melodramas. Whenever there was a children's

---

* "Terror and Utopia of Form: Robert Bresson's *Au hazard Balthazar,*" in Roy Grundmann (ed), *A Companion to Michael Haneke* (Wiley-Blackwell, 2010).

film, that was even better. Later, for the first CinemaScope film, *The Robe*, a new cinema was built in Wiener Neustadt, and I still remember the sensation of seeing that enormous screen. Everyone fought for tickets. There was a real desire to see films. Throughout my youth, whenever I had a bit of money, I went to the cinema. But I wasn't the only one. My friends did the same.

There must have been a lot of American films to see.

When the James Dean films came out, it was like a kind of cult, just as it was with *Blackboard Jungle* starring Glenn Ford, which, with *Rock Around the Clock*, introduced us to rock music. I remember I wasn't old enough to see it when it was released. There were plainclothes policemen at the entrance checking the IDs of anyone who didn't seem to meet the age requirement. We tried to sneak in, but I never made it past them. I saw *Blackboard Jungle* only much later. In reality, there weren't that many American films; it was mostly German films that were screened. Similarly, I only discovered auteur films once I got to university, with the exception of Ingmar Bergman, whose films were well known and which I saw in high school. At the time, Bergman wasn't considered an elitist filmmaker. His film *The Silence* caused such a scandal that everyone wanted to see it. To this day I've never seen such a long queue outside a cinema in Vienna. That success allowed me to see all of Bergman's subsequent films, as well as others like *The Virgin Spring*, which were widely distributed in Austria.

Did you go to see his films because people were talking about them or because you had read about them?

At first it was because people were talking about them. You would hear that people found them interesting, so you went along, but not for cinematic reasons. We went for the content, for the issues related to religion. I only became aware of aesthetic approaches once I was a student, through courses that introduced me to them.

Earlier, you mentioned that you read a lot during your youth. Do you remember any titles?

I don't recall what I read as a child, but I know that as a teen-ager I read a great deal—mostly love stories. I was very impressed by Dumas' *La Dame aux Camélias*. At school, we studied some French writers like Francis Jammes, but the book I loved most was

Le Grand Meaulnes by Alain-Fournier. It remained my bedside book for a very long time. Of course, I also read Heinrich Heine and all the classics we were required to study, which I enjoyed. I kept going on my own with Eichendorff and other Romantic writers, the kinds of books that speak to you at that age, when everything feels intense and beautiful, but are rarely read after that, even though they are excellent books. At the age of 15, I adored Dostoevsky. Finally, someone who understood me!

Do you remember the first Dostoevsky novel you read?

The one I've always thought was the best: *The Demons*. It's incredible. But there isn't a bad Dostoevsky book.

Were you one of the most cultured in your group, or perhaps even the intellectual?

We were all bourgeois, all at the same cultural level. But it's true that within our group, I was a bit of the "artist." I wanted to form a theatre troupe, which I never managed to do.

Did you show the little poems you wrote to your friends?

Not to my friends. To the girls!

And did they appreciate them?

They were flattered. I also wrote a small collection of poems for my mother, which a friend with beautiful handwriting calligraphed for me—one poem per page—as a Mother's Day gift.

Despite her demanding career as an actress, were you still able to spend time with your mother?

No, but I visited her very often in Vienna.

Did you see her perform on stage at that time?

Rarely. The first time, I was very young. I went with my grandmother to see her in a play by Ferdinand Raimund called *Der Verschwender*, an Austrian classic in which she played the Fairy Queen. When she appeared in a flying carriage, I shouted, "Hey—it's mummy!" The whole audience burst into laughter. After that, I saw her on stage several more times, but not very often.

Haneke's mother, Beatrix von Degenschild.

Tell us more about that theatre troupe you wanted to start.

That was mostly to make myself look interesting.

Did acting and directing interest you?

It was all interesting to me. Lead actor, troupe director, stage director, even playwright. There were ruins about five kilometres from Wiener Neustadt, a beautiful spot where we often went by bicycle. That's where I wrote a version of the Electra story for a woman I knew. She was supposed to learn the text and it turned into a bit of a disaster, but at the time, I was very proud of it.

Did you keep any records of your poems or that play?

No. I might still have a few of my early writings, but we lost a lot over the course of our moves.

Did you take theatre classes?

No, because as a teenager I hated every form of school. I was a rebel.

A rebel against what?

Everything. I hated everything. I felt an unbearable pressure weighing on me. I wanted to be free! I had decided I wouldn't stay in Wiener Neustadt and that I would become an actor. My parents were actors, so I could become one too. I was sure I had talent. One morning, I left school and hitchhiked to Vienna to audition at the Reinhardt Seminar, the drama school I had heard about. Before mentioning it to anyone, I had already auditioned in front of my mother to see if she thought I had talent. Naturally, she thought I was amazing, so I was convinced I would succeed. I wrote to the school to register. We had to prepare three pieces, and I chose a monologue from *Hamlet*, a comedic excerpt featuring the Devil from Hugo von Hofmannsthal's *Jedermann*, and Beethoven's *Heiligenstädter Testament*, a letter that had deeply moved my mother. For the audition, I decided to start with the Devil, as that was my weakest piece. The moment I began, I knew I was terrible. I thought things would improve with *Hamlet* but they didn't even give me the chance. I had barely finished my first performance when they dismissed me with a curt, "Yes, thank you…" Once I stepped outside, I knew I hadn't done well. I had to wait the entire day for the results. When they finally posted the list, my name wasn't on it. I couldn't believe it. I went home without saying a word, except to my mother. I asked her why they hadn't accepted me. She inquired through her colleagues and learned that I had a very poor vocal technique. I think, actually, I was just very bad. That was the end of my acting career. Since I couldn't stand school, I decided to quit altogether. I had already repeated a grade because I had refused to use notebooks.

Was it authority you couldn't accept, or the subjects themselves?

Haneke's father, Fritz Haneke.

Everything. I hated everything.

Even literature?

No… When it came to that, I was a star pupil. Same with music. In those two subjects, I always had my notebooks and got the best grades. But in all the other subjects, I got nothing but zeros.

How long did that attitude last?

Quite a while. And it only got worse as I got older. At 18, I got my motorcycle licence because I had bought an old one cheaply. It was March, and I had decided to go to France. I left when it was snowing, and it took a whole week to reach Paris. I stayed for three months with a very kind family. The father had been a prisoner of war in Austria and had worked on my uncle's estate, where he had been treated well. In gratitude, he would occasionally visit my uncle, and he had offered to host me in Paris anytime. Despite their modest means—they had seven or eight children in a small house—they gave me a room, squeezing their children into another, as a token of thanks for what my uncle had done for their father. After three months, I ran out of money and returned home.

What did you do with your days?

Not much. I was staying far out in the suburbs, and would ride into Paris and wander around. When I finally returned to resume my studies, I wasn't exactly welcomed back at school with open arms. My aunt was very diplomatic. She spoke with the teachers and told them they had to understand this boy who was so sensitive. That's when I realised I had to pull myself together and start studying to get my diploma. And that's what I did.

So it was this trip to Paris that made you decide to work seriously?

Yes, more or less. I remember thinking, I've come so far, and yet nothing has changed. That's when I realised that everything depended on me.

Your family—your aunt and mother—seemed quite relaxed about it all, letting you discover things on your own.

It wasn't easy for them, but with someone as stubborn as me, what else could they do? It was smart of them to react that way.

Once you had your equivalent of the baccalaureate, you had to think about the future, including university.

Yes, and it was the best vacation I ever had. I chose to study philosophy.

Because you were asking yourself a lot of existential questions at the time?

We had a lot of discussions about French existentialism, which was in fashion. Today, young people look toward America, but for us, the dream was France. Anyone interested in culture was fascinated by France, by Sartre, Camus, the *Nouvelle Vague*.

As a teenager, you were very drawn to religion.

That happened before all those urges and confusions of adolescence really kicked in. For a while, I toyed with the idea of becoming a pastor. It was never a serious calling, more of a passing thought. But looking back, I suppose the questions I was asking even then were already existential.

There's still a difference between wanting to be a pastor and being an existentialist.

I was never an existentialist, and my spiritual evolution was like that of most teenagers. At first, you look for an answer to your fears and desires. Then you discover the opposite sex, and everything shifts in another direction. At first, it was God, then it was girls. Put that way, it might sound frivolous, but most young people go through similar phases.

Was your family very religious?

Not at all. No one in our household went to church. But we never spoke badly about religion either. It just wasn't a central part of our lives.

Were you not taught to pray?

Yes, at school. Among Protestants, there is confirmation at 14. We are prepared for it; we have to learn things, not just pray. I found it all very interesting. I remember feeling a real inner tremor the first time I took communion in a packed church. I was kneeling and shivering with emotion. It was extraordinary. One rarely experiences moments as intense as that. But it lasted for a time, then it was over.

Did your brief vocation as a pastor stem from this intense emotion?

No, I think it was more of a flirtation with the idea of being chosen. At that age, you're serious, but in a rather simple, naïve way.

Even if you gave up the idea of becoming a pastor, you didn't let go of your existential questioning?

Once you start asking the big questions, they don't just vanish overnight. And it's not like I gave up on becoming a pastor the moment I met a pretty girl. It faded out gradually, over time.

With thoughts like those, you must have been a pretty good philosophy student.

Not really. To be a good philosophy student, as in all university disciplines, you need an enormous memory, which wasn't something I had. Anyway, I didn't enrol in university to become a professor or secure a job. I didn't care about the future or how I would make a living. I wanted answers to my existential questions at the time. In the end, the only answer I got was that there are no answers, which is already a big step. When I got to university, I imagined that these very learned people would explain the world to me.

Which philosophers did you study at university?

I had to study Schopenhauer, Kant and Hegel, who gave me a lot of trouble because his language is barely decipherable. But I loved Pascal and Montaigne, even though they weren't on the syllabus. Pascal's thought is refreshingly clear. Though I'm no believer, I have always read him with great pleasure. He answered my questions better than Hegel, who is too abstract. You have to dig through so many layers just to understand him. Later, I moved on to Wittgenstein. In fact, all the philosophers who interested me I read outside the official curriculum.

What did Wittgenstein do for you?

He made me realise that I could never become a philosopher. I remember a seminar organised by another professor where a student gave a presentation which mathematically challenged Wittgenstein's theses using formulas from the *Tractatus*. That student was so brilliant that I realised I would never be as good as him. I was quite depressed really.

Another philosopher you appreciated at that time was Theodor Adorno.

Haneke, aged 18.

Another philosopher not studied at the university. Around 1968, he became very well known, but before that, at the University of Vienna, no one talked about him. I discovered him when my neo-Hegelian professor gave a semester-long course on Nietzsche and Thomas Mann's *Doctor Faustus*. Adorno gave Mann guidance on that book, which made me want to read some of his many works. He quickly became my intellectual guide on matters of art and society. As for *Doctor Faustus*, it remains, to this day, my favourite book.

Why did it leave such a mark on you?

Because Mann examines what remains of culture's resources after the horror and barbarism of fascism. His protagonist, Adrian Leverkühn, is a great composer who pushes his art so far that it ends up negating traditional culture, culture that had lost its credibility through the very events it witnessed. In his final work, the music collapses into nothing more than a scream, a howl. One of the keys to the novel is the parallel Mann draws between Germany's collapse and that of his hero, who, in despair, makes a pact with the devil. At the same time, Leverkühn's fate echoes that of Nietzsche, whose writings — through tragic misreadings — ended up paving the way for fascism. You can read *Doctor Faustus* as a kind of indirect biography of Nietzsche, translated into the realm of music. Mann's message is so layered, so dense with references and ideas, that you really can't sum it up in just a few lines.

How far did you go in your university studies?

Up to the fourth year. But in the last year, I had already started earning a living. I had to meet my obligations because I was married and we were expecting a child. I started as a factory worker, then a heating technician, and finally a post office cashier. At the same time, I was also working for radio and newspapers.

How did you manage to get into radio and newspapers without any experience in the field?

I had already contacted various newspapers to offer them short stories I had written. For radio, I had a letter of recommendation from someone I had known in Wiener Neustadt, who had since become a professor of literature at an American university. During my studies, I had shown him my writing, and he had supported and encouraged me. Through him, I was able to contact the head of the cultural department at Austrian radio, who had me write book reviews and, on Sundays, produce radio adaptations of novels in half-hour serialised episodes. At the same time, I was writing film reviews for newspapers. That's how I started making a very modest living. I enjoyed it a lot. Later, through my father, who was no longer an actor but had become a casting director for TV films on the German channel ZDF, I got a three-month internship at Südwestfunk in Baden-Baden. That was in 1967, and I went from a completely apolitical world to one that was in turmoil. I found it fascinating because I was discovering entirely new perspectives. My lucky break was replacing someone who had retired. He was a script editor. It involved reading scripts submitted to the network, selecting the best ones, and then overseeing their production until completion. They had been searching for a replacement for a year, and since none of the candidates had been any good, they kept me on. At the end of my internship, I became the youngest script editor in German television, and from that moment on, I was able to live a normal life. I had a real salary and regular office hours.

How did you experience the turbulent period of 1967-1968?

As I mentioned, everything was new to me in Baden-Baden. Much later, I learned that in certain circles a similar protest movement had also existed in Vienna. Since I wasn't part of those groups and their activities weren't very public, I knew nothing about it. In Baden-Baden, however, everyone my age was engaged in these debates. Our programme director was a famous journalist named Günter Gaus, who had launched a show called *Zur Person*, on which he interviewed prominent figures. He acted like a judge, and was extremely precise in his remarks. His guests were always people with complex personalities, like [the German political activist] Rudi Dutschke, who turned out to be brilliant. Everyone loved that encounter.

Did you personally get involved in these protest movements?

Not really. I sympathised with many of their ideas, but I was never someone who went out into the streets to fight. I'm too much of a coward for that. In fact, I can tell you a story about that, which happened much later in France, in Avignon. At the time, I was separated from my first wife and living with an actress. We found ourselves in the middle of a farmers' protest, where they were throwing apples onto the streets. Suddenly, the police charged in with their transparent shields. I ran as fast as I could. Then, after a while, it hit me: "Wait... where's my girlfriend?" She was furious with me. Rightly so. I was really quite ashamed.

Did you encourage radio listeners to take action?

No, because even though I shared those ideas, I wasn't someone who took a keen interest in politics. It's the same with my work as a filmmaker. I deal with society, but not from an ideological perspective.

According to our sources, you signed a petition against Jörg Haider, the Austrian far-right leader, at the 2000 Berlin Film Festival.

I actually don't remember that at all. But one thing is certain: Haider was a disgrace to our country. In general, I rarely sign petitions. Many of my colleagues sign everything, everywhere. That creates a kind of inflation, and I don't like it. But Haider must have irritated me so much that I felt compelled to take a stand in some way, perhaps in various interviews. Even today, Austrian politics is a disaster. I'd rather not talk about it.

Looking back at the late 1960s, the protest movement generally broadened your perspective.

Yes, much like my encounter with Ulrike Meinhof, who was a truly remarkable woman. The TV network had commissioned her to write a screenplay, and when she arrived, all the executives came to meet her. She was brilliant, very assured in her opinions, yet also charming, with a great sense of humour and self-deprecation. We spent time with her throughout the period she worked on her script, about girls in a juvenile detention centre. She was deeply committed to helping those girls, even taking some of them into her own home. At the same time, she was becoming increasingly radical. Each time she returned to the office, she seemed more bitter, convinced that real reform was impossible because the system wouldn't allow it. Then came the moment when she participated in her first violent action with the Red Army Faction. We never thought she would take that step because she had children and was highly cultured, and was a real star in journalism. But we should have seen it coming. Her moral rigour and intransigence were bound to lean her toward radical methods.

How do you explain this contradiction in Ulrike Meinhof's behaviour, starting from humanist ideas and then becoming a terrorist with the Baader-Meinhof group?

It's the eternal problem posed by any ideology. When an idea is transformed into an ideology, it creates antagonisms, and personal relationships quickly become inhuman. That's the theme of *The White Ribbon*.

It's a theory that has been proven repeatedly: Jesus had good ideas—

Exactly.

—but the Church turned them into Christianity.

It's exactly the same problem you find today with Muslims and Islamism.

And, in a way, the same was true with Nazism. How did the legacy of national guilt, so strongly felt by the generation of German-speaking artists born during or just after the war, affect you?

Unconsciously, it must have left a mark on me. But not consciously. Of course, I have thought about this issue a lot, but I have never felt personally guilty about Nazism. I feel guilty about a thousand things in daily life. I actually think you can't really live without guilt. That's an idea that runs through all my films. And even if I don't feel personally guilty, I do think the German collective guilt over World War II is entirely justified. Yesterday, I saw a short report on a German film festival where the lead actor, Moritz Bleibtreu, said: "The heroes of German cinema are all antiheroes and losers." It's true. A German screenwriter still can't make the protagonist a winner, as the Americans do, because of this lingering collective guilt. And I think that's a good thing.

What was your view of the Baader-Meinhof group at the time?

On one hand, I was surprised; on the other, I understood very well why Ulrike Meinhof turned to terrorism. I didn't think she had made the right decision, but she had become so radical in her opinions—much more than anyone else I knew at the time—that she was no longer capable of the slightest compromise. That's the problem with all radicals, but it was especially surprising in someone with such a sharp sense of humour and irony. She once told me, with a mischievous smile, that since her daughters were often late for school, she had instructed them to tell their teacher, if asked why: "It's because of capitalism!" That made her laugh a lot.

During those years working in German television, were you still doing radio?

I hosted a programme on theatre criticism, focusing on regional theatre in southwest Germany. I had to find local actors from theatre troupes for minor roles, so I had to stay informed about productions in the area. That gave me the idea for this radio program, which enabled me to attend all the premieres of new plays in the region.

Did you develop close relationships with anyone in the theatre world at that time?

Not particularly, except in Baden-Baden, when I was working in television. I had a close collaboration with the city's theatre and also a more personal relationship with an actress. That's also where I started directing my first stage productions.

Did you see theatre as a new form of expression that might lead you to abandon television?

No, for twenty years, I worked in both theatre and television. I didn't make my first feature film until I was 46. Every year, I staged a play and wrote a script for a television film, though there was variation, with certain years focused more on theatre and others more on television.

Before we delve into your work during those two decades, a question about your early cinephilia. How did you discover auteur cinema?

At university, I took a course with a Danish professor who specialised in theatre but had organised a film seminar, supported by the French cultural institute, which had an extensive film collection. It was wonderful because the seminar gave us the opportunity to watch a film and then discuss it afterward. If you spoke well, if you were outspoken like me, that was enough to get an excellent grade. I attended that seminar for several years, and it was through it that I discovered Bresson. We also watched Truffaut's *Jules et Jim* and Agnès Varda's *Le Bonheur*, films that for us became cult classics. And of course, we jumped to see every new Godard film.

Among the Nouvelle Vague filmmakers, which ones influenced or inspired you the most?

When I saw my first Bresson film, *Au hasard Balthazar*, I was deeply impressed. It was a new kind of cinema, different from anything I had seen before, and I thought it might be a path worth exploring. But there was also *Bande à part* and other Godard films, which were not as complicated as the ones he made later in his career. All young people went to see them; it was all very fashionable. We also loved Italian films. Every Antonioni film had students rushing to the cinema.

When watching all these auteur films of the 1960s, did you consider a possible career as a filmmaker?

Before moving to Germany, I was more inclined to become a writer. I had already published several short stories, while the chances of breaking into cinema seemed very slim to me, since I didn't know anyone in the industry. Even later, when I was working in television, I wrote a screenplay called *Wochenende* [*Weekend*], which foreshadowed the future story of *Funny Games*, but it didn't include any distancing effect, and the criminal wasn't a torturer. The script must not have been too bad since I received German funding in advance, a grant of 300,000 DM — a substantial amount, but not enough to produce the film.

Were the worlds of cinema and television very separate at the time?

Not that much. For example, Westdeutscher Rundfunk co-produced many films, including those of Jean-Marie Straub and Danièle Huillet. ZDF as well. But I didn't know anyone in the film industry and I didn't know who to approach, so I had to return the grant money. That was unfortunate, but it reinforced my determination to one day make a film. I knew that if I remained a television script editor, no one would ever think of offering me anything else, so I started directing my own theatre productions at the Baden-Baden theatre, where I invited my superiors to see my work. That's how I got the opportunity to direct my first television film.

In 2002, Sight and Sound *magazine asked you, among many others, to list your ten favourite films. You ranked them as follows:* Au hasard Balthazar *(Bresson),* Lancelot du Lac *(Bresson),* Mirror *(Tarkovsky),* Salò, or the 120 Days of Sodom *(Pasolini),* The Exterminating Angel *(Buñuel),* The Gold Rush *(Chaplin),* Psycho *(Hitchcock),* A Woman Under the Influence *(Cassavetes),* Germany Year Zero *(Rossellini), and* L'Eclisse *(Antonioni). Do you still agree with this list, considering that you later said you would have gladly added* Once Upon a Time in the West *by Sergio Leone?*

It's such a well-made film that it deserves to be on such a list. It's truly a masterpiece, perfect on every level, but I wouldn't watch it ten times. It's not my kind of film.

You probably don't like genre films.

No, not really.

You have always preferred auteur films. But when you were a critic, didn't you have to watch everything released in cinemas?

No, only the films that interested me. In reality, I wrote far more about books than about films for that newspaper. Of course, I was assigned certain books, which I read, even if I disliked them, but once I had a bit of standing on the team, I made it clear that it was better if I only wrote about books that interested me. I don't think it's good to read or watch just anything, even for the sake of reviewing it. In my view, one of the great challenges of criticism is avoiding cynicism, avoiding coming to hate your job because you waste time on books and films you find idiotic. Criticism is a really difficult profession. Fortunately, it wasn't my main job, so I could afford to be selective, but from time to time I did enjoy tearing apart a film I hated, because, as everyone knows, it's always easier to criticise a film than to praise it.

Apart from the Sight and Sound *list, the films you mention most often in interviews are* Au hasard Balthazar, Mirror *and* Salò. *Are these still your favourites?*

Yes, these films remain very important to me, but if I had to make a new list, I would put *Mirror* at the top. I don't know how many times I've seen it; far more often than *Au hasard Balthazar*. Each time, I discover a new nuance that I hadn't noticed before. And each time, I end up in tears, overwhelmed by the beauty of it. That's something that happens to me very rarely with a film. At the University of Vienna, where I teach cinema, it's the first film I show to every new class of students. They don't understand it at all because they're not used to this kind of film. It's shameful, but 90 percent of film students today have never seen a film like that, and they are completely unable to decipher it. They aren't just surprised; they're also frustrated. Over time, as they watch it again and analyse it in detail—as they do with all the films I screen for them—they eventually begin to understand it better and even appreciate it. That doesn't mean they'll want to make films like that, but at least it opens their minds to a kind of cinema that exists.

Returning to your three favourite films…

It's purely emotional. Those are the films that have left the greatest impression on me. With *Salò*, it's a special case because it's terrifying. I saw it once, and never again.

You don't have it in your large DVD collection?

I do, but I don't dare watch it. That film completely devastated me at the time, yet I still consider it an extremely important film.

So you don't show it to your students.

No, because some people, especially young women, are very sensitive, and I don't want to traumatise them. However, I do emphasise its importance and recommend that those who feel strong enough should watch it. It's up to each person to decide; I don't want to force anyone.

Did it amuse you when people compared Funny Games *to* Salò?

Yes. The two films have the same goal but take very different paths to get there. *Salò* is, as far as I know, the only film that depicts violence as it exists in reality. In most violent films, particularly American ones, violence is staged for consumption, as part of the spectacle. You feel safe in your seat, and when the film ends, it's as if nothing happened. With *Salò*, it's something else. You truly grasp the reality of violence, and it's unbearable. I had hoped to approach that same level of intensity with *Funny Games*, but I can't really compare the two films, because one was made by Pasolini and the other by me.

Two

Let's talk about your theatre years. From the start, were you able to direct plays of your choice?

No. In fact, I directed my first play thanks to my girlfriend at the time. She was an actress in the Baden-Baden theatre troupe and often complained about the notes given to her by directors. When I offered to help her rehearse lines, she initially declined, saying that I was just an amateur. But I persisted, and eventually she agreed to let me assist. She found my suggestions insightful enough to mention them to her colleagues. Being the young star of the company, her opinion carried weight, and they trusted her. This led me to approach the theatre's director to express my interest in staging a production. He was surprised at first, then told me, quite frankly, that the theatre had no money. I replied that I wasn't concerned about that; I simply wanted the opportunity to direct. He added that there was also no budget for sets, so I proposed reviving *Des journées entières dans les arbres* by Marguerite Duras, which had recently been adapted for television with Heinz Bennent and Roma Bahn. I knew where I could get access to the existing sets from that production. Eventually, and perhaps out of resignation, he agreed. The play was a success, and it gave me the chance to continue.

This time, with the ability to choose your own play?

Yes, from that moment on, I always chose the plays myself. I started with smaller works, then moved on to classics like *The Prince of Homburg*.

Still with the Baden-Baden theatre troupe?

Yes, which was a challenge. Since we were in a provincial town, it was very difficult to get anyone from a major theatre to come and see what we were doing. These people assume that no talented artist will ever be discovered in a small town like Baden-Baden. I wrote countless letters, none of which received a response, and in the end, an actress I had recently worked with at the theatre convinced the script editor of the renowned Darmstadt theatre— who she knew personally—to attend one of our performances. He liked it and made me an offer, but nearly three years had passed between my first play and his visit. I learned a lot about actors during that time. When you have to work with the same group of performers, at least half of whom aren't very good, you gradually figure out how to help them improve.

So how did you help an actor improve their performance?

That's a question my film students ask me constantly. They are quite intimidated by that part of the job, whereas technical aspects don't scare them at all. It's true that debut films are often technically polished but lack strong performances. How do you fix that? There is no one-size-fits-all answer. Every actor is different, and only experience allows you to determine how to approach each one. Some actors need to be handled very gently, while others need to be pushed. Some require explanations, even concrete demonstrations of what they should do, others have to be left to figure things out on their own. Directing actors is always a case-by-case process.

Do you think a solid understanding of behavioural psychology is necessary for aspiring filmmakers?

I don't think so. You don't make a film with theories. What matters is practice. Even though the idea that you can only learn to make a film by making one is a cliché, it's also true. The same goes for all artistic or craft-based professions. You don't learn to paint by applying theories. If that were the case, all university professors would be great artists. There is also, in the making of a film, a deeply artisanal dimension in which I firmly believe. Like a craftsman, I have to be precise and know exactly what I am doing. Whether what I do is considered art isn't for me to decide. That's where talent comes in, and talent can't be taught. It's like music. Take someone without talent. They can work obsessively on a simple sonata and still achieve only a mediocre result. Someone else might spend just an hour on it and leave everyone in awe. Talent is unfair, and directing actors depends on talent.

So theatre allowed you to learn how to direct actors. Did it also teach you other things, such as lighting?

Yes, because even though lighting is done differently in theatre than in cinema, a stage director, like a film director, must know what needs to be lit and how. This isn't a matter of scientific knowledge or practice. Even after twenty years in the profession, some directors will still get it all wrong. And even if you explain to them why their lighting doesn't work, they won't understand. It's a question of talent and sensitivity.

Were you very interventionist in your productions when you weren't satisfied with certain aspects, like the lights and the scenic design?

Yes, I got involved in everything. Maybe that's why, unlike my time spent in cinema, I never felt truly comfortable in theatre. From the very first day of rehearsals, I would arrive with a very clear idea of what I wanted, and from that moment on, I wouldn't rest until I achieved it. That approach may work well when it comes to giving technical instructions in advance, but with actors, it's more complicated. Some of them would follow my direction either because they felt obliged to or because my reasoning convinced them. But they were often frustrated that the ideas didn't come from them, and they made that known. Several of my productions didn't work because of the actors. The German director Peter Zadek, who died in 2009, developed an excellent method. He started rehearsals by letting the actors show him everything they wanted to do. Once they had exhausted their ideas, Zadek would begin guiding them, making them believe the adjustments were their own. This motivated them for the rest of the process. I was too impatient to work like that, even though theatre gives you time, unlike cinema and opera, where rehearsals are limited by budget constraints. I did succeed with some productions, but there were many where I failed to achieve what I wanted because I didn't know how to give the actors enough space. When I finally realised this—and it took me a while—I stopped working in theatre. As I always say: "You shouldn't ask a shoemaker to make hats." And that, in a way, was my situation.

When was your last theatre production?

During the filming of my first feature film, *The Seventh Continent.*

You directed plays by very different authors, including Strindberg, Goethe, Bruckner, Kleist, Hebbel and Duras. What are your best memories from these productions?

I think my best productions were von Kleist's *The Broken Jug* and Friedrich Hebbel's claustrophobic *Maria Magdalena*, which works like a relentless pressure cooker. In his diary, Hebbel wrote that he was satisfied because he had managed to "seal off every mouse hole" through which the characters could escape. It's a brutal, deeply pessimistic, and depressing play, but also incredibly powerful. Kleist's play, on the other hand, is a bitter comedy written in an extraordinary language. But my most rewarding theatre experience was probably *Intrigue and Love* by Friedrich Schiller. I adore that play. It was one of my first productions in Baden-Baden, and even though I was a bit overwhelmed by its complexity, I took great pleasure in directing that bourgeois tragedy. It's incredibly sad, but also incredibly beautiful, largely thanks to the language, which is just magnificent. I remember being really nervous on opening night— I even scratched my hand raw from anxiety—and instead of watching the actors, I kept my eyes glued to the audience. When I saw people in tears at the end of the final act, which is truly heartbreaking, I felt an enormous sense of relief. It made me genuinely happy. That moment has stayed with me as a beautiful memory.

Is it true that you directed only one vaudeville play, and that it was a failure?

That was a disaster, yes. It was a play by Eugène Labiche called *Le Plus Heureux des Trois* which the theatre management suggested I stage for New Year's Eve. I wasn't convinced I was the right person for it, but I wanted to give it a try. From the very first day of rehearsals, I knew I was in trouble, and after two or three days, things only got worse. I could tell that the play relied entirely on

Haneke's production of Schiller's *Intrigue and Love* in Baden-Baden.

comedy and I had no idea how to translate it into staging. I wanted to quit, but they told me that was impossible because there was no replacement production for New Year's Eve, so I had to go through with it. It was a disaster. My staging was so dull that there was no chance for laughter. Everything felt heavy. The audience had come to have fun, and at each curtain rise they applauded enthusiastically because the sets were beautiful. But their enthusiasm quickly faded. At the end of the performance, the actors left the stage to polite applause, and at the reception afterward it was as if no one knew me.

Couldn't the actors take the lead and make suggestions during rehearsals?

Everyone was just as disheartened as I was. It was the only time that happened to me. However, I did very much enjoy directing the comedies of Carl Sternheim. His humour was sharp, biting and, above all, realistic. Not that realism has to be a must, of course. There were also two Westerns I directed—world premieres, no less—one written by a well-known film critic from Munich. We were offered the play because no prestigious theatre wanted to stage a Western, but everyone ended up having a fantastic time. Even actors who weren't in the play would come to watch the rehearsals.

Were there horses on stage?

No, it was more in the style of a Spaghetti Western. We used Ennio Morricone's music and leaned heavily into the references. It was all a bit tongue-in-cheek, a kind of playful riff on all the clichés.

Did you ever direct Shakespeare?

Never. Nor did I stage Greek classics, as their aesthetic didn't seem to fit my style of directing. I also never directed Chekhov, but for different reasons. First, I had too much admiration for this god of theatre to imagine staging a production worthy of his genius. And I couldn't seem to assemble the ideal cast, with a great actor in every role. That's why it's so rare to see a truly convincing staging of Chekhov. Recently, I saw a magnificent production of *Uncle Vanya* with Jens Harzer as Astrov, an actor so brilliant that he made up for the inconsistencies in the rest of the cast. Watching that, I felt like a child at the foot of a Christmas tree. It was a great and rare moment of joy. Today, I go to the theatre very little because I'm so often disappointed.

Did you bring actors from your stage productions into your television or film work?

Mostly in my television films, as I was still directing theatre productions at the same time. I should mention my collaboration with Josef Bierbichler, an actor I adore and who had one of his first screen roles in *Sperrmüll*, my worst TV film. I was delighted to work with him again as the stage manager in *The White Ribbon*.

Before making your first television film, did you ever shoot amateur films in Super 8?

No, but I did act in two short films. When I was still in Wiener Neustadt, there was a businessman obsessed with Super 8. His films were silly, but he had a white Jaguar that fascinated us. Since he knew I was "the artist" of the group and the son of actors, he asked me to act in two of his films. They had no artistic value, but it was a fun experience.

Did your experience in radio adapting novels help you with theatre directing?

No, because my radio work was limited to writing adaptations of novels and literary reviews that I read on air. My best training came from reading bad scripts as a television script editor. Every morning, I would find a pile of scripts on my desk. That taught me how to quickly identify what didn't work in a text. Today, my approach to structuring a screenplay owes a lot to that experience.

Did painting play a role in your artistic development?

Not really. I'm a man of the ear. In theatre rehearsals, I would often sit with my eyes down, listening to the actors. They frequently complained that I wasn't looking at them. I would explain, "I see you better when I'm not looking." I can immediately hear when a line sounds false, when the emotion isn't right. It's harder to detect that when I'm watching them. Similarly, in my writing, I never start from an image, but rather from a situation that I try to express with maximum intensity. For me, that process rarely involves pictorial references.

When you were a student, did you often visit museums?

Not often. I only really came to understand the importance of painting in recent years. Before that, there were paintings that amazed me, but it never went much further than that. Although, when I was in Baden-Baden, I discovered Renaissance painting. At the time, we smoked a lot of hashish, and one evening, while I was stoned, I looked through a book on Renaissance painting. Of course, I already knew the paintings and thought they were beautiful, but for the first time, I began to see connections between the images. They started telling me a story. Later on, I experienced the same sensation again, this time completely sober, when I looked at those paintings anew. And that was that, until these past few years, when for reasons I can't quite explain, I started to really enjoy looking at paintings from the 15th, 16th, 17th, even the 18th centuries. The 19th century—the Impressionists and so on—is lovely, but I don't find it particularly moving. For me, the Ghent Altarpiece with Van Eyck's *Adoration of the Mystic Lamb* is extraordinary, as are Velázquez's paintings, which I revisited at the Prado a few months ago.

Looking at Egon Schiele's paintings, one might see an approach to melancholy that resonates with some of your films.

Perhaps, but that's for you to say. I can't look at my films from that perspective. There is, indeed, an Austrian melancholy, both in literature and painting, which has been widely analysed, but I don't know where it comes from, and I don't even want to think about it. It wouldn't be good for me to try to analyse it, just as I don't believe psychoanalysis can help an artist.

Do you think your cinema is closely linked to Austrian culture?

As I say, there is a certain melancholy in Austrian culture, especially in the work of several writers I admire. Joseph Roth, for example, whose novel *The Rebellion* I adapted, is the quintessential Austrian writer. He embodies that taste for melancholy and an extraordinary formal mastery, expressed through the elegance of language. But if you asked me to define the "Austrian soul," I wouldn't have more words than the ones I just used: melancholy and elegance. And even then, in literature, that only applies to the late 19th and early 20th centuries. Austria doesn't have a great literary tradition. During the classical period, nothing exceptional emerged, unlike today, when Austrian writing represents a significant part of German-language literature, despite our population of just over eight million compared to Germany's more than eighty million.

Returning to your theatrical career, apart from Baden-Baden, where else did you stage productions?

At first, I went to Hildesheim, then to Darmstadt, Düsseldorf, Hamburg, Berlin, Vienna, Frankfurt and Stuttgart.

Working in television at the same time, did you struggle to manage everything?

We had to establish a strict schedule. Sometimes it didn't work out, and there were times when I had to give up projects I cared about. But I was fortunate. Aside from the very early years when I had left my stable television job to focus solely on directing and struggled to gain recognition beyond Baden-Baden, I was able to work continuously. That's why I started making films so late; I simply didn't have the time. Between theatre and television, I had plenty of opportunities and could more or less do what I wanted. If a project fell through, I would just take a vacation.

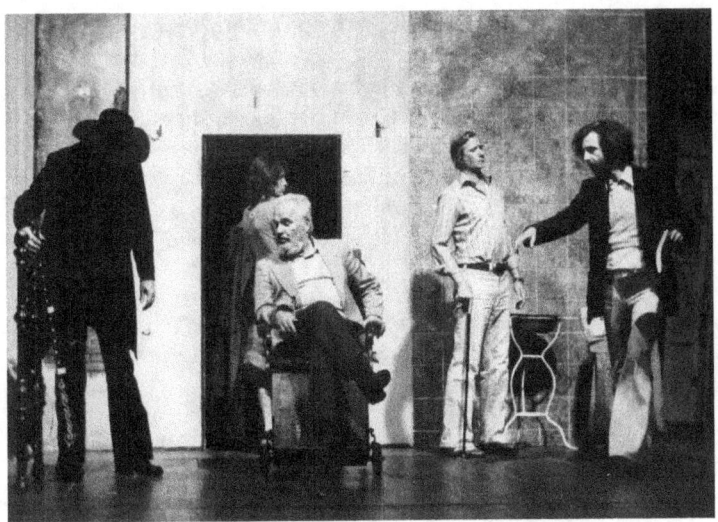

Haneke (right) directing a production in Baden-Baden.

Nowadays, I no longer allow myself that luxury, but at the time, it was wonderful to spend three months on a Greek island.

Speaking of Greece, you wrote a short story entitled "Persephone." What was it about?

It was a kind of fable about three tourists facing a series of problems in a convent on a Greek island. The woman ends up killing one of the two men with an arrow, and the survivor wonders if it was his fault. I wanted the language to be very sophisticated, and the story anticipated a theme that runs through my films: What really happened? Does my perspective align with reality?

Did you publish other short stories?

Just one more, though I've forgotten the title. It was a story somewhat similar to "Persephone." All I really remember is the ending, which left me feeling quite bleak. One character says to the other: "But that's my story! What can you do with it?" And the other replies: "Nothing. Exactly."

Where can these short stories be found today?

Nowhere. They were published in collections that competed for an Austrian literary prize and are now impossible to find. "Persephone" must not have been too bad, because after its publication, I received several invitations to write more short stories. That was around 1967, a time when I would have been very happy to have a salaried job at a publishing house, but they only wanted a collection of short stories from me. I had only two or three stories in mind, and it would have taken me at least two years to write enough for a full book.

Before discussing your television films, can you tell us about the role of music in your life after you gave up on becoming a concert pianist or composer?

As soon as I arrived in Vienna, I found myself without a piano, and I could only play when I visited Wiener Neustadt. Naturally, my playing deteriorated, and it frustrated me so much that I preferred to stop completely. I became just a consumer of music, buying a lot of records.

Do you often go to concerts?

Not often. As for opera, I hate going because the productions are rarely good. I don't like being surrounded by too many people when I'm engaging with a work of art. And today, if I go to the theatre, everyone knows me. If I attend a premiere, I'm expected to give my opinion afterward, which I hate. If there's a play I want to see, I'll go later in the run so I can watch it in peace, without being asked to comment. Also, in Vienna, I know all the actors and most of the directors, and it's uncomfortable to tell them what I really think of their work. As for music, I often travel to hear Bach's *Passions* because large choirs can't be fully appreciated at home. Even though I have excellent sound systems in both my country house and my office, I go out to listen to music all the time.

In your youth, did you stick to classical music, or were you also interested in other genres, like rock?

Rock interested me when I was growing up. We loved to dance to Little Richard, Elvis Presley, Bill Haley and everyone else. Then, when I moved to Baden-Baden, during the hashish era, the popular music I listened to the most was Pink Floyd. That's where it stopped for me. Of course, I know who Michael Jackson is, but I know nothing about his music.

Do you remember how you discovered your favourite composers?

I remember the emotion I felt when I first heard Handel's *Messiah* or, as I've already mentioned, Mozart's C minor sonatas, in the film with Oskar Werner. I liked Bach very early on, but I can't say how or why. His music exists outside of everything. It transports you into another realm, something that feels close to the divine.

Do you place Bach above Schubert?

Bach, Mozart, and Schubert are undeniably my three favourite composers. But it's difficult for me to rank one above the others.

Three

Und was kommt danach?: my first television film — Godard, McLuhan and the Beatles, to a Rolling Stones song — The virtues of the long take — *Sperrmüll* is rubbish — The cinematic writing of *Drei Wege zum See* — Adapting for television — God, luck, and inspiration — My most Austrian film? — I don't believe in happiness

Und was kommt danach? (1974)
(And What Comes Next?)

A couple in bed after making love. The woman admits that she felt little pleasure during the act. This is followed by other vignettes involving the same man and woman, both in their thirties, in their apartment, confronting the frustrations—both material and emotional—of daily life. These scenes are intercut with various quotations that comment on the action and prompt the viewer to reflect. Among the cited authors are Marshall McLuhan and the Beatles ("The word is love"), Wittgenstein and Hunter Davies, Andy Warhol and Thomas Wolfe, Siegfried Lenz ("All human conflicts obey the law of war") and Norman Mailer ("Neither knowledge nor imagination is innate. They are closely tied to the sufferings of a past we have forgotten"). These quotations, like the many conflicts between the protagonists, aim to provide—as Jean-Luc Godard would say—"a worldview characteristic of a generation." Most of the time, they appear over an image of the Beatles in concert, while the soundtrack features the emblematic Rolling Stones refrain "(I Can't Get No) Satisfaction." The couple gradually realises that, in their need for connection, they can only manage to talk to each other without ever reaching mutual understanding. The

woman grows bored. The man distances himself, con-
firming Theodor Adorno's statement that "Love is the
ability to perceive similarities where none exist."

In 1974, for your first television film, Und was kommt danach?,
you adapted James Saunders' radio play After Liverpool. *Under
what circumstances did you transition to directing for television?*

At the time, within the artistic hierarchy of Baden-Baden, television was seen as superior to theatre, so I invited television
producers to come and see my theatre work in the hope that I
might persuade them to let me direct something for them. What
they saw convinced them to give me a chance on the regional
network. Of course, they had no budget. The only resources they
could offer me were gigantic Apex video cameras, a studio, the
network's set designer, and this radio play by Saunders, for which
they owned the rights. I accepted all the more willingly because I
found the dialogue amusing.

Were you able to choose the actors?

Yes. I was very pleased with Hildegard Schmahl's performance,
less so with Dieter Kirchlechner. He was the partner of an actress
I had previously worked with in theatre. In his text, Saunders
explicitly allows for different actors to be used for each vignette,
but for budgetary reasons, I had to do the whole thing with just
two performers.

*You retained only twenty-two of the original twenty-six vignettes.
How did you make this selection?*

The choice stemmed from the decision to work with only two
actors. I then took advantage of the author's permission to reshape
the text by making cuts and rearranging scenes to construct a
narrative. The original play treated male-female relationships in a
more abstract way.

You also added intertitles.

The play's title gave me that idea. I thought Saunders named it *After
Liverpool* because he was depicting a generation influenced by the
cultural revolution that originated in Liverpool, with pop music
and the Beatles. That's why I chose to introduce each sequence

with a popular 1960s quote and accompany these intertitles with excerpts from the Rolling Stones song "Satisfaction."

You quote the Beatles in your intertitles, but why do your characters never refer to them?

Because this reference to Liverpool is more about atmosphere and cultural climate than musical taste. With this film, I had the somewhat naïve ambition of portraying my generation, those in their thirties, so I chose actors who were the same age as me. We weren't influenced by Beatles music because we were already too old when they appeared.

But then why the constant use of the Stones song, which doesn't quite fit the characters' age? Is it because, even in its full title— "(I Can't Get No) Satisfaction"—it points to a major theme in the film and in your cinema in general, that of—

—existential frustration. Yes, of course. But it also connects to the Andy Warhol quote I include, where he says that from one generation to the next, only the clothes change. The fundamental problems remain the same.

Did you consider using this Stones song from the moment you wrote the script?

Yes, I thought of it right away, but everything depended on securing the rights. That was much easier for television than for cinema. For example, in *Wer war Edgar Allan?*, another one of my television films, I used music that Ennio Morricone had composed for Bertolucci's *1900*. But later, when a distributor wanted to release the film theatrically, Bertolucci's rights holders demanded such a high fee that we had to abandon the idea.

The other major cultural reference in Und was kommt danach? *is Jean-Luc Godard. You open the film with a quote from him.*

I was a huge fan at the time, and looking back, I would even say that I see this first television film—which, by the way, I don't think is very good—as a rather naïve attempt to "do Godard."

What did you particularly like about him?

His intellectual sophistication. You could say he institutionalised what I would call cinematic self-reflection, the idea of film examining itself. No one had done it to that extent before him. It had the same impact on me as discovering Bresson. It was a kind of cinema that, until then, I couldn't even have imagined.

In Und was kommt danach? *you make at least two other references to Godard. You show the poster for* Masculin féminin, *and in the third sequence you film your characters in a lateral tracking shot from right to left, then back again, just as Godard did with Anna Karina and Sady Rebbot, filmed from behind at a café counter in* Vivre sa vie.

Yes, that was a nod to him.

The quotations in your intertitles are quite varied, from Adorno to Henry Miller, including Norman Mailer, the Beatles and Andy Warhol. One from Marshall McLuhan—"Television images constantly require us to tighten the mesh of our net with active sensory participation"—seems to foreshadow your later cinematic work.

I became interested in the idea of television's manipulative power very early on. And, of course, I had read McLuhan, who was well known in Austria at the time.

On language and the difficulty of communication, you also cite Wittgenstein: "The tacit agreements underlying language comprehension are enormously complex." That's another idea you would explore later.

Those quotations aren't there by accident. Since childhood, I had the feeling that communication between people is difficult. In daily conversations, we don't try to be precise. Everyone speaks without always listening to what the other person is saying, or they listen only half-heartedly That's where most of the trouble comes from when we try to communicate. And even if we do make an effort to be clear, my red and my blue won't ever be quite the same as anyone else's.

Your intertitles function in two ways. Sometimes they introduce the upcoming scene, sometimes they conclude the previous one.

That was a way to avoid the formulaic feel of one scene just following another. I wanted to play around with the format a bit.

Hildegard Schmahl and Dieter Kirchlechner
in Und was kommt danach?

There's quite a bit of irony in all of it. In that first film, I touched on themes that interested me, like how hard it is to communicate. But I also didn't want to start out with something too ambitious. Two characters, one location, three weeks of shooting… I figured I could keep that under control. I didn't feel like I was making a major film, and that helped me stay within my budget. The film ended up doing well. It was originally meant for local broadcast, but it ended up being shown nationally, and then got several repeat airings.

You only had three weeks of shooting. Were you very limited in the number of takes?

No, because we were shooting on video, and it cost nothing to do multiple takes. But we didn't need many because the actors were quite good, especially Hildegard Schmahl.

Did you rehearse much beforehand?

We didn't rehearse, but we had long discussions about the changes made to the play, and the actors contributed significantly to these modifications. Since the dialogue could be placed anywhere within the set, everything was possible. For example, it was the actress who came up with the idea of setting one scene at Christmas.

This preparation with the actors was almost like a table read in theatre.

Yes, you could say that. In fact, my directing style was somewhat theatrical. Specific cinematic techniques, like shot/reverse shot, are rare in the film.

And they appear quite late. It seems that your mise-en-scène unfolds gradually. The first scene is a static long take, then comes the lateral tracking shot we mentioned earlier. In a way, we're witnessing the genesis of Michael Haneke's future cinematic style. When we hear the line about ping-pong, it even brings to mind a key scene from 71 Fragments of a Chronology of Chance.

That sounds good to me.

We were struck by your decision, in the opening scene, to frame the couple in bed after making love from an almost perfectly vertical overhead angle. You would go on to use similar shots in your later films, like the close-ups of hands on the piano keys in The Piano Teacher, *but it's still a rarely used perspective. Do you remember why you chose to introduce your characters that way?*

Starting the film from that angle was a way of introducing the overarching idea, the perspective of a detached, almost scientific gaze on communication, through a series of model examples.

Another striking shot is the final one. The couple appears in the background, in a wide angle, while the camera slowly moves toward them in a fourteen-minute-long tracking shot.

That tracking shot was made possible by those enormous video cameras, which had to be moved very slowly due to their weight. If I had been shooting on film, I couldn't have held the shot that long, as I would have been constrained by reel changes.

But why did you choose to move in so slowly on the couple for that final scene?

Hildegard Schmahl and Dieter Kirchlechner in the opening scene of
Und was kommt danach?

That choice wasn't based on any theory. I just felt it was the best
way to serve that farewell moment. At the start of the shot, I needed
a wide frame to show how small and lost they are in the space.
Then, gradually moving in on their faces allowed me to capture a
certain kind of beauty, one that comes from the sadness of the situation. As for the length of the shot, it simply follows the rhythm
of the story the man is telling the woman. To recreate the feeling of
reading a story that seems to go on and on, I didn't want to break
the flow with any cuts.

*Even in your first television film, you use the long take, a technique
you would frequently employ in your later work on the big screen.*

There are two reasons to use long takes. First, it helps the actors;
it gives them time to develop an emotion, a feeling. For me, the
performance is fundamental. When I shoot shot/reverse shot,
I always let the actor restart the scene from the beginning, even
if the camera starts rolling partway through. If a scene has any
emotional weight, it's absurd to have an actor deliver only a single
line at a time. The second reason for preferring long takes is related
to manipulation. A long take manipulates less, as it doesn't cheat

Und was kommt danach?

with time. This, in turn, builds tension. The long take plays on the viewer's impatience and uses it to keep them engaged.

Why did you have three cinematographers on this film?

They were the three operators of my electronic cameras. At the time, it was standard practice in television productions to credit all the cameramen, regardless of their level of responsibility, even if only one of them was truly the cinematographer.

Your sets are both highly realistic and somewhat stylised.

Yes, they're a bit theatrical, but that comes from the original play. It calls for that approach. The characters, like the situations, are types, though they can still carry realistic elements, so I had to work on both levels, leaning into stylisation without becoming too abstract, so as not to lose the sense of reality. It was a delicate balance to strike.

Watching your television film today, we are struck by its formal mastery. But at the time, did you think this first attempt would quickly open the doors of cinema for you?

I did certainly hope that this first experience would take me a little further. But I wasn't thinking about directing for the cinema yet. Until I wrote *The Seventh Continent*, I always felt that I hadn't found my own language yet. I was searching and learning what my strengths and weaknesses might be.

In 1975, you directed your second television film, Sperrmüll, *which you have already described as terrible and which we haven't seen—*

—and which I forbid you to watch. Fortunately, no copies exist.

Why is the film so bad, and how did you come to make it in the first place?

After the success of my first film, produced by SWF, I was contacted by Germany's second major television network, ZDF. They offered me an adaptation of a two-character play by a South American writer, intended to air in a late-night slot. This time, I was given four weeks to shoot. But just as the casting was final-ised, the network informed me they were cutting one week from the schedule. I told them that with only three weeks, I wouldn't be able to manage. They urged me to reconsider, saying that this adaptation was my way into ZDF. I did think it over, and still said no. At the time, I figured I would never hear from that network again, but a year later, a production exec from ZDF got in touch and said he would like to make a film with me. The catch was that I first had to direct a different project he was already contracted to produce. When I read the script, it was immediately clear it wasn't very good. The story was about a retired high school teacher whose children want to put him in a care home. He refuses, because he doesn't want to live in two rooms when he's always had five, but in the end he is forced to go, and insists on taking all his furniture, most of which ends up on the street. It was a melodrama, and a boring one at that. Still, I figured if I turned this down too, I would never get another call from the ZDF, so I thought maybe I could try to improve it a little. I did, slightly, but it was still a bad film. On top of that, unlike at the SWF where I knew everyone and could work with the best cameramen and crew, in Munich I didn't know a soul, and they stuck me with lousy technicians, and the network couldn't afford the actors I wanted. That said, the film actually did well when it aired and even won an award. As for the man who had promised to produce a film of my own after-ward, he passed away before that could happen, and I never got the chance to work with the network again. That's when I told myself: everyone's allowed one mistake, but not two. And from then on, I became very demanding when working in television. I've always insisted on getting everything I wanted, because if something doesn't work, it inevitably comes back to bite you.

What does the title Sperrmüll *mean?*

It refers to the municipal collection of bulky waste. The title is metaphorical. By the end of the film, the "bulky waste" isn't just the furniture but the protagonist himself.

Drei Wege zum See (1976)
(Three Paths to the Lake)

Elisabeth Matrei goes to spend her holidays with her widowed father in Klagenfurt, the capital of the state of Carinthia. She plans to rest and swim in the nearby lake, but discovers that the three hiking trails that once led there have become dead ends. Her stay becomes a time for introspection. She tells her father about her brother Robert's wedding in London, which he had refused to attend. Robert married a woman younger than himself, though the age gap is smaller than the one between Elisabeth and her current partner, Philippe. She makes a living as a photojournalist, a passion that had always puzzled Trotta, the great love of her life. What was the point of photographing war and misery? After many arguments and misunderstandings, they had eventually split at the end of the Algerian War. Elisabeth has had many other lovers, but now she knows that only Trotta truly mattered. More than Hugh, her American husband, from whom she agreed to divorce too quickly. More than Manes, with whom she had a passionate affair after Trotta's suicide. Her father updates her on life in Klagenfurt: the neighbours, the shops closing or being bought out. After a chance encounter with a former schoolmate, bitter about her own life, Elisabeth decides she no longer wants to stay. She has Philippe send her a telegram ordering her to return to Paris for work reasons. While changing trains in Vienna, she meets one of Trotta's cousins, recently married, who secretly slips her a note confessing that he loves her and has always loved her. She reads the note at Orly, just before meeting Philippe, who has come to pick her up. He tells her he has promised to marry a young woman who is pregnant with his child. Elisabeth seizes on this as a reason to break up with him. She knows that the next day, she will accept the dangerous assignment in Saigon that her boss has offered her.

In 1976, you adapted Drei Wege zum See *from a short story by Ingeborg Bachmann, published in 1972. How did you come to direct this television film, co-produced by SWF and the Austrian network Österreichischer Rundfunk?*

I have always adored the work of Ingeborg Bachmann, who is now considered the quintessential Austrian poet among postwar authors. I had read all her short stories, but I was particularly keen on adapting this one because it had a very cinematic structure.

What makes it particularly cinematic?

It's built around temporal back-and-forths that link different moments in the protagonist's life. Most of Bachmann's other short stories are so interiorised that they don't lend themselves to cinematic storytelling. Among the other works of hers that have been filmed, the most famous is her novel *Malina*, with Isabelle Huppert, adapted by Werner Schroeter. It's beautiful, but it's closer to Schroeter or Elfriede Jelinek, who wrote the screenplay, than to Bachmann.

One of the striking choices in your film is that you entrusted the voiceover of heroine's inner voice to film director Axel Corti.

I never thought of using a female voice. I don't really know why. I immediately ruled out using Ingeborg Bachmann's own unique voice, which is very recognisable because of all the recordings that exist. I remember one of her readings at the Auditorium Maximum of the University of Vienna, where she captivated twelve hundred people with such a fragile voice that we feared at any moment she might break down in tears. But that wouldn't have worked for my film. Axel Corti was a well-known voice in Austria. He had a 15-minute radio show every Saturday called *Der Schalldämpfer*, a reference to the mute used to dampen a trumpet's sound. He spoke about all sorts of things in an ironic tone and very elegant language, which made me think he was the best person for the voiceover.

Why a voiceover?

In all my television films adapted from literary works, I tried to preserve as much of the original text as possible. There's a big difference between adapting a book for television and for cinema. To me, cinema is an artistic form, and the literary work being adapted must submit to it. Television, on the other hand, treats the book as the work of art; the goal is to make viewers want to read it, and to achieve that, my job is to highlight the beauty of the language.

Was Austrian television in the 1970s concerned with producing high-quality artistic programmes?

Yes. Austrian television was very different from what it is today. You could take risks because, due to a lack of funding, there was no Austrian cinema to speak of. The Film Federation, which would later give rise to a national film production scene, had not yet been established. Occasionally, some clever person would manage to secure funding to make a film, but anyone who wanted to create serious films had to go through television. It wasn't the place for experimental cinema, but for a while producers were keen on adapting major works of German and Austrian literature. I think that all of Joseph Roth's novels were adapted, and I was even offered *The Man Without Qualities* by Robert Musil, but I declined... because I'm not suicidal. In any case, most of my television films are adaptations because they were easier to get produced. Over the years, though, I could see how increasingly difficult it was to finance television projects that weren't purely entertainment, and when I suggested a film adaptation of Kafka's *The Castle*, the channel's director asked me if it was "really necessary." As for *Drei Wege zum See*, I was still in Baden-Baden, though no longer working for SWF, when I got the idea. I went to Vienna to find a co-producer, and that's where I met a script editor who immediately backed the project. That was the beginning of a long collaboration with ORF.

Beyond the voiceover, another striking aspect of the film is its structure. You managed to translate the novel's interiorised discourse into cinematic form through "mental editing" effects, reminiscent

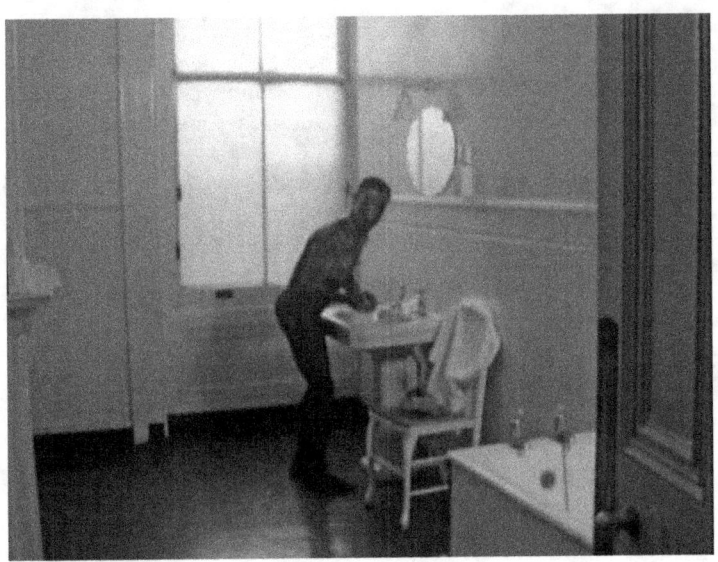

Drei Wege zum See.

of what Resnais pioneered in the 1960s with La guerre est finie *and* Je t'aime, je t'aime. *A good example is at the beginning of your film: the young woman, Elisabeth, arrives at the Klagenfurt train station, where her father is waiting to take her home by taxi. They drive past a large sculpture of a* Lindwurm, *a dragon—the emblem of the city—when suddenly there's a flash cut to a naked black man bent over a sink. The young woman opens a door and he shouts at her to get out. At that moment in the film, we viewers don't yet know that this is a flash-forward, so we can't understand who he is or what this moment means. This association between the dragon and the man who frightens her isn't in the original story, but it stays true to the spirit of a narrative built around the protagonist's thoughts, memories and sensations.*

That's a good example of what I've always tried to do in my literary adaptations. People often ask me whether it's easier to write an original screenplay or to adapt an existing work. I would say that when starting out, adaptation takes longer. The story already exists, so it's not easy to make it your own. It always takes more time than developing a story you've invented yourself. For an adaptation, I first read the text multiple times, highlighting passages in different colours. Each important character has their own colour. Then, slowly, I restructure the original material in a cinematic way. I don't want to reproduce 100 percent of the text's structure because film is a different medium. In *Drei Wege zum See*, I came up with flash-forwards to create tension and engage the viewer in an interiorised narrative.

Even bolder is the moment later in the film when Elisabeth, on her way to the lake, suddenly has to stop because—due to construction below—the path leads to a sheer drop. You then cut directly to her memory of Trotta's suicide. Your cinematic approach is much more abrupt than Bachmann's literary style, which is more fluid.

That makes sense, because in just one sentence you can bring together multiple characters and jump across different time frames, whereas in a film scene, all you have are contrasts or juxtapositions. The end result feels much more abrupt than it would in a book. But that can actually work in your favour, as it helps keep the viewer on their toes.

It's also very close to the brain's own associative process, which is instantaneous, and abrupt in the same way. When you were working like that, did you think that emotion could come from telling the story this way?

I admired this short story so much that I felt the need to proceed in this manner. It seemed to me the most appropriate way to respect the interiority of the text. I didn't know if it would actually work during filming, but after producing the disaster that was *Sperrmüll*, I couldn't afford another failure, so I imposed formal safeguards on myself through this mental montage.

Were you interested in this mental structuring beyond its application to Ingeborg Bachmann's story?

Yes, because it is something intrinsic to cinematic language. It came very naturally, not because I was searching for an original structure at all costs. I simply thought that I needed to find a form capable of telling this rather complex story. And once I found it, many possibilities opened up to me.

Did you map out clearly defined timelines in your script?

I always create diagrams when writing and dedicate a separate timeline to each character. When I have five timelines in front of me, I can see if the timing for any given scene is too long or too short. At the beginning, I always work with multiple structures. For each scene, I use small cards that I move around on a large board before transferring everything to a computer. At first, it's not always clear how it will work, but by shifting the structure—even if just in diagrams—you always learn something new. That's what I try to teach my students, who tend to rush because they're impatient. Personally, I go through several trials before everything fits together. Of course, sometimes a structure presents itself immediately, but such gifts are rare. There's a Jewish joke I love: Moshe goes to the rabbi and complains that he never wins the lottery, while all his friends do. The rabbi replies, "But you have to give God a chance... To win, you have to buy a ticket!" That's what I always tell my students. You have to give inspiration a chance. But luck only comes if you work hard on your subject. If you examine it from every possible angle, you will eventually find something. If you just sit around waiting for inspiration, you might be waiting a long time!

You prepare extensively, but do you often find yourself having to change things during the shoot?

It rarely happens, and when it does I feel miserable. Generally, when you're forced to make last-minute changes, you don't have the entire film in your head, and that's when mistakes happen, unless the change comes from an actor's suggestion. That can enrich the film, and I make a point of considering it, but it happens only two or three times over the course of an entire shoot. Most of the time I change almost nothing. I think that if you make films where the form is dictated by the content, improvisation is difficult.

You filmed Drei Wege zum See *in different locations: a small town, the countryside and Paris. Were all your transitions planned?*

Yes, of course. Even if I were making a film set in a single room, I would make sure to plan everything. It gives me security, and makes it much easier to judge whether an actor's suggestion, for example, is a good one or not. After that, it also depends on the style of the film. If I were making a documentary, I would need to react to situations and the people being filmed. But that's not my strength, and for that reason, I've never made a documentary.

Ursula Schult in *Drei Wege zum See*.

The third aspect that struck us in this film is the exceptional perfor-
mance of Ursula Schult. Was she well known?

She was a star of the Josefstadt Theatre in Vienna, and I chose
her because she physically matched the character of Elisabeth
perfectly. My father, who had acted with her years before, warned
me that she was very difficult, and she was, indeed, very difficult…
She wasn't used to performing in front of a camera and we didn't
get along. During editing, I was still very critical of her because of
the challenges we faced on set, but in hindsight, I recognise that she
was good. Even so, I still find Guido Wieland, who plays the father,
more moving. He has since passed away, but he was an extraordinary actor, who also worked at the Josefstadt. I was also pleased to
work with Yves Beneyton, who I discovered through my colleague
Peter Patzak. Patzak had cast him in the lead role of a crime film he
had just shot for television, *Zerschossene Träume*, and he recommended Wieland. I watched a clip and was impressed. I later loved
him in *The Lacemaker*. I haven't seen him since, which is curious,
because he was a good-looking man and a very interesting actor.

In the airport scene where Elisabeth meets Trotta's cousin, played
by Bernhard Wicki, she makes a very beautiful gesture after he

Bernhard Wicki in *Drei Wege zum See*.

leaves: she picks up the ashes from a cigarette and places them in the ashtray. Was this small gesture something Ursula Schult came up with?

No. Things like that are always directed.

It's a beautiful idea that accurately reflects her state of mind at that moment.

I do occasionally have good ideas. You always have to look for external signs to express internal emotions.

Why did you choose Wicki for the role of the cousin?

He was better known as a director than as an actor. As a filmmaker, he had a terrible reputation; some even called him sadistic. When he arrived at the airport in Vienna, the producer, who was also the head of SWF's film production department, Rolf von Sydow, personally came to greet him. He was afraid that Wicki, seeing how young I was, might try to streamroll me, but everything went smoothly. The same thing happened when I cast him in *Lemminge* and everyone came to welcome him in Vienna. But what followed was funny. His first task was to have a mould made of his face for the death mask we needed for the second part of the film. I was busy shooting when my production manager suddenly rushed onto the set in a complete panic. He explained that they had hired a specialist, someone who had worked on death masks for famous personalities, but the special liquid he had developed adhered so well to Wicki's beard that, once it hardened, they couldn't remove the mask. Wicki started suffocating, and they had to put him in a bathtub, peeling off the mask piece by piece with a suction pump. Wicki was furious, but by ten o'clock that evening he came out of his hotel room, his face still a bit swollen, and invited us all to dinner. After that, there were no more problems. As a director, he may have been difficult, but as an actor, he was wonderful. To answer your question, Wicki wasn't a great actor, but he had a strong presence, which made it immediately clear that his character was important. I always say that even for the smallest role, you need the best actor you can get, which isn't always easy.

Like the role of Trotta, for example.

Walter Schmidinger, who played him, was a great theatre actor, at the time, my favourite among German-speaking performers. As soon as I decided to make this film, I knew I wanted him for Trotta.

What about Udo Vioff, who played Manes?

He was a rather handsome actor, well known in Germany, who mainly worked in television. His role was quite thankless, but working with him was a pleasure.

At that time, did you personally choose the extras, like the black man in the bathroom scene?

Yes. I remember the casting session in London. The team there knew we needed a black extra who would appear nude on screen, and we selected one of the candidates. I don't recall if there were rehearsals, but it wasn't a complicated role. I had already spotted that very white bathroom in a hotel, and it was that whiteness that gave me the idea to cast a black man for the contrast.

For the music, you used Mozart and Schoenberg in very different ways.

Mozart was used for moments of harmony in the father-daughter relationship, like the scene at the lake, whereas Schoenberg's *Verklärte Nacht* [*Transfigured Night*] corresponds to Elisabeth's more painful inner life. There's also a piece by Purcell in the scene just before the one with the black man in the bathroom, an excerpt from *Hark! The Echoing Air*, sung by Kathleen Ferrier, which I chose both for its lyrics and because it was a well-known English piece that fit well with a trip to Britain.

We feel that this is the film where you express the most of that Austrian melancholy.

Perhaps, but that wasn't intentional. Everything Austrian in the film comes from the short story. There's a melancholy that Ingeborg Bachmann conveys with such rare elegance and beauty in the German of that time, and then there are all her many references to Austrian literature, which she weaves into all her books. The character of Trotta, for example, is a nod to von Trotta from Joseph Roth's *The Emperor's Tomb*. I was never trying to make a statement about Austria; I was simply adapting the text based on what I felt. If, like Bachmann, I include references to Austrian culture, it's not to convey a message but simply because I grew up in that country and have been immersed in it my whole life. For instance, I see the father's character as a representative of the old Austrian regime.

When he says that everything ended in 1914 and that the Nazis were merely a consequence, he anticipates The White Ribbon.

Absolutely, yes. That was in the short story already, but I share that perspective. The fact that I revisited it in *The White Ribbon* is no surprise. As I like to say: it's always the same mind making the films.

Several other ideas reappear in your later films, such as the notion of impossible happiness.

Put that way, it seems exaggerated, but it's connected to melancholy. I don't really believe in happiness, though that doesn't mean there aren't moments of happiness. For me, happiness is something that belongs to a moment. If I fall in love with someone, for example, I'll be on cloud nine for a while, but it won't last. It's not a lasting state, just something you experience briefly. This idea recurs in several of my films. They depict a series of moments of

Guido Wieland and Ursula Schult in *Drei Wege zum See.*

happiness, but nothing like the naïve optimism of the vast majority of films, which try to sell us the idea that everything will work out. That has nothing to do with reality. Reality is complex, contradictory and not necessarily pleasant. If you're asking whether that makes me pessimistic, my answer is: I'm a realist.

The film isn't pessimistic, and neither is the short story—

They're sad.

…but they invite us to consider the possibility of being less unhappy by opening up more to others. Trotta tells Elisabeth: "I never knew what life meant. I'm not really alive at all. Life is what I seek in you."

That's Bachmann's beautiful text. Many Austrian intellectuals can identify with Trotta and his morbidity. Joseph Roth embodied this attitude throughout his deeply unhappy life. It's a mentality that's both Czech and Slavic, the deep exhaustion from the weight of a once-great empire.

The only glimmer of hope in the film comes from an idea suggested in the voiceover: "At the very least, we could be kind to one another, even just for a moment."

I don't remember that exact line, but it could be mine. I've addressed that idea in several films. It's both true and beautiful.

A moment ago, you said happiness isn't possible, but listening to Ingeborg Bachmann, kindness could be a way to improve human relationships because it's simpler.

It's not that simple, but it is accessible to everyone. It's a matter of will. If we were all kind to one another, the world would be a very different place. And yet, it's always up to me to decide whether to be good or bad toward someone. If the other person is an idiot, that doesn't mean I have to be one too.

In the film, communication is an extremely difficult challenge for Elisabeth. When she's swimming in the lake, she suddenly says to her father, "Papa, I love you." But he doesn't hear her. She has the chance to repeat it, but she doesn't. This situation appears again in Lemminge. *Every time, there's a blockage, we're afraid to be kind.*

Exactly. For example, I adored the aunt who raised me, but I was never able to tell her, "I love you." It's very difficult with parents. With a woman, it's different, though still difficult, but with parents, you go through so many mundane daily routines together. Even people with very strong relationships can only express their affection through small gestures. In theatre and cinema, this restraint is an asset because it forces you to be creative in expressing emotions indirectly.

In Drei Wege zum See, *Trotta criticises Elisabeth for photographing suffering, just as the photojournalist in* Code Unknown *is later criticised. Since this idea was in Bachmann's short story, we wondered if reading her had inspired this critical stance in your films.*

I don't know. The things we invent, the things that haunt us, we never really know where they come from.

Why is the story set in Klagenfurt?

That's Carinthia, where Ingeborg Bachmann was born. I wanted to film in the real locations and landscapes she described and stay as close to reality as possible, but we couldn't shoot in her actual house. She had already passed away when we started filming, and her sister, after reading the script, found it "pornographic" and refused to let us film there, so we had to use another house in the same neighbourhood. This sister behaved like Nietzsche's sister or certain writers' widows, but when she saw the film she thought it was wonderful and wrote me a letter saying she regretted her refusal.

How was the film received when it aired?

The reviews were quite good, but it's always difficult to know how television audiences respond to a film.

Four

Lemminge: my first personal film — Arcadia, my youth, and Julien Duvivier — A blend of characters I knew well — Suicidal little rodents — I enjoy using suspense — Indifference and glaciation — A youthful flaw — Bad publicity for the Church — Memories of my blonde schoolteacher

Lemminge (1979)
Part One: Arkadien (Arcadia)

The chronicle of a group of young people in the small town of Wiener Neustadt, Austria, in the autumn of 1959, begins with anonymous acts of vandalism against parked cars. The young Eva Wasner is dating Christian Beranek, who she met at her dance class. Fritz Naprawnik, meanwhile, is having an affair with Gisela Schäfer, the wife of his private Latin tutor. When the affair is exposed, a scandal erupts at school, affecting the families involved, especially when Gisela confesses to her husband that she is pregnant by her young lover. In desperation, she violently harms herself to terminate the pregnancy. Eva also becomes pregnant, which is catastrophic since, at the time, single mothers were harshly judged and abortion was illegal. She is forced to leave school. Eventually, it is discovered that the vandals were Sigurd Leuwen and his sister Sigrid, the children of wealthy parents who had been severely wounded during the war while trying to protect their offspring. Once unmasked, Sigurd throws himself to his death in front of his sister. When confronted by their father, who calls them "lemmings," Sigrid can only explain their actions as deriving from the thrill of destruction. Fritz leaves Gisela for Bettina, a girl his age. Eva attempts suicide. Christian does not intervene. She survives. He then decides to marry her, and they commit to passing their exams by studying on their own. Christian shares this with Sigrid on the train taking her to Vienna. He is tempted to follow her but ultimately returns to Wiener Neustadt to face his fate.

Part Two: Verletzungen (Wounds)

A car crashes into a tree. An ambulance arrives, but the passengers are indistinct. At home, Eva wakes up. Her husband Christian, now an army officer, complains of stomach pain. Their son has had another nightmare. Eva, now a housewife, takes up horseback riding as a hobby. She also has a lover who informs her that he is soon leaving for Norway. Sigrid has returned to town following her father's death. She refuses to see his body at the hospital where Fritz now works. The priest in attendance accidentally breaks the deceased's death mask. Sigrid weeps. She invites her old friends—Fritz and Bettina, Christian and Eva—to a dinner at her family's grand house. The evening turns into a bitter reckoning, with Bettina lashing out. When Eva's lover leaves her, she sinks into depression. A visit to the hospital prompts her to suggest an affair with Fritz, who accepts. When Christian discovers her infidelity, he confronts her. Meanwhile, Sigrid is pregnant. Observing the hatred and anger around her, she wonders how she can raise a child in such an environment. She turns to the priest for guidance, but he has no answers, only piles of empty wine bottles cluttering his small apartment. Christian reveals to Eva that he has a terminal illness and blackmails her into taking a two-week trip with him, without their children, to "reconnect." Fritz seems indifferent to their affair, so Eva agrees. Christian drives their car into a tree (this is the scene from the beginning). Eva dies. He survives but is injured. As Sigrid gives birth, she screams in agony. Recovering, his arm in a sling, Christian watches a group of young army recruits. Their behaviour irritates him. He berates them, forcing them into line, while questioning what still matters in life.

With Lemminge, *you moved away from adaptations and wrote an original story. Did you face challenges getting the film produced for television?*

Yes, *Lemminge* is indeed my first personal film. After the success of *Drei Wege zum See*, its producers expressed interest in working with me again. I always tell my students that when you're young, you should focus on stories drawn from personal experience, and I suggested a portrait of my generation. At first, I only planned a single feature film, what is now Part One, subtitled *Arkadien*, but then I was summoned by the director of ORF, who had admired my adaptation of Bachmann, and who told me that if I truly wanted to portray my generation, I had to go bigger, and proposed a three-part story. I immediately agreed, but as I left his office—where I thought I was going for a quick meet-and-greet—I suddenly found myself responsible for two additional feature-length films, with no idea what to include in them. During the meeting, I had thought of structuring the first part around the characters' youth and the second around their adult lives. I initially thought about setting the third part in the future, but that concept never really clicked into focus, so I started by writing the first two parts before tackling the third. After thinking about it for a long time, I ended up dropping it because nothing I came up with felt convincing.

The first part, Arkadien, *is a time of great hope before moments of harsh disillusionment.*

It is, of course, a highly ironic title, and I can tell you how it came about. When I was younger, I was deeply moved by Julien Duvivier's romantic film *Marianne of My Youth*. Wanting to trace its origins, I went to the Vienna library, where I found the book by Peter de Mendelssohn on which it was based. Mendelssohn, who also wrote a biography of Thomas Mann, was a German Jewish writer who emigrated to England in 1936 and wrote in both German and English. The book—which I, in fact, stole—contained both his novella *Schmerzliches Arkadien* [*Painful Arcadia*], which inspired the film, and a piece about the making of Duvivier's film. That's where I learned that the filmmaker had originally wanted to adapt *Le Grand Meaulnes* by Alain-Fournier—a book I adored in my childhood, as I've already mentioned—but the writer's sister, Isabelle Rivière, refused to grant him the rights. Duvivier then searched for a subject that would allow him to tell *Le Grand Meaulnes* without relying on Alain-Fournier's novel. That's how he came across this

Haneke directing *Lemminge.*

novella, which Peter de Mendelssohn had written at a very young age. I still had its title in mind when I began *Lemminge*, and that's why I named the first part after a story that no one knows. I recently rewatched *Marianne of My Youth* on television and was very disappointed. Duvivier made some truly great films, but that one is just plain kitsch.

How did you structure your screenplay around five young people who are meant to represent a microcosm of your generation?

I portrayed people I knew, though naturally with some modifications. The story of the high school student having an affair with his teacher's wife, for example, was something I knew about. I think it's the only one of my films that is so deeply autobiographical, though parts of *Variation* are also very personal.

The story of Sigurd and Sigrid, the brother and sister with physically disabled parents, who are strongly drawn to each other and turn to vandalism—was that based on real events as well?

It's a composite; not everything happened within the same family. The bedridden mother, for example, was loosely inspired by my own. After two fainting spells on stage, she could no longer act and had to retire in her early forties. She was always in bed, in the dark, lost in cigarette smoke. The authoritarian father played by Bernhard Wicki, however, is definitely not based on my own father. As you know, I grew up without a father figure; my uncle never took an active role in my upbringing. But you can imagine that I didn't have to look far to find an example of such a father. As for the relationship between the brother and sister, that's one of the few elements that is entirely fictional.

Why did you name them Sigurd and Sigrid, two similar names that earn them the same nickname, Siggi?

Those names were very popular during the Nazi era because they referred to Germanic mythology, like Siegfried.

And their relationship with their parents, who were left disabled after throwing themselves over their children to shield them from a bombing?

That story of disability was something I heard about. As for their relationship with their parents, it reflects a dynamic typical of children of that generation, who had to grow up under the shadow of parents who returned from the war—guilty or not.

That's a theme that recurs in several of your films, such as Caché, *where children feel guilty about the actions of their parents.*

They aren't guilty, but they are still the heirs of their parents' actions. There's a phrase that sums it up well: the sins of the parents are the neuroses of the children.

The first part of Lemminge *has something of the tone of your previous film. The young romantic couple, Eva and Christian, is particularly touching. She wants to lose her virginity but hesitates. Then, after it happens, she wants to kill herself but fails. It's at the same time beautiful, simple, and foolish.*

But that's who we were… There wasn't much to invent for this film. Anyone who lived through those years had stories like this in some form. There's nothing in the script that's particularly out of the ordinary, and if the film has any significance, it's in the way these characters are brought together to create a portrait of the unease of that time, especially since everything was shaped by me, whereas in my adaptation of Bachmann, I was simply following the course of her narrative.

The great originality and boldness of Lemminge *lies in the decision to revisit all the characters twenty years later, using different actors, which is unsettling for the audience.*

At first, it's a bit confusing, as with any film where you're suddenly thrown twenty years into the future. The only way to avoid that is by casting actors who have children who resemble them and can act. We did our best here by choosing performers whose physical appearance closely matched the earlier cast, but even so, it takes a little while for audiences to figure out who's who.

Did you shoot both parts consecutively?

Yes.

And was the television broadcast structured the same way?

It aired over two days. Before the second part started, there was a short recap of the first to help viewers get their bearings.

The overall impression Lemminge *leaves is of a generation that wanted to live differently and therefore rebelled, but too timidly, leading to failure twenty years later. Hence the title of the second part,* Verletzungen.

Already in the first part, Sigurd commits suicide and Eva tries to as well, though she doesn't succeed. The film's title refers to lemmings, those little rodents known for their collective suicides, and, by metaphor, to young Austrians, who, according to statistics at the time, had a particularly high suicide rate. But the meaning of my title has faded over time, since other films have used lemmings as a reference without any connection to the idea of collective suicide.

You incorporated those youth suicide statistics into the priest's dialogue at the end of the second part. He's quite an unconventional clergyman, given that he's an alcoholic.

The character was inspired by a monk I knew, who taught religion. He was very kind, offering free Latin lessons to everyone, even Protestants like me. You could visit him at home, and just like in the film, he had one room filled with full bottles and another with empty ones! He was also quite funny, always referring to himself in the third person. After every lesson, he would "sample" a new

Walter Schmidinger, Elisabeth Orth and Christian Spatzek in *Lemminge*.

bottle, which he would inevitably finish. We all liked him a lot. He made such an impression on me that I worked him into the film, though I did tweak the character a bit, of course.

One of the film's most striking moments is the final scene with Sigrid, who is about to give birth to the child she wanted, yet can't imagine raising it in a world filled with hatred. She is shown alone in the delivery room, suffering intensely. Why such a harsh ending?

That birth doesn't offer a happy ending. At the time, I felt we were living in a world where bringing children into it was almost unjustifiable.

But that scene doesn't conclude the film. You end with Christian, who, at the end of the first part, had taken responsibility for his actions and fatherhood. Twenty years later, as a military officer and betrayed husband, he has sought revenge by crashing his car into a tree, killing his wife in the process. We then find him with his arm in a sling, furiously berating young soldiers who don't recognise him.

First, let me share a funny anecdote. For that final scene, we wanted to shoot at a military base, but the Austrian Ministry of Defense asked to read the script and denied us permission. Their reasoning? An Austrian officer could not possibly be cheated on by his wife, nor would he ever react as Christian does. According to them, the film was an attack on the Austrian military. That said, my ending is certainly too heavy-handed. The point had already been made earlier, and today I wouldn't shoot it that way. Better to avoid being too on-the nose. However, I do still feel connected to the first part of the story, where things are presented more indirectly. I was telling stories in a way that allowed each viewer to take what they wanted from them. The second part suffers from my youthful determination to hammer home what I wanted to say at the time. That's a common flaw when you're young. You're so certain of your assertions that you lose all sense of restraint. Still, the film's message about a generation's downfall and the loss of values was clearly heard. When *Lemminge* first aired in 1979, some critics were outraged, accusing me of ignoring 1968. But I had deliberately left out the protest movements because, ten years later, in Austria, people were still searching for their lasting impact.

In this final scene, Christian appears to have become the very image of his parents, echoing the Andy Warhol quote from your first television film, Und was kommt danach?, *which suggested that generations and problems repeat themselves, only the clothes change.*

But isn't that exactly what happens?

Visually, there were several things that must have seemed daring for the time: the depiction of sexual intercourse and full-frontal nudity, for example.

And the abortion scene, a taboo subject on television, which wasn't easy for the actress, Elisabeth Orth, to perform. She had a great reputation at the Burgtheatre and was the daughter of the renowned actress Paula Wessely. With Attila Hörbiger, Paula Wessely formed *the* quintessential acting couple in Vienna. She had acted in Nazi-era films, which she later apologised for. It's a rather complicated story. In any case, after our film, Elisabeth Orth received a flood of letters from people reproaching her—as Paula Wessely's daughter—for playing that scene and appearing completely nude. It was a real scandal.

Did the producers react when they read the script?

No, there was no censorship. I should say that I never had any problems like that when I worked in television. For this film, there was only one thing imposed on me. At the end, when Christian laments the loss of values and adds, "Austria is dead!" I was told that such a statement couldn't be made on Austrian television, so I had to add the sound of a passing airplane at that moment to make the phrase inaudible, a bit like Buñuel did in *The Discreet Charm of the Bourgeoisie.*

We assumed that the airplane noise was intentional, a harsh sound that brought an extra layer of despair and added weight to the ending,

You're not wrong. Actually, from the outset, I planned to use that airplane noise, but in the end, I moved it to cover the actor's voice. The producers wanted me to dub the actor saying something else, but I preferred to keep the original line and drown it out with the sound of the airplane.

Even at that time, your films showed strong thematic consistency. The motif of nostalgia, very present in Drei Wege zum See, *is powerfully echoed here. Fritz directly expresses it when he says, "The only things one can truly feel are sadness or maybe nostalgia."*

Yes, in German, one would say *Sehnsucht*. Like *Heimat, Sehnsucht* is a typically German word, with no exact equivalent in French or English.

Your characters in Lemminge *are constantly contradicting themselves. For example, Eva, the romantic teenager in the first part, has to get married because she's pregnant, and in the second part, disappointed by her husband, she takes one lover after another.*

I know a lot of people like that. At least Eva is a positive character who keeps trying to form real relationships even after every failure. It's more the men in the second part who are negative. The husband, Christian, is certainly in pain, but his suffering drives him to hurt others. It's like the doctor in *The White Ribbon*. When he says horrible things to the midwife, she replies that he must be suffering a lot to be so cruel. I believe it's always like that: people become cruel when they're in too much pain, and once that cycle starts, nothing can really stop it.

The two parts of Lemminge *are structured according to the same principle. They open with a shocking scene — cars being vandalised, another crashing into a tree — the meaning of which will only become clear at the end of the film.*

It's a way of creating tension, like in *71 Fragments of a Chronology of Chance*, which opens with a text about a massacre we don't understand until we've seen the entire film.

But unlike 71 Fragments, *where the identity of the future criminal quickly becomes apparent,* Lemminge *maintains the suspense. It's almost like a whodunnit.*

I enjoying using suspense to keep viewers glued to their seats. There's nothing better to keep their attention.

When you wrote the two parts of the script, did you deliberately create parallels between them in the structure?

Not really, because the structure of the second part is much simpler than the first. There are fewer characters, and it becomes clear pretty quickly how they're going to develop. That said, starting both parts with a scene involving the destruction of cars was definitely a deliberate choice.

Some character traits remain consistent across both parts. For example, before making love for the first time, Eva asks for a cognac, and later, in the second part, when she visits her second lover, she asks for one again.

Yes, I always find it fun to include such callbacks. It also helps the audience track the character's evolution from one part to the next.

Do you create character profiles before writing?

Yes. As soon as I have my characters, I create a profile for each, gathering everything that might be useful for their future behaviour. In the first part of *Lemminge*, for example, is Fritz, a working-class boy who later reappears in the second part as a doctor whom Eva asks to become her lover. He was inspired by a friend who was exactly like the character, and I made a very precise profile of his development. But it's not always that simple. Often, at the start, I don't even know how many characters I'll need, and very often, a single idea or situation could apply to three or four characters.

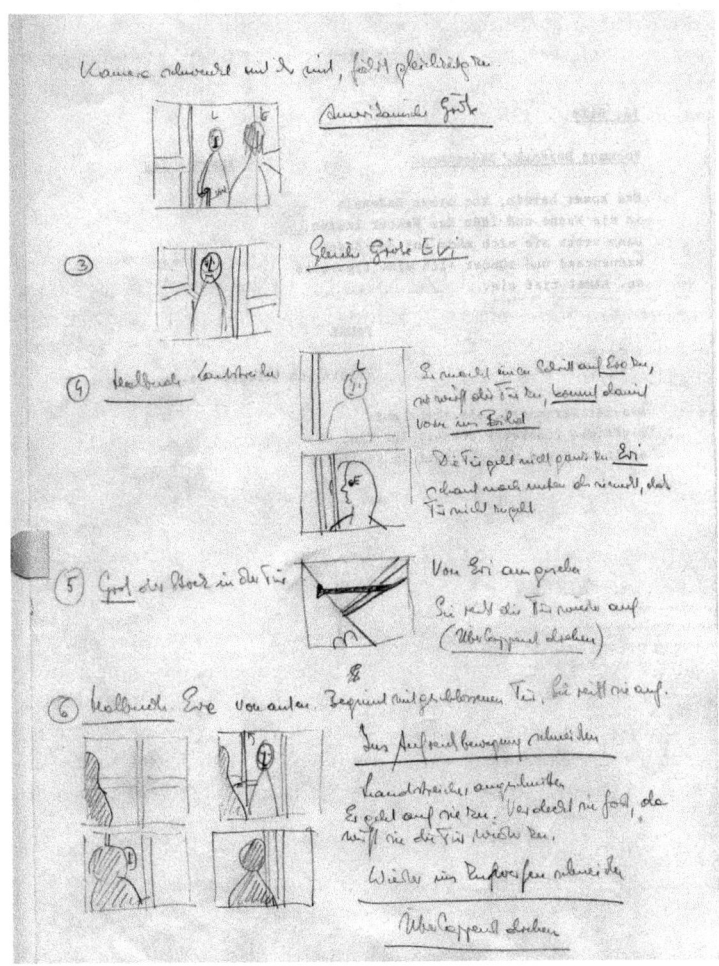

Storyboards for *Lemminge.*

Then I have to decide who will do what. These are the pleasures—
and challenges—of writing.

Did you do any research for the characters in Lemminge?

No, I only had to sift through my memories. The only thing I
actually did was visit my former schoolmates to ask if they had
kept any of the clothes we used to wear at the time: jeans, a white
shirt, a black sweater that was always thrown over the shoulder

and tied around the neck. It was important for me to get hold of a few of those sweaters because they weren't being made anymore when we shot the film. Besides that, we were lucky to be able to shoot in the actual locations where the events took place.

In general, do your characters pre-exist before you structure the drama?

No, both aspects have to be worked on simultaneously. As I always tell my students, the hardest part is the structure because that's where you decide who stands for what. If you make the right choices at that stage, writing becomes easy, because then it's the character who speaks and acts, and you really come to know that character. But if you haven't prepared properly, you don't know them well enough, and once you start writing, it can quickly turn into a struggle. That said, it's not always easy to know for sure that you've got the structure right before diving into the actual writing.

When do you write the dialogue? As you go along with the scenes or after you've established the entire structure?

I don't start writing dialogue until the overall structure is set. Of course, sometimes I hit a block and have to change something in a scene, which can have consequences for the ones that follow. When that happens, I go back and make all the necessary adjustments before diving back into the dialogue. That's just part of the process. I don't think you can write a screenplay or a play the same way you write a novel because you have to keep the viewer from getting bored. In a book, you can get away with a few slow patches. In a film, the audience drifts off immediately, and once you've lost them, it's very hard to win them back.

Take Sigurd and Sigrid. Do you remember how you imagined these two characters? Did you conceive of them first and their parents afterward?

These two characters are actually a reference to a novella by Thomas Mann, *Wälsungenblut* [*Blood of the Welsungs*], the story of an incestuous brother and sister, Siegmund and Sieglinde, who themselves refer to Wagner's *Die Walküre*. I started with these characters to construct the two Siggi in my film: their ambiguous relationship, their noble family with a German name in Austria, their beautiful home, which is nonetheless filled with deep sadness

- 17 -

Bild 13

Wohnung Beranek. Vorzimmer.   Innen - Tag

Anschluß.
Eva geht, indem sie den Morgenmantel
ordnet und die Tür zum Wohnzimmer
schließt, sodaß die Stimme der Gymnastik-
tante ausgesperrt ist, zur Wohnungstür und
öffnet.
Draußen steht ein vollkommen zerstört und
verkommen aussehender Mann. Mit der linken
Hand stützt er sich auf einen Stock. Als er
Eva sieht, grinst er zahnlos und schmierig.

                              Der Landstreicher:
                              Grüß Gott, gnä Frau. Hättens net was
                              für mi ?

Eva ist erschrocken und verstört.
Sie stottert:

                              Eva:
                              Ja..was..was wollens denn ?

Er grinst, streckt die Hand aus
und macht einen Schritt auf Eva zu, die
erschrocken zurückweicht und ihm die
Tür vor der Nase zuzuwerfen versucht.
Aber da ist der Stock des Mannes in
der Tür. Eva reißt die Tür nochmals
auf, faucht ihn wütend an:

                              Gehn sie weg !

Er grinst, kommt noch näher

                              Der Landstreicher:
                              Aber, gnä Frau..

From the script of *Lemminge*.

since the mother is paralysed, though the cause of her condition is
unknown. The children are left to themselves, which brings them
closer and closer together. Are they in an incestuous relationship?
Even though their emotional closeness is greater than usual for a
brother and sister, the question remains open. One of my favourite scenes in the film is with these two characters. When Sigurd
returns and Sigrid stops playing a piece by Schubert on the piano,

something powerful happens between them. In fact, when we shot that moment, by the end of the take everybody was absolutely still. We were all clearly very moved.

Did Eva Linder, who plays Sigrid, know how to play the piano?

No, she had to learn.

And Paulus Manker, who plays her brother?

He also had to learn. He spent three months studying the cello with a musician from the Vienna Philharmonic Orchestra. It's even harder to fake playing that instrument than the piano. They both worked extremely hard because if they wanted the roles, they had to be able to play.

You took a risk in casting actors who didn't know how to play an instrument.

Yes, which is why I insisted from the very beginning: "You absolutely must learn!" I can be very persuasive.

In the second part, there's a striking sequence with a homeless man who seems to want to enter Eva's home while she's alone. He puts his foot in the doorway to stop it from closing, but she manages to push him out.

He represents poverty, the Third World, everything we fear and can only get rid of by destroying "the other." We would rather break his foot or hand than let him in.

There's also that scene where Eva sees two children fighting near a church, then a dead cat on the sidewalk that no one pays attention to until a bucket falls from a construction site above.

Yes, but that really was a bit too much. I wanted to create a sense of *Entfremdung*, a feeling of alienation and fear, the idea that we're just small, insignificant things. It's like that scene in Bresson's *The Devil, Probably* where a boy gets on a bus and the doors won't close. No one knows what to do, and then someone says, "It's the devil, probably." That scene is much better than mine. If I had seen that film before making mine, I would never have shot my scene that way, but I had to create an atmosphere that explains why this woman is so broken by the end. It's also a question of perception.

Eva Linder and Paulus Manker in *Lemminge*.

There are moments in life when we are oblivious to everything, and others when we notice such things, when they hit us out of nowhere and it becomes almost unbearable.

In fact, the second part opens with this theme of indifference. Sigrid feels nothing in front of her dead father, but she breaks down in tears when his death mask is accidentally shattered by the priest. It makes us wonder if the world has lost its humanity.

Has the world ever been humane?

With progress and the evolution of the modern world, one might hope for a better life, but you show the contrary.

Yes. And on top of that, all the characters in both parts of *Lemminge* are privileged people who have no financial problems.

Privileged individuals who fall victim to what you later called "emotional glaciation."

I greatly regret coining that expression. It haunts me everywhere I go.

Monica Bleibtreu and Wolfgang Hübsch in *Lemminge.*

*You're wrong to regret it, because it perfectly encapsulates an atti-
tude that is self-evident today.*

I was asked so much about this topic at the time of the trilogy
[*The Seventh Continent, Benny's Video* and *71 Fragments of a
Chronology of Chance*] that I needed a term to sum it all up, a
kind of keyword. But that's dangerous: a keyword simplifies the
complexity of the idea it expresses. It's like putting a label on something; it inevitably reduces it. As soon as you name something, you
strip it of its complexity. That's what makes me unhappy. Every
time I have to talk about my films, whatever I say limits their scope.
So yes, *Lemminge* is a film about emotional glaciation, but not only
that. If you reduce it to that single interpretation, you create a false
hierarchy. Glaciation becomes the central theme at the expense of
everything else. The same goes for violence. Contrary to what is
often claimed, I don't address violence in itself but rather its representation and how the media exploits it. But that's less problematic
because it's a subject, not an attempt to summarise feelings, which
can't be reduced to a single word.

That said, looking back at your work, it's undeniable that
Lemminge *marks the genesis of your major cinematic films.*

Yes, I believe so too.

*So regardless of whether you like the term "emotional glaciation,"
indifference—the first step toward that glaciation—is central to*
Lemminge. *Similarly, in your earliest television films violence often
begins with something as simple and direct as a slap. Up through*
Amour, *there are reportedly twenty of them.*

Really? You sound like my wife... One day, she pointed out that
several of my characters urinate on themselves and told me I
needed to stop. As for the slaps, that doesn't surprise me. A slap
is a simple way to create the impression of humiliation. More than
physical violence itself, what matters is the meaning of the act. In
Lemminge, Georg, the Latin teacher, slaps his wife Gisela when he
learns that she is pregnant by her student, Fritz. Fritz, in turn, is
slapped by his mother when she finds out about the situation.

*So violence begins naturally within the family, with a slap, before
escalating on a broader social level.*

Someone once asked me for a single word to sum up all my work,
which was a ridiculous request, but I played along and answered:
"Civil war." Because that's exactly what it is. Not in a political
sense, of course, but in the everyday sense, the war we wage against
each other all the time.

With Lemminge, *it seems that, philosophically, you were already
denouncing the failure of Christianity, something you would continue to do, always symbolically.*

I honestly never thought about that.

*Not in a religious sense, but strictly on a human level. Christianity,
at its origin, was a beautiful call for tolerance.*

In that case, one could just as well say it's the failure of human
culture, not just Christianity. Let's not use the word "glaciation"
again. "Coldness" is a sign that all these values we constantly talk
about no longer really work. They still have their place now and
then, but they function less and less in our society. At least, that's
how it seems to me. The end of the second part—the scene with
the alcoholic priest—is a key one for me, philosophically. He says
that the Middle Ages are over but that no one has absolved us of
our guilt, so we will now have to live with it, which will be diffi-

cult. The fact that a priest says this gives the statement even more weight. A terrible advertisement for the Church! But if you read the writings of all the French Catholic existentialists, you'll find that we're more or less in the same realm. Religion today has been reduced to a mystical dimension but no longer functions as a social system.

Which is why Fritz, the former lover of Gisela—now a deeply lonely doctor—has a Francis Bacon painting in his home: Study after Velázquez's Portrait of Pope Innocent X. *Eva, equally lost, comes to visit him there.*

Yes, but that's an exaggeration. How could an ordinary doctor afford such a painting?

We assumed it was a reproduction.

Perhaps. But today, I would avoid doing that.

Why that particular painting, which depicts a screaming clergyman?

For me, Bacon's painting *is* the embodiment of the situation. It's a figure that screams, but no one hears. In fact, this symbolism applies to nearly all the characters. But I'll say it again: showing it in the film was *artistically wrong*, because it's too explicit.

The two parts of Lemminge *feel very different. The first presents a series of events, the second is more symbolic, with few major incidents, aside from Christian's car crash.*

The first part is more elegant, more successful. For the second, I was a bit overwhelmed by the challenge of representing, in artistic terms, such an elevated level of discussion between the characters.

Earlier, you mentioned that in the second part, the male characters aren't very admirable, but in the dining scenes, for example, your framing of solitary women and the way their loneliness is emphasised through the editing is very striking. Here, the mise-en-scène itself conveys the message.

That happens instinctively. I know that the way I film will guide the audience toward feeling sympathy or antipathy for a character. Every shot carries a judgment in its composition. But it's not always a rational process. People have often told me I'm a "director of women," and I admit that I'm more interested in women than men. They interest me because they are more complex than men, and also because they are often victims. For me, victims are always more interesting than perpetrators. It's the complete opposite of American cinema, where the hero is supposed to be strong.

You also used a significant number of close-ups, which wasn't very common on television at the time.

Actually, it was quite common back then. Close-ups largely depend on the director's confidence in the actors. If you look at Bergman's *Scenes from a Marriage*, for example, it's filmed largely in close-ups because Liv Ullmann and Erland Josephson are extraordinary, and Bergman knew it. In such cases, the face says everything. Of course, there are situations where the body is more important, but for expressing emotions—everything that comes from within—the close-up is essential. That's something I've always tried to do.

Even though you say painting hasn't influenced you, with these close-ups you create true portraits of your characters, as seen head-on. This individualises them at key moments and highlights the difficulty of communication when their interlocutor is also isolated in the frame.

Traditionally, there are two ways to approach this. If I want to show that communication is working between two characters, I frame them in over-the-shoulder shot/reverse shot compositions, always with the other person's head partially visible in the frame. But if I want to show their difficulty in communicating, I isolate them in the shot/reverse shot.

Before wrapping up Lemminge, *we wanted to mention a scene that surprised us, because it appears again in* The White Ribbon. *In the second part, Fritz tells Eva how, as a child, he killed his father's bird and left its dead body in the cage to make it seem like it had died naturally.*

I had completely forgotten that this scene was already in *Lemminge*. But I have a good explanation for that: I actually first told this story in the very first short story I ever wrote, about a 10-year-old boy who adores his teacher. One day, he is standing by the classroom door when he sees her coming down the hallway. Inside, his classmates are making a ruckus, so he orders them to calm down.

Rüdiger Hacker (centre) in in *Lemminge.*

When they don't, he starts shouting at them. Just then, the teacher walks in and reprimands *him* for making so much noise. Shocked, he goes home and falls ill with a high fever. When he is nearly recovered, he goes into his father's room and kills his bird. I personally experienced something similar in school when I was wrongly accused by a teacher, a beautiful blonde woman I adored. I didn't kill a bird, but I was so upset that, when I started writing, this was the first story I wanted to tell. That's how I create. I use experiences I have lived which resurface over time.

Why did you choose to direct your son, David, in the final scene of the second part, where he plays Christian's eldest son?

I needed a boy of that age, and I thought it would be easier to use someone I knew well. That and he had a good presence. Plus, I found it amusing.

Five

Variation on a ménage à trois — Always the same first names — Art and the end of ideologies — I'm no moralist — Nudity as an expression of despair — The deaths in Venice in *Wer war Edgar Allan?* — Horses in the labyrinth — I feel no hatred toward fathers — Music hides the flaws — The ironic gaze of *Fräulein* — Münchhausen and the story of Germany — An anti-Fassbinder film — Editing tricks and the shift to colour

Variation (1982)

Georg has just seen *Stella*, Goethe's play, with his wife Eva. As they return home, they discuss the performance with Sigrid, Georg's sister, who lives with them and studies the cello. Initially, Goethe had envisioned an optimistic ending with an idealised ménage à trois between the count, the young woman he has brought back from his crusade, and his faithful wife. But thirty years later, Goethe wrote a second ending in which, overcome with despair, all three commit suicide. Georg soon becomes the lover of Anna, a journalist. He does not tell Eva, who nonetheless suspects something. Anna, in turn, lives with Kitty, an alcoholic actress who takes the affair very badly, causing frequent scenes. One night, Anna calls Georg for help. As he leaves to meet her, he wakes Sigrid and Eva. The latter warns him that if he leaves, it will be for good. Anna and Georg move in together. After several months, they agree to meet Kitty and Eva to talk about what they are all going through. The atmosphere is already tense when Eva reveals that Sigrid has attempted suicide by slitting her wrists and is still in the hospital. Georg becomes agitated. Anna cannot bear it and runs away, leaving

Georg a note explaining that she does not understand what is happening, but she is sure she loves him. The five characters are left to face themselves.

The screenplay for Variation *is very loosely inspired by Goethe's play* Stella, *which you had already staged.*

Except that I no longer remember whether I staged the play before or after the film. Probably after, since it was in Vienna. But it doesn't really matter.

How did the project come about?

While filming *Lemminge*, I felt very comfortable with the actors and wanted to make another film with them, but I had only a vague starting idea: a couple suddenly confronted with a serious problem... This is the only time, during the writing stage, that I asked actors to contribute to the plot by sending me ideas, documents, memories—that kind of thing. They responded with enthusiasm, and I incorporated everything they suggested, down to the smallest details. Initially, I cast Walter Schmidinger, who played Trotta in *Drei Wege zum See*, in the lead role, but once the character was more clearly defined, Schmidinger backed out, claiming that, as a homosexual, he could not convincingly portray a man in love with two women. I told him that I thought that was a ridiculous argument, but I ended up replacing him with Hilmar Thate, a close friend and a well-known theatre actor in East Germany. He was married to Angelica Domröse, my future lead actress in *Fräulein*, and together they were a star couple there. They were eventually allowed to move to West Germany, where both became major figures in theatre and film. Elfriede Irrall, Suzanne Geyer and Eva Linder, who had acted in *Lemminge*, were my first choices for their respective roles.

How did Goethe's text influence the final screenplay?

Stella is the quintessential German-language play about a love triangle, the utopian dream of a man living with two women. But, sadly, it just doesn't work!

Goethe wrote two endings: one utopian, where the ménage à trois is realised, and one tragic, where all three commit suicide.

Eva Linder in *Variation*.

I chose the tragic ending when I staged the play. When Goethe first wrote it, he had only considered the utopian ending, but audiences rejected it, and thirty years later, he added the tragic conclusion. In *Variation*, the characters seem to live through the first ending, but the film ultimately asserts that such a utopia really isn't possible.

Why that title?

It's ironic. This story is so commonplace, so often told, that what we're watching is merely a variation on the theme.

This is only your second original screenplay, and already you're using the same names: Georg, Anna, Eva, Sigrid.

I always reuse them. I find it tiresome to come up with new ones.

That's what you always say.

It's a common literary device. Thomas Mann, for example, uses names that tell you something about the characters, but with a realist medium like cinema, that isn't possible. Mr. Big might turn out to be short, so I went for simple, common, short names.

In Variation, *we find another Sigrid.*

It's a self-reference to *Lemminge*. She even has the same last name: Leuwen.

Do these two-syllable names have a musical quality?

You could interpret it that way, but mostly it's just my laziness in finding alternatives. Bergman also reused the same names. Since he always explored the same themes, why give the illusion of a different subject by changing names? You might as well keep them.

So you admit it's not laziness! It's perfect continuity, a genuine throughline.

If you say so.

Let's talk about a setting that plays an important role in your films: the kitchen. In Variation, *it's in the kitchen that Georg and Eva discuss* Stella, *the play they've just seen, and where Sigrid, Georg's sister, joins them. Why this attachment to this domestic setting?*

Because, as in real life, the kitchen is a busy meeting place where people talk about all sorts of things, so it makes sense that I set a lot of scenes there. Too often in films, it feels like everything happens in the bedroom or the dining room, when actually life unfolds in other places too—like the bathroom—and the kitchen.

As in Lemminge, *the credits arrive late, after a long prologue.*

I begin by introducing the source of the screenplay, *Stella*, before starting the variations on the theme of the love triangle. That's why I placed the title between the two. First the thesis, then its application.

Up until now, your films have mostly focused on adults and teenagers, but Variation *opens with the world of childhood and its almost apocalyptic relationship to the environment, shown through a display of drawings. Why the shift?*

In 1982, there seemed to be a kind of apocalyptic feeling in the air. Looking at children's drawings, I realised they had absorbed that mood, so we asked some schoolchildren to draw what fear felt like to them. The selection shown at the start of the film comes from their work.

In Caché, *too, children's drawings express fear or vengeance. What is striking in your work is that as soon as children appear, they seem associated with fear.*

A child is born with a very weak sense of security, which is severely tested as soon as their parents are absent. At such moments, the child feels powerless, everything seems dangerous. I was very fearful as a child, and I tend to think all children are like that. A child is a potential victim with no means of defence.

What's beautiful in Variation *is that some unsettling emotions are resolved with great simplicity. For example, Sigrid, feeling abandoned by her brother Georg, leaves him this note: "These furious tears that Icarus sheds upon seeing a jet plane. You know how much I love you. Your sister, Sigrid."*

That was indeed a beautiful idea, but I must admit it wasn't mine. Credit goes to the actress, Eva Linder, who fully embraced the process of contributing ideas to enrich her role. I liked her suggestion, and I kept it.

In a conversation between Anna and Georg, you allude to the creative crisis in the West. What did you mean by that in 1982?

I don't remember exactly, but just look at cinema. Today, the most vibrant films come from Asia and Africa. It's not a recent phenomenon, but the trend has only grown stronger over the years. In the United States, France, and even more so in Italy, aside from a few filmmakers, there's nothing left, whereas in the 1960s and '70s, there was an extraordinary richness.

How do you explain this decline?

It would be presumptuous of me to attempt an explanation when people much smarter than me have struggled with this question, although it's clear that the media have played a significant role in this process, particularly cinema and television, because education is transmitted through them, and young people today have no cultural foundation. They can't read complex texts and don't even want to try. Sure, it's easy to blame the media, but they foster a kind of discouragement. People convince themselves that trying to understand the world is no longer worth the effort, so they turn inward. It wasn't always that way. Back then, not every theory had been discredited, but today, we don't believe in any of them. And this whole postmodernist approach is so hollow. If people are so desperate for distraction, it's because their frustration levels are sky-high.

You already touched on this decline of culture in Christian's dialogue at the end of the second part of Lemminge, *where he claims that the modern world no longer offers new ideas to replace those once defended by 20th-century ideologies.*

If I wanted to be even a little optimistic, I would say that the only thing that remains is art. But for whom? To truly see an image, to truly hear music, you need a certain level of education. If you don't have that, you're lost.

You are seen as one of the last great filmmakers who encourage audiences to reflect on how we live in a world adrift. But some criticise you for being a moralist.

Yes, I know, and that bothers me, because there's a great deal of confusion about what people mean by "moralist." If being a moralist means giving lessons, then I certainly am not one. I do have a moral perspective, but I don't impose it on anyone. In my films, I address uncomfortable truths without offering answers to the questions I raise. The people who call me a moralist are often those who don't want to confront these questions. So be it. There are plenty of young people who do appreciate my work.

To us, you seem more like a humanist. A humanist is not a moralist. A humanist is a lucid observer. This seems to align with your cinema, which blends observation and reflection. This also connects to Georg's comment in Variation: *"I know utopias exist. What interests me is how people deal with them."*

Dass es Utopien gibt, weiß ich selber [*Utopias exist, I know that*] was actually the subtitle I gave to *Variation*. It's like Kant's "categorical imperative": a fine system, but not one that actually resolves anything. Georg is right, but that doesn't explain much. Every relationship with another person, or even with an animal, involves a decision you make on your own, and that decision shapes who you are. One person acts decently, another doesn't.

Suzanne Geyer, Monica Bleibtreu, Elfiede Irrall
and Hilmar Thate in *Variation*.

Why is that? Because, as a child, one was loved too much and the other mistreated? That's too simplistic. We're all responsible for what we do. But, of course, that goes against what the media keep hammering in, that all that matters is money, success and pleasure. Nothing else. That's why Spenden—those public donation drives for humanitarian causes—are so popular, raising massive amounts of money. It's just like the Papal indulgences Luther protested against: money given to ease your conscience. I'm not saying it's a bad thing. On the contrary, it's commendable to give to worthy causes. But the real motive isn't helping others, it's trying to silence your guilty conscience.

In the long restaurant scene at the end, you once again allow yourself some bold strokes of cinematic writing. The alternating shots between the guests at the table and Sigrid, who begins to slit her wrists in the bathtub, maintain ambiguity about the exact nature of the suicide attempt. Are these imagined images playing out in someone's mind, or is it a real suicide attempt taking place during the reunion at the restaurant?

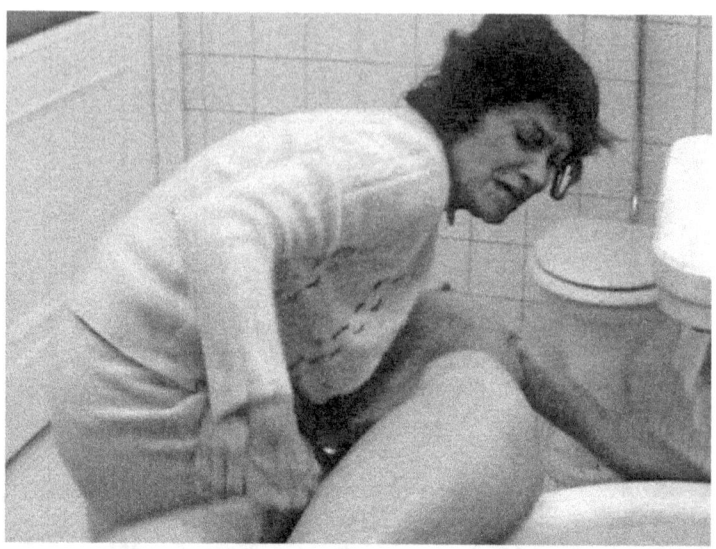

Monica Bleibtreu and Eva Linder in *Variation.*

The dialogue in that restaurant scene is also laced with irony. The characters are fully aware of how bleak their situations are, but they poke fun at it in a roundabout way. That kind of humour is very Austrian; it's all a bit sarcastic. As for the shots of Sigrid, yes, that's me manipulating things. The narrative is rigged. At first, you might think it's a projection of Eva's guilt, but as the scene unfolds you start to realise that the cross-cutting with the suicide attempt is actually anticipating the verbal revelation Eva eventually shares with her friends. That said, when I rewatch the scene now, I find it too slow, and the dialogue a bit heavy-handed. If I were editing it today, I would go for a tighter cut. I've grown increasingly impatient with age.

Sigrid's suicide attempt also revisits a recurring visual motif in your films: the depiction of the nude female body in moments of extreme despair.

Vulnerability is heightened when you're naked.

Yes, but in your films the depiction of nudity is never erotic. When Eva and Christian make love in the first part of Lemminge, *for example, they're naked, yet their genitals aren't shown. But as soon as Eva regrets this first sexual encounter, you frame her fully nude.*

Yes, because it's very difficult to show genitalia in an erotic scene. It quickly becomes either uncomfortable or obscene. Likewise, I never show explicit sex or acts of violence in my films because the audience knows it's not real, that it's being performed. For me, it's not about puritanism but about preserving the illusion of cinema.

Wer war Edgar Allan? (1984)

In Venice, a countess is found dead after falling from a window. Murder or accident? A student, whose father has just died, unwittingly becomes entangled in the affair. While reading a newspaper article about the death at the Caffè Florian, a peculiar American, Edgar Allan, sits beside him and starts discussing the case. As days pass, the story takes another turn. A marquise, a friend of the countess, is also found dead. All those involved are linked to drug trafficking and blackmail. Is Edgar Allan part of it, too, or does he exist only in the student's mind? Accompanying Edgar Allan to a betting shop, the student later realises that the horses they bet on don't match any actual race, and Carlo, the clerk who took their bets, doesn't recognise either of them. Carlo recounts a strange tale: he once framed a friend of his as an adulteress in her husband's eyes, even though she had remained faithful. She ultimately fell into the arms of Edgar Allan, who had been after her but insists he had no part in the deception. The next day, Edgar Allan vanishes. The police release a composite sketch that resembles him. Is the student still dreaming?

In 1984, for ORF and in co-production with the German network ZDF, you directed Wer war Edgar Allan? [Who Was Edgar Allan?]. *Was this adaptation of Peter Rosei's novel a personal project or a commissioned one?*

The script editor of *Lemminge* suggested it to me. We had a good rapport, and he encouraged me to read the novel to see if it interested me, which it did. There was already a screenplay adaptation written by Peter Rosei himself. I read it and didn't like it at all. Not that it was bad, but it was a completely different film, and I understood why: the author didn't want to simply remake his book, he wanted to tell another story. The situation became complicated because there was already a signed contract with Rosei and his publisher, while I was only willing to make the film if I could write my own screenplay. The script editor supported me, despite resistance from the publisher and the director of ORF, who tried to block it. In the end, I was able to make the film the way I wanted. Rosei saw the finished film and thought it was good, though he regretted it wasn't the one he would have made. I went through the same thing again with *Fräulein*, my next film, which is what convinced me never to co-write a script with anyone again.

The credits list Hans Broczyner as a co-writer. Is that a pseudonym for Peter Rosei?

Yes. I said that I didn't mind being credited alongside a co-writer, even though I had written the script alone. Rosei, who had already been paid for his version, didn't want only my name listed in the credits, so he chose this pseudonym as a way to be credited while signalling his disapproval of my adaptation, which he probably never even read.

Were you faithful to the original text?

Yes. But I also invented a lot after scouting locations in Venice. I went there with Rosei, who, having lived there, knew the city well. For about a week he acted as my guide before I returned to Austria to write. I then imagined elements that weren't in the novel, like everything surrounding the student protagonist's drawings, the sculpted head on the wall, and the reference to Morelli's writings.

Why did you make reference to Giovanni Morelli?

That was an idea from Paulus Manker, who plays the student. He discovered Morelli and suggested using him.

It's not a neutral reference, as Morelli was a very particular art critic and historian who invented "attributionism."

Yes, Morelli developed a method based on analysing small details—a selection of recurring objects or body parts like nails and ears—to authenticate works and identify forgeries. This resonated with our subject. In *Wer war Edgar Allan?*, form and content work together so well that it's probably the most aesthetically accomplished of my television films. I haven't rewatched it in a long time, but I remember it as a successful piece of work.

The film was shot in Venice. Did you have a large budget?

I don't recall it being bigger than for my previous films. Of course, shooting in Venice was more expensive than in Vienna, but there were only two characters, and we filmed exclusively in natural settings. The main costs were tied to the time we spent there.

How much time did you have for filming?

Not much. For my early television films, I never had a lot of time. Between five and six weeks of shooting.

What was your angle on filming Venice?

It's a difficult city to film because it's been shown in cinema so often that you can't hope to reveal something entirely new. My challenge, for instance, was to find a fresh way to shoot St. Mark's Square. I opted for a high-angle shot from the Campanile, then through a curtain being lifted. When you actually visit Venice, you see not just all the famous postcard sights but also the labyrinth of streets, away from the main thoroughfares, where it's easy to get quickly lost. That's what I tried to capture.

There is a sequence where the camera follows the protagonist for a long time through narrow streets and across small bridges. Did you use a Steadicam for those shots?

Yes. It was my first time. We had no choice. At the time, using a Steadicam was still quite rare because it was so expensive. We even had to bring in a camera operator from Germany.

There's also an unusual circular tracking shot around the boat carrying the four horse statues along the Grand Canal which initially seems subjective before shifting to the character. What was your intention with that shot?

I wanted to reinforce the idea of a film where you never quite know where you are. Is it reality or the protagonist's delusions? It's like the little wire horse hanging on the student's wall, a rather kitschy decorative object that was very popular in Austria in the 1950s. I first show the horse at rest and later in motion. Is the student actually seeing this, or is it an image, since the horse is a classic symbol of madness? As for the shot you're talking about, we were very lucky with the four St. Mark's horses on the canal. The originals were under restoration, and they had made replicas, which we were able to film. This fit perfectly with all the variations I had imagined around the horse motif. In the novel, the only reference was to horse racing.

There is an evolution in the representation of the horse, from the static object on the wall to the short film of racing horses in the betting shop. Between these, various horse figures—gliding on the canal, galloping on the wall—mark the transition from still to moving images. Some commentators saw this as a reflection on cinema. What do you think?

And why not? But it wasn't my intention, at least not consciously. Maybe it was instinctive. It's true that all these horse images connect to the fundamental question cinema always asks: what is reality?

The theme of reality's illusion underpins the entire story. Was it the same in the novel?

Yes, of course. Like the film, the novel remains open-ended. In the famous horseracing passage, we don't know whether Edgar Allan is giving betting tips to unsettle the young man or even if Edgar Allan really exists.

Hence the long tracking shot through the alleyways, where the student loses sight of him. Just as in St. Mark's Square, when the curtain opens, he seems to appear as if by magic.

And if he does exist, why does he frequent the Caffè Florian so regularly?

Was the play on mirrors in Edgar Allan's apartment, which contributes to this distortion of reality, present in the novel?

I don't remember. Thinking about it now, I don't think it was. There were a lot of elements we changed, like in Edgar Allan's apartment, the photo of a chubby baby that looks like the cherub's head in the alleyway. For me, this was an integral part of the psychological destabilization inflicted on the young man.

The student is seen standing before the cherub's head on the alley wall four times. Beyond its almost musical recurrence, does this leitmotif relate to the four seasons?

Rolf Hoppe in *Wer war Edgar Allan?*

No, it represents four different states of his mind. The snow, the rain and the sun are there to suggest that this story unfolds over a relatively long period, without making it clear exactly how long.

It feels almost dreamlike when it rains and he stubbornly continues to draw without seeking shelter, as the raindrops gradually erase his sketch.

That was meant to show that he's obsessed, that what he is doing is utterly irrational.

Were the curtains in the windows, opening and closing on the action, a reference to a theatre curtain?

No. The idea was rather to repurpose a set element to simulate a fade to black or a fade-in during scene transitions.

Seeing all those curtains, one might wonder if you were alluding to Shakespeare's famous idea that "All the world's a stage."

One might just as well reference Racine, who said that God watches a performance, and that we are that performance. I have no problems with those interpretations, but that wasn't my original intention.

Yet when you suddenly shrink the frame in the final scene, it's clearly to create a sense of distance.

Yes, to highlight the artificiality of the film and remind the audience that we haven't been watching reality, only a performance.

Regarding the illusion of perceiving reality, the final scene echoes what a character says at the beginning of the film: "When you find a wallet full of money on the ground, you might think you're dreaming!"

If I remember correctly, that was how the novel ended. The novel also cited Edgar Allan Poe's short story "Hop-Frog." The challenge in my adaptation was figuring out how to bring that fantastical tale of revenge and deception into a film that otherwise has a realistic tone. That's how I came up with the idea of a scene that breaks away from any sense of reality, where the student recounts the story of "Hop-Frog" directly to the camera, as it slowly zooms out to reveal a strange set and the flashing light of the ambulance that's about to take him away. We shot that scene on Giudecca Island, in Venice's old film studio, which had long been abandoned. I hadn't even known it existed, but when I came across it during location scouting, I immediately knew it was the perfect place for that sequence. The place was in terrible shape, with dangerous holes in the floor, and we had to wear masks because of the asbestos. The idea was to gather several of the film's key objects there, like the phone booth and a gondola, and turn the space into a kind of convergence point for the story.

With the story of the faithful woman, abandoned by her husband because he's convinced she's cheating on him, you show how the inability to grasp reality can make you lose everything you believe in: love, art, even God.

That's all in the novel.

Yes, but this theme greatly interests you, to the point of it being placed at the heart of Benny's Video.

It is indeed one of my favourite themes.

It's also the first and only time you explicitly explore this confusion between reality and virtuality through drugs.

Paulus Manker and Haneke
on the set of *Wer war Edgar Allan?*

I think Peter Rosei used that device in his novel to help the reader accept the protagonist's loss of bearings. But I still believe the student didn't need to be drugged for it to work. In the film, I didn't want to deviate from the novel, but I treated the drug element as discreetly as possible. You only see the student snort something once. In my original scripts, I always try to create situations that don't rely on drugs or other tricks to be believable. In *Funny Games*, and also in *Caché*, you don't know whether what you're seeing is reality or a video. And I don't feel the need to explain or justify that.

There is a curious scene when the young man sees a ray of sunlight on the floor of his room and lies down on it. How do you interpret that gesture?

It's a kind of symbolic representation of death. Since the ray will move with the sun, the light will leave him and he'll be left in darkness. But lying down like that is also a way of feeling the warmth of the sun.

This gesture also suggests the idea of a quest.

Yes. With the visit from the manager of the family business at the beginning of the film, it becomes clear that the student has come to Venice to escape his father's world. He has rejected a life that was laid out for him in advance, and now he's losing himself while trying to find himself. It's a coming-of-age story. The fact that, at the end of the film, he finds an empty wallet is, of course, a metaphor, but I have never asked myself whether that open-ended finale is a hopeful one or not.

As in Lemminge, *the relationship with the father is confrontational. This is a recurring theme in your work.*

Perhaps... I never really noticed. When *Lemminge* came out, my father actually asked me where this hatred of fathers came from. But I don't feel any hatred, neither toward my biological father, who had no part in my upbringing, nor toward the fathers in my fiction. It's just that when I write a film, I always feel more sympathy for female characters than male ones, which is why, in June 2010, when I was in Graz receiving an award for *The White Ribbon*, I was surprised to hear a feminist activist praise it. She said it was the most feminist and anti-machismo film she had ever seen, and that it was unimaginable that a man could have made it. I laughed a lot because I can't stand feminists.

Is it their activism that you dislike?

Mostly their ideology, which leads them to invent enemies, which is foolish—as foolish as machismo.

With you, is everything that ends in "-ism" to be avoided?

Yes. It's really not my thing.

Otherwise, do you like Hitchcock?

Absolutely. But "like" isn't the word. He is, in my opinion, the greatest of the masters, and "master" is the right word. I don't know any creator who has mastered his craft as well at Hitchcock. Every one of his shots serves the film. For every problem, he has a convincing cinematic solution. And that led him to invent a lot of things.

We ask because in Wer war Edgar Allan?, *we find what Hitchcock termed a "MacGuffin."*

It's a device I often use in my films.

We're thinking of the mention of the countess' death at the beginning. Is it suicide or murder?

That's also in the book.

Yes, but in your films, the manipulation of the viewer often involves elements that only seem important to the plot, which is exactly what Hitchcock called a MacGuffin.

The MacGuffin is a way to create the kind of tension I'm always aiming for in a film. But it's not that easy to come up with a good one. If the viewer ends up feeling cheated once they realize they've been following a false lead, it just doesn't work. The MacGuffin has to have enough realism to stay believable in hindsight. It's the same when you want to invite the audience to think through an open ending. You have to first build a story that could genuinely go in several different directions. But there's no point offering five possible endings if four of them don't hold up.

The opening of the film is beautiful and mysterious. It is night time. We see a policeman on a balcony above the canal, then a young woman appears, a man joins her and leads her inside. Her scarf slips off at that moment, and the camera follows it as it falls, all the way down to the surface of the water, where rescuers in boats are searching the canal. All of this happens in a single shot. We immediately sense that something serious has just happened. Then we learn about the death of the countess, and we realise that the scarf—although it wasn't hers—symbolises her disappearance.

Exactly. You see those two people looking down, but there's no mention of the countess at that point. It's only later, thinking back, that the viewer pieces it all together: the countess vanished that night, but we don't know how. By the way, I should mention that the two people looking down at the rescuers were actually the set designer and the costume designer, and that shot was incredibly difficult to get right. We filmed it at least twenty-five times because the scarf kept landing in the wrong spot. Luckily, I had planned ahead and asked for a large supply of scarves.

The second shot, where the scarf sinks, is just as remarkable.

It cost us a few more scarves…

The mysterious beauty of the scene is heightened by the music, taken from Ennio Morricone's soundtrack of Bernardo Bertolucci's 1900. Why did you use this piece?

I spent a long time looking for music that had a sense of mystery and remember feeling quite desperate when I couldn't find anything suitable in the classical repertoire. Then someone at ORF suggested I listen to some of Morricone's records. When I came across that particular piece, I instantly knew it was exactly what I had been searching for, even though, in *1900*, it wasn't used in a mysterious context at all.

Some filmmakers edit their films with temporary music until the composer provides an original score. Have you ever worked this way?

I have never commissioned an original score for any of my films. In my theatrical features, there is no music, except for what is played within the scene. For my television films, I always used music I already had in mind, like Schoenberg and Mozart for *Drei Wege zum See*, or, in *Lemminge*, songs from my youth that I was happy to hear again. Only once did I use music from another film as a leitmotif, and that was Morricone's piece from *1900*.

Why didn't you work with a composer?

Because I couldn't be sure I would like what they composed for me, and I would have felt trapped, so I preferred to search for existing music myself. And it was a great pleasure to spend hours listening to beautiful music.

How do you explain the absence of music in your feature films?

Music is often used to cover up flaws in the direction. It's what people turn to, for instance, when the tension starts to drop. For me, not using music is a matter of honesty. On television, it's a different experience because people watch in a totally different way than they do in a cinema, where they have made the effort to go out and paid for a ticket to have an experience. At home, people get up, go to the bathroom, answer the phone, yell at their kids—they aren't really watching, so you have to find ways to force them to focus when something important is happening onscreen. I always say that cinema can be an art form, but television can't because it relies on the crudest of tools, like using music to grab attention. Of course, that doesn't apply to genre films, like those by Hitchcock or Sergio Leone, which simply wouldn't work without music. Me, I use the tools of genre cinema to make films that are more or less realistic, and that doesn't require music.

After your early work in cinema, you returned to television for two adaptations, The Rebellion, *based on a novel by Joseph Roth, and Kafka's* The Castle, *both of which contain almost no music whatsoever.*

It always depends on the subject. You can't adapt Kafka and add music.

Orson Welles used Albinoni's Adagio *in his adaptation of* The Trial.

That's a great film, but it has nothing to do with Kafka.

In your depiction of the young man's room, there is a series of tightly framed shots on various objects, reminiscent of Bresson or Godard in the 1960s. You later used this technique in Fräulein *and applied it systematically in* The Seventh Continent. *What led you to that aesthetic choice, aside from those well-known influences?*

It mostly comes from everyday experience. We never really see the whole picture. Focusing on something is always a kind of fragmentation. The moment I concentrate on you, everything else is still there, but I'm not seeing it. I wanted to find a way to express that on film.

That's quite similar to Impressionist paintings or a piece of music, with small touches that follow one another and create an impression.

Yes, but in painting and film, you can only show things one after the other. In theatre—or in wide shots in cinema—you can place several things side by side at the same time. *Gleichzeitigkeit,* the simultaneity of different actions, is something very hard to show on screen, because you're confined to a single flow of time that you can't step outside of. You can handle this in experimental cinema by using multiple screens, but in a regular film you're usually forced to show separate actions one by one. It's only through editing that you can really convey the idea of simultaneity.

Paulus Manker in *Wer war Edgar Allan?*

You gave the lead role to Paulus Manker, who had already appeared in the first part of Lemminge *and would go on to appear again in* Fräulein *and* The Castle, *and to whom you later entrusted the direction of your screenplay* The Moor's Head.

He comes from a well-known family here, and at the time of *Lemminge* he was still studying at the Max Reinhardt Seminar, the theatre school in Vienna. His mother was an actress and his father was a renowned stage director. We hit it off right away, and from the very start it was obvious that he had to play the student character, with whom he shared a certain morbidity. He's a very intelligent young man, and very sensitive too. He was very young back then, but already an exceptional actor for his age.

Fräulein—Ein deutsches Melodram (1985)

1955. In her small German village, Johanna runs the local cinema and has raised her son, Mike, and daughter, Brigitte, on her own, ever since her husband, Hans, went missing on the Russian front. Hans' brother, Karl, wants him declared dead, both to simplify matters for his business and to allow Johanna, now living with André, a former French prisoner of war, to move on. André makes a living as a wrestler under the stage name The Black Mask. But following the Adenauer accords with Moscow, Hans returns from a Russian camp. He is exhausted, ill, and unable to work. Johanna and André, who had sworn never to see each other again once Hans came back, break their promise and begin an affair in secret. Then André vanishes. Mike, now a delinquent caught up in various illegal dealings, dies in an explosion in a building where he and his gang had been cornered by the police. Brigitte follows an American GI and marries him in the United States. Johanna decides to end her husband's suffering by turning off his IV drip. She then travels to the small Breton village in France from which André had once sent a postcard to his old wrestling club. There, she discovers he has a wife and two grown sons. They meet in secret at a hotel. But Johanna must leave because André's wife knows what is going on. On her way back, Johanna stops at a roadside restaurant, and her life—like the film, which until then had been in black and white—suddenly shifts into colour. On the television, Hans Albers, star of *The Adventures of Baron Münchhausen*, seems to wink at her. At that moment, André enters the restaurant, smiling, and tells her he did the same as she did: he killed his wife. Johanna bursts into hysterical laughter. A black-and-white shot shows her at the police station confessing to her husband's murder, leaving the end of the story open to doubt.

You shot Fräulein *for Saarländischer Rundfunk in 1985, around the time Edgar Reitz was making* Heimat. *Did you also feel a need to revisit German history?*

No, it was more banal than that. The origin of the film was a more or less true story that was told to Bernd Schroeder, who then told it to me. I found it interesting and wanted to film it.

Who is Bernd Schroeder?

A television screenwriter who pitched his first script, *8051 Grinning*, to the Südwestfunk channel when I was working there as a script editor in the early 1970s. That was a time when the network was looking for new writers, and since his script was quite good, my boss hired him. Schroeder was from Bavaria, but he had just met

Peter Franke in *Fräulein*.

a new woman and moved to Baden-Baden with her. That's when we became friends, and years later he told me the story of *Fräulein*.

How did your collaboration on the script unfold?

Actually, we wanted to make an anti-Fassbinder film. I had just seen *The Marriage of Maria Braun*, which I didn't like at all. I found the story of this suffering German woman, who nevertheless leads us toward a better future, too sentimental and quite unbearable, so the idea was to do the opposite. I joined Bernd in Italy, where he had a house, and we spent several days discussing and structuring the story. Then he stayed behind to write it. Our conversations were very fruitful and I thought it was going to be a great film, but two months later, when he showed me his script, it was nothing like what I had hoped for. We worked on it again together, and once again I was very satisfied. I had already started preparing the film when I received his second version, which was just as bad as the first. At that point, there were only two options: either drop the whole thing or write my own version. I didn't have time to wait for more drafts from Bernd. The channel's script editor gave me the green light, so I wrote my version, which is the film you saw. It was a big disappointment for Bernd because, after all, it was still his story, but even though he was my friend, I just couldn't shoot his script. As I told you, that was the moment I decided never to co-write with anyone again. I'm simply not built for it. The script has to become something of my own, otherwise I can't do anything with it.

What was the nature of your disagreement?

In the end, he had still written a Fassbinder-like story. It's true that the plot contains elements that feel close to Fassbinder's world, but I wanted an ironic perspective. The entire ending, for example, is exactly as I envisioned it. Johanna's character is rather negative. She's a victim, but she's also cynical, just like the film as a whole. That was my way of pushing back against the fake sentimentality in Fassbinder's cinema, so it wasn't so much about the twists and turns of the plot; it came down to sensibility, the tone of a scene, or how a line is delivered. That's where Schroeder and I didn't see eye to eye. Take the scene halfway through the film, when Johanna comes home late at night and finds her husband building a church out of matchsticks and, in a very harsh exchange, he calls her a whore. That's my dialogue. Schroeder's script was more straightforward and somewhat sentimental.

How did Schroeder's script end?

Like a tragedy. The heroine was imprisoned for her husband's murder.

Your film's ending is more mysterious.

Not mysterious—ironic. Everything literally takes off.

One could imagine that the real ending is the black-and-white shot where she is at the police station.

One could imagine that. Or she could imagine that. Maybe that's what will happen to her, unless the immensely popular German film *The Adventures of Baron Münchhausen* carries us all away toward a happy ending?

It's at that precise moment that the film shifts to colour. What meaning do you give to this effect?

It's a reference to the passage of time and the arrival of colour in cinema from that era. But it would be too narrow to stick to that realistic reading. The shift to colour at that precise moment is ironic

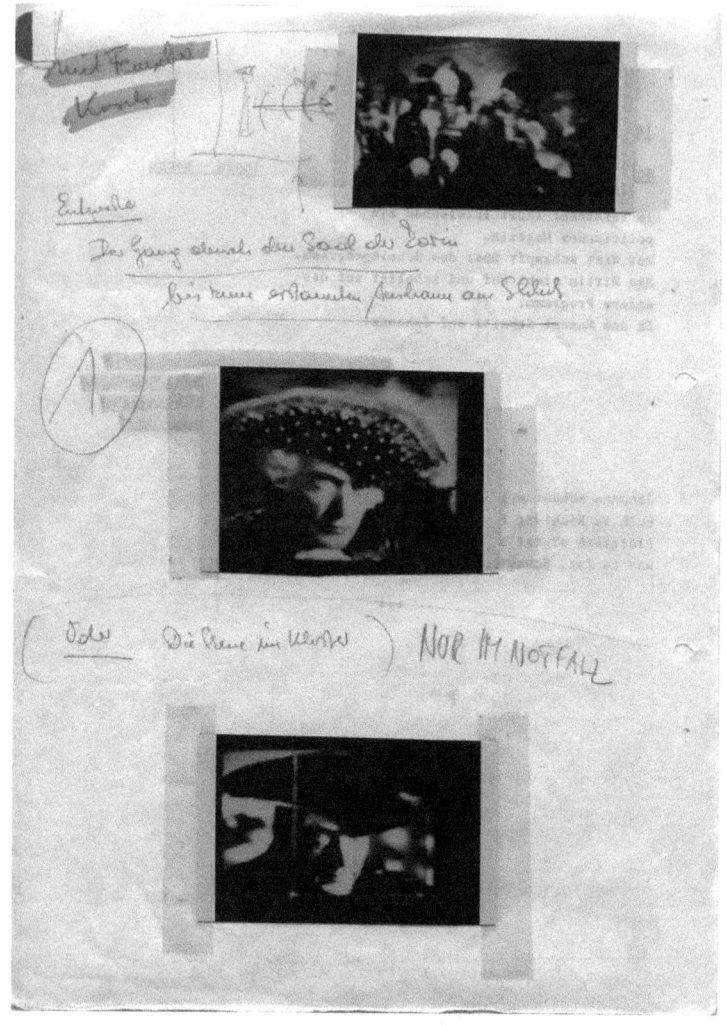

A storyboard college for *Fraulein.*

because it coincides with Münchhausen's entrance into the story. In other words, the melodrama is upended by a kind of fairy tale.

Was Hans Albers, who plays Münchhausen, an important German actor?

More than that—he was like a god to audiences. He had acted under the Nazi regime, but he managed to keep his distance from the Reich and never appeared in any direct propaganda films. In the immediate postwar period, he took on major roles one after another and remained a major star in Germany until the 1960s. Besides the excerpts from *Münchhausen*, I also made sure to show a scene from ...*Und über uns der Himmel* [*And the Heavens Above Us*] a film shot amidst the ruins of Berlin around 1947, which he wanted to make to lift the spirits of regular Germans. Albers is actually inseparable from *Fräulein*, since the story Bernd Schroeder first told me was about a woman who owned a cinema and was a devoted fan of his, which is why there's a large poster of him hanging in the lobby.

For the director of photographer, you brought back Walter Kindler, who had shot Lemminge *and* Variation.

Yes, though for *Lemminge* he only shot a few scenes as a replacement for Jerzy Lipman, the cinematographer of Polanski's *Knife in the Water* and Wajda's *Ashes and Diamonds*. Lipman was Jewish and had emigrated after enduring terrible experiences in a concentration camp. He was a broken man and once told me that I terrified him when I criticised him for not working fast enough. When he was shooting in the East, he had much more time for his shoots. He told me that for the banquet scene in *Ashes and Diamonds*, he was given almost a week just to set up the lighting! That obviously wasn't an option for us. In the end he had to be replaced by Walter Kindler for part of *Lemminge* because of a scheduling conflict. His availability didn't line up with Elisabeth Orth's, and she had to move straight on to another shoot.

We brought up Walter Kindler to get to the question of the loyalty you show toward your collaborators. Later on, you worked regularly with cinematographers Christian Berger and Jürgen Jürges and set designer Christoph Kanter, unlike your first three films, where you changed crews each time.

For my first three films I had to work with foreign crews. It was only when I started directing in Austria that I had the chance, from one film to another, to reconnect with people I got along well with. That's often not possible because of other commitments. But generally, I like working with the same actors and technicians.

Since everyone already knows each other's strengths and weaknesses, it makes things easier. Communication is more fluid.

How did you choose your actress, Angelica Domröse?

She was a major star in East Germany. I don't remember how I met her, but I do remember that after the film, I directed her in two plays: *Krankheit der Jugend* by Ferdinand Bruckner, which I staged in Berlin, and *Who's Afraid of Virginia Woolf?* in which she acted with her husband, Hilmar Thate. To me, she was the character of Johanna. She fit the role perfectly. And we got along very well.

Why cast Lou Castel in an anti-Fassbinder film? That's something of a paradox.

The first actor I really wanted was Gérard Depardieu. He would have been perfect for the role. His agent was enthusiastic but told me he wouldn't be available for another three years, so we started looking for someone who could convincingly play both a wrestler and a lover. Lou Castel came to the audition claiming to be French, but once we started shooting it became clear his French wasn't all that strong. He's actually of Scandinavian origin. On set, he didn't get along particularly well with Angelica Domröse, but things still went smoothly overall.

Did you have any trouble finding the German village where you shot the film?

Actually, we ended up shooting in a French village near Saarbrücken. If you look closely, you'll notice the telephone poles aren't the kind you would have seen in Germany at the time, but since digital effects didn't exist yet, there was no way to change them. During location scouting, we crisscrossed the entire Saar region and couldn't find anything convincing. All the German villages had new buildings, and we didn't have the budget to make major changes to the sets, so we had to settle for France.

Nevertheless, you still tell the story of Germany through the excerpts and posters of films from that era.

That was our original concept and one of the reasons I wanted to make this film. It also allowed for a reflection on German cinema and on what audiences liked back then. And, of course, it contributed to the film's overall ironic tone.

Angelica Domröse in *Fraulein*.

Among the amusing references is a poster for the film Law and Order *with Ronald Reagan...*

...who was President of the United States at the time we were shooting the film.

You also refer to several popular films of the era, like East of Eden *and* Johnny Guitar, *but also a German film we know nothing about,* Die Lüge.

Die Lüge, from the 1930s, is a story of deception. All the films mentioned have something to do with the situations in *Fräulein*. I was lucky enough to find a man who used to paint film posters onto walls for a living. The ones he had kept didn't match the films I wanted, but he had no problem repainting all the posters I needed.

Was it difficult to obtain the rights for the film excerpts?

For the television broadcast, everything was easily arranged, as were the rights for the music extracts, through an office that handled these matters, but for the screening at the Munich festival we had to cut the excerpt from Walt Disney's *Snow White and the Seven Dwarfs* because of rights issues and replaced it with black frames. From the start, we knew that including all these excerpts would make distributing *Fräulein* in cinema or on video nearly impossible. Since then, I've had a falling-out with the television network that produced it because they treated me poorly on my next project. As a result, it's complicated to screen the film at retrospectives today.

Why did you turn the excerpts from Johnny Guitar *and* Snow White, *which are in colour, into black and white?*

Primarily to emphasise the artificial nature of the film and to push audiences to take a step back from what is, after all, only a performance. Plus, it would have disrupted the impact of the ending, when my film itself suddenly transitions to colour. To establish that distance between the film and the audience from the outset, I planned an opening shot that I still regret not being able to shoot. It was supposed to be a vertical crane shot, with the camera moving up and then down again, but on the day of filming I didn't have a crane. They had set up something that allowed me to shoot from above, but without any movement, so I had to rethink my shot list. That ended up affecting how the audience perceived the two other overhead shots, the one with Hans and Johanna in bed and the one of the murder, which I had already filmed. When the first of those shots appears, about twenty minutes into the film, it feels a bit off, and some audiences probably wonder why I suddenly went with such an unrealistic angle, especially after everything that came before was so grounded.

Did the full-frontal nudity scene cause any issues, at a time when cinema had already become quite liberated in erotic content?

No issues, except for Angelica Domröse's husband, who was rather upset when he saw the film.

Understandably so, especially since there's also the brothel scene where Lou Castel penetrates her, and later, the scene in Brittany where she lies on the bed and spreads her legs for her lover. Were you aiming for realism in the way you showed sex, or were you trying to provoke?

I wasn't trying to provoke. I wanted to show that this is passion that's both sad and intense. If you decide to show sexuality, it has to feel like something real is happening, otherwise you risk falling into clichés.

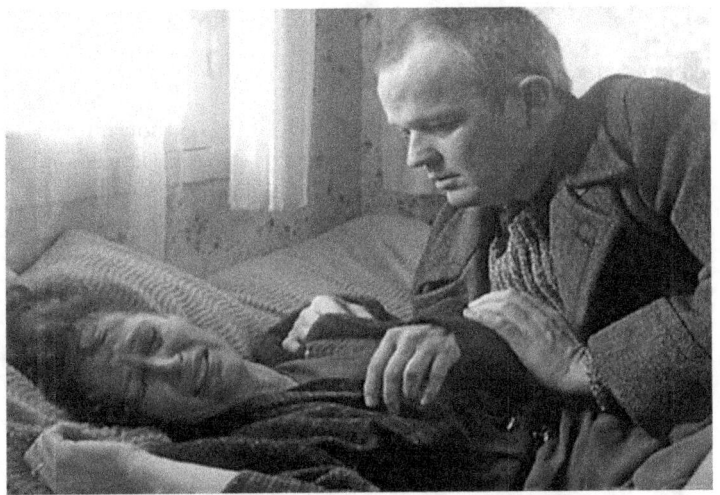

Angelica Domröse and Lou Castel in *Fraulein*.

With this kind of bold filmmaking, did you see yourself paving the way for other directors?

I never think in those terms. I focus on the most effective way to tell my story, without worrying about whether I'm advancing cinema in some way.

In Fräulein, *you revisit a situation from* Drei Wege zum See, *where Elisabeth, who is swimming, calls out a touching "I love you" to her father, who doesn't hear her.*

Ah! I'm repeating myself...

It's less repetition than a recurring theme: the difficulty of expressing kindness to those we care about. When you write a scene like that, are you aware that you have done something similar in a previous film?

Yes, but it's not about redoing a scene I've already shot. It just comes naturally, and later I realise it fits. I generally forget about my films once they're finished. Once a film is made, I lose interest and focus on the next one, which is why I don't like rewatching my films, unless I'm watching with someone whose reactions I want to see.

When you finish a film, do you test by showing it to anyone?

My wife Susie is always the first to see a finished film.

Do you ever change it based on her reactions?

Yes, but I also show it to other people, like Alexander Horwath, the curator of the Filmmuseum in Vienna. He has a very clear mind and knows everything about cinema. His feedback is helpful. He often points out things I was already aware of, which reinforces my sense that I need to rethink the edit. When I finish editing a film, I usually know where its weaknesses lie.

So you have a clear perspective on the finished film, unlike some filmmakers, who only see the flaws much later?

It's easier for me because the editing is already mapped out at the script stage. The problem is when a scene doesn't work. I only shoot what's written in the script, unlike in America, where they cover everything from multiple angles just in case and the editor ends up shaping the film. I don't want that, so I only shoot what I've planned. But if something doesn't work, I'm in trouble and I have to find a way to patch it up so the audience doesn't notice. Worst case scenario, I cut the scene altogether, like in *Time of the Wolf*, where I took out nearly twenty minutes that wasn't working because I had made a casting mistake.

So with your way of working, is cutting the only option when a scene doesn't work?

You can't always cut because certain story elements need to be there, and sometimes those elements are in a scene that doesn't work. Now and then, that can actually spark new ideas. I have even ended up coming up with something better than what I originally planned. Quite often the scenes that don't work turn out not to be essential. When a scene is really good and the actors are highly skilled, the chances of it not working are low. If something feels off, we try to work around the difficulty and eventually find a solution. The key is recognising that the scene was poorly written in the first place. The older I get, the more rigorous I have become, cutting out anything that doesn't feel right at the writing stage. When you're young, you treat every written line as if it's a masterpiece. I see this in my students today, and I was the same at their age, but with time, it gets easier to throw things into the bin.

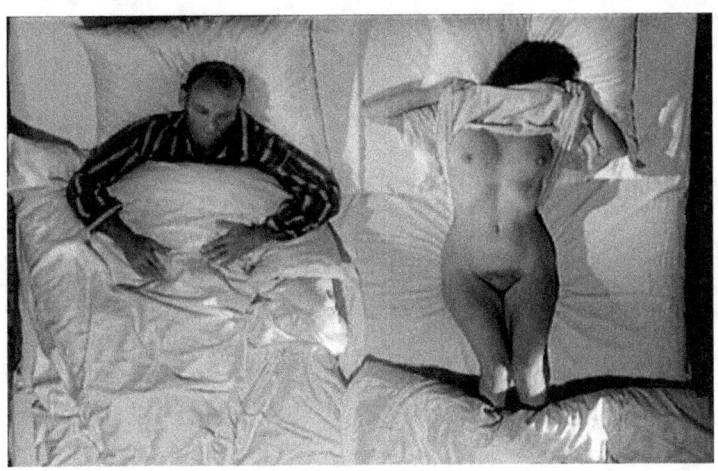

Peter Francke and Angelica Domröse in *Fraulein*.

*Since you show the finished film to Susie and then to others, do you
do the same with the completed script before filming?*

Yes, I have Susie read it. In the past, my first reader was my aunt,
a fairly simple woman who had nothing to do with art or cinema,
but who was very sharp. I could have shown her anything and
she would have liked it because she adored me. But she would ask
questions like, "I didn't understand this. Why does he do that?"
And she was always right because ordinary people often have a
more relevant perspective than professionals, who tend to be
blinded by film theory. Regular people ask themselves whether
they understand and whether they're interested. Unfortunately,
it's not easy to find people like that, who you trust completely. My
wife is also very sharp in her reactions. I don't take her comments
into account when it comes to violent scenes, which she can't stand,
but in general she immediately understands what I'm trying to
convey, and when she criticises my work, she's right about 70% of
the time. That helps me a lot, especially since she's the only person
I let read the script. By the time I consider the script finished, it's
already the film I'm going to make.

What role does the producer play in your creative process?

None. He just has to find the money. Of course, I'm exaggerating
a little. It depends on the producer. The late Margaret Menegoz
from Les Films du Losange, for example, was very intelligent.

I had complete trust in her and would give her the script as soon as it's ready. She would give feedback like, "Don't you think this part is a bit too long?" or "I didn't quite understand this…" Since she knew her profession very well, I always took her opinion into account. But I do what I want and she never tried to interfere. If I disagreed with her, she accepted my reasoning. Here in Austria, it's the same. Even in television, I have always been allowed to do things my way, which is no longer the case for my younger colleagues. Television networks today have so much power that you can't push back. When young filmmakers are told their script is too complicated, they have to comply, or they won't be able to make their film. If you want to start out today at a certain level of quality, it has become extremely difficult, at least in Austria, and since television is increasingly involved in financing theatrical films, its influence over cinema keeps growing worldwide. That's the worst thing.

In terms of style, Fräulein *stands apart from your previous films. It has a faster, more sustained rhythm.*

Because it's is a melodrama, as indicated in its subtitle, "A German Melodrama."

Melodramas are generally a bit slow.

Yes, but mine is a parody of melodrama, with many cross-cutting scenes that were already in the script. That speeds up the narrative.

In addition to its fast pace, Fräulein *features bold editing choices for a television film. For instance, in the cinema scene where the 3D version of* Creature from the Black Lagoon *is being shown, we see Johanna's daughter wearing the 3-D glasses of the time. Then there's the outdoor scene where she tells her mother she plans to marry Bill, before cutting back to her crying with the 3-D glasses still on. Her tears, of course, aren't because she is watching the Jack Arnold film.*

Exactly. It's a visualisation of her thoughts in that moment, because for her it's a tragedy. She loves her father and is about to leave her family.

That kind of editing really helps give the film its brisk rhythm.

At other times, it's also a chance to use a *Schlager*, a popular song that adds an ironic commentary on the action.

Coming back to the ending, you completely re-edited the excerpt from Münchhausen. *When Lou Castel tells Johanna he has killed his wife and is now free to be with her, the Baron gives us a wink.*

I like that bit a lot. But I could only allow myself that kind of re-editing of a quoted film at the end when it's no longer clear what is real and what exists only in the heroine's imagination.

Six

Nachruf für einen Mörder, my only foray into experimental film — A sensational news story — Violence on a TV talk show — The elegance and depth of The *Rebellion* — Colour and black and white — Bresson's donkey in Murnau's toilet — *Tatort* and the dangers of nuclear power — *The Castle,* or the necessity of incompleteness — Adapting Kafka — My first meeting with Susanne Lothar

Before moving on to your beginnings in cinema, we would like to discuss your three other films produced for television between 1990 and 1997. Where did the idea for Nachruf für einen Mörder [Obituary for a Murderer], *which you shot between* The Seventh Continent *and* Benny's Video, *come from?*

There was a programme on ORF called *Kunststücke* made up entirely of small experimental productions. It was the perfect platform for students hoping to make their first films on a shoestring budget. The person running the show was the same script editor I had worked with on my earlier films, and he kept encouraging me to get involved. I always turned him down, telling him I didn't have the time, that the pay was lousy, and that I only made fiction films, never anything experimental. But then, on September 8, 1990, something happened in Vienna that made headlines. A drunk young man got kicked out of a party. He went home, grabbed a gun, and shot his parents in their bedroom. Then he went back to the party and killed four more people, and injured several others. He ended up shooting at the police and managed to flee before eventually killing himself. The newspapers covered the story in detail, and a week or two later, it was the topic of a popular late-night debate show on TV called Club 2. This programme aired just before the final news broadcast of the day, the segment that wraps things up and signals the end of programming. That night's episode was titled "But Why Did This Happen?" and featured, among others, a psychiatrist and the sister of one of the victims. She seemed on the verge of breaking down, but the host handled her with extraordinary sensitivity. Thanks largely to her—she was really quite moving—the programme got to me. Of course, it didn't answer the question in the title, but it stuck with me, so I called the script editor back and told him I was ready to make a *Kunststück* on the subject. My idea was to replay the entire debate programme, but only show the image for the first minute. After that, the sound would continue, but the visuals would be replaced until the very end, when the original picture would return for the news broadcast and the closing sequence with the Austrian flag. In between, I wanted to cut together a kind of collage of everything broadcast on both ORF channels the day the shooting happened. Every single show, even adverts, would be included, proportionally, according to how much airtime they got. My assistant and I watched the entire day's programming on VHS and calculated everything meticulously. If a film ran for two hours, we would include about ninety seconds. An advert got maybe three frames. We didn't do any internal editing; we always just chose the most violent moment from each program. I kept some of the audio, but we didn't include the subtitles with the dialogue. The result was an extremely violent film, made even more intense by the fast-paced editing—every clip was incredibly short—and, of course, by the provocative title. Normally, you don't write obituaries for murderers, only for decent, upstanding people. When it aired, it caused an uproar and ORF received a flood of complaints. A lot of viewers didn't even understand what they were watching, even though we had clearly explained our approach at the beginning. The head of cultural programming, the one who had greenlit the project, was a smart guy. When we screened the finished film for him, he just sat there, frozen, and said, "Technically, I ought to resign after airing something like this. But I promise you we'll broadcast it. And I'm willing to put my job on the line to defend it." I was really impressed, until he added, "Actually, I do that all the time."

What exactly was the scandal? Was it that people didn't understand what you were trying to do, or was it the violence being shown on a public channel?

I think it was both. That said, I did receive a great number of messages from people who thought it was brilliant and very unusual. For me, too, it was exceptional; my only foray into experimental cinema. I'll never do anything like that again... The film was my reaction to a television broadcast I had stumbled upon and that moved me, though I also found it naive to think we could get to the bottom of such horrific violence just by throwing sociology and psychology around on a TV set. What my film did—at least what I hope it did—is hold up a mirror to all the violence that pours out of the media nonstop and ends up numbing us. It's a theme I returned to immediately afterward in *Benny's Video*, though in a different register. *Nachruf für einen Mörder* was more about reacting in the moment, to the killings and the debate they sparked. If I had waited, everyone would have forgotten the shock and emotion stirred by the entire affair.

With this young killer, one gets the impression that murder had replaced speech. Alienated by society, his sole form of expression is violence.

I think it's always been that way. Violence is what happens when communication breaks down. It's a fundamental human issue; it's been with us since the beginning. But if people genuinely try to connect, there's always another way. There's always an alternative to violence.

I'm sure we'll come back to that later. But for now, let's move on to your second-to-last film for television, your 1992 adaptation of Joseph Roth's novel Die Rebellion. *What drew you to that book?*

It was actually the network's idea, and I said yes right away. I love Joseph Roth, and beyond that, it's a story that really lends itself to a TV adaptation. Roth's stories have weight and substance that go well beyond the elegance of the writing.

The Rebellion (1993)

Andreas Plum returns from World War I with an amputated leg. Proud to have served the Emperor on the battlefield and of the price he has paid, Plum is convinced that he will now be able to lead a decent life, and he is quickly rewarded when the City of Vienna grants him a license to play the barrel organ in the streets. Good fortune continues to smile upon him when he befriends Willi, a second-hand dealer, who offers him food and shelter. Added to this is a chance encounter, made during one of his musical performances, of a widow, Frau Katharina, who takes a great interest in his earnings. Their marriage is swiftly celebrated. But Andreas' fate takes a sudden turn. On a tram, he confronts a bourgeois man who is hostile to a protest by disabled veterans demanding their pensions from the city. A policeman arrests Andreas and confiscates his license. From then on, his wife treats him with contempt and replaces him with a neighbour who had been courting her for some time. Summoned to appear before court, Andreas is unable to attend because he gets into an altercation with a narrow-minded policeman and ends up in prison. There, he feels a kinship with the birds that land on his window ledge, but he is not allowed to feed them. Upon his release, he reconnects with Willi, who has since become the owner of a public restroom business. Willi gives him a job in one of these facilities. Increasingly isolated, Andreas lashes out at God, reproaching Him for allowing so much suffering and injustice. He collapses and his body is donated to science. Willi comes to pay his last respects, then walks away, whistling as always.

Did you know that the novel had already been adapted for television once before, back in 1962, in a version directed by Wolfgang Staudte?

I had no idea. What I do know is that *The Last Laugh*, Murnau's film, inspired Joseph Roth for the final part set in the public restrooms. At least, that's what I read somewhere. Roth was a journalist at the time. He wrote extensively for the press alongside his novels. *The Rebellion* isn't even his most famous work.

That journalistic background is reflected in the level of detail throughout the novel.

Perhaps, but it's also very poetic. All of Roth's novels are beautifully written. Few other German-language writers possess his elegance.

Once again, you used a voiceover, this time spoken by Udo Samel, who you had already directed in Variation.

I asked him because he has one of the finest voices I know.

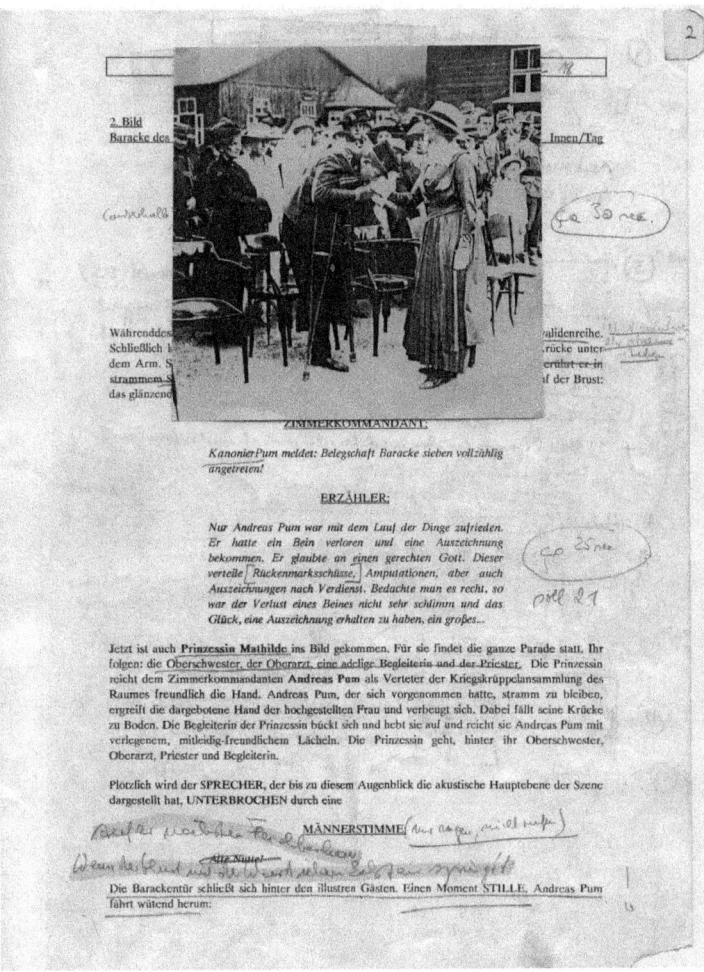

A vintage photo in the script of *The Rebellion*.

You opted for a sepia-toned image. How was that achieved?

We shot in colour and then removed the colour to obtain the tinted black-and-white look I wanted. The film included archival footage, and I wanted the texture of our footage to match it.

The effect really works. At first you can clearly tell which shots are archival, but then you get caught out by the parade of the wounded where, astonishingly, we suddenly recognise the protagonist. Why did you choose to include some scenes in colour?

I wanted colour for that brief period of happiness in his life, from the moment he meets the woman he marries to their wedding, and then again in the moments when he dreams of a better life or looks back on happier times, especially when things are going badly for him. I wanted the shifts between black and white and colour to reflect his emotional state.

You stayed very faithful to the novel, but also added some personal touches, like the scene in the toilets where we see his donkey carrying the organ, the two things that brought him the most happiness.

The ending of the novel was hard to adapt because so much is conveyed through language, like his speech to the birds in his prison cell, and later, his revolt against God, which really only works as voiceover. I needed to find images that corresponded to these passages. It was the first time in my career that I was working in a more metaphorical register, and it wasn't easy for me, but I think it turned out quite well. It's one of my favourite television films because I stayed true to the author while also making it my own. I'm also happy with the performances. There's a real tenderness that comes through. Branko Samarovski, who plays Andreas Plum, is quite brilliant.

How did you find him?

He is an important actor at the Burgtheatre in Vienna. Whenever I have a role for him, I cast him. He has an extraordinary face. He plays the farmer in *The White Ribbon*. *The Rebellion* is undoubtedly his best role. He's very moving in it.

We also really liked the Luxembourgish actor Thierry Van Werveke.

Sadly he died in 2009. I adored him. He was a very warm, very likable, slightly crazy guy. You could never be sure he had actually learned his lines, but with me, that was never a problem. He was also a rock singer. At the wrap party — or maybe it was for *Time of the Wolf*, I can't remember — he came and played with his band.

And your lead actress, Judit Pogány?

Haneke directing Branko Samarovski in *The Rebellion.*

I searched for a very long time without success. Judit is Hungarian, well-known back home as a film actress, who didn't speak a word of German. She sent me a scene from the film that she had worked on with her coach and recorded on video. The moment I saw it, I knew she was who I had been looking for. She was the only one who really defended the character. In the novel, the character isn't particularly likable, and every actress I auditioned played up that unlikable side. Judit wasn't ideal—she was very focused on getting the pronunciation right—but even so, she's completely convincing from beginning to end.

It's true that your film presents a more ambiguous image of this woman. In the novel, she marries a disabled man just to have control over him.

It's the same kind of adjustment I made with the character of Walter in *The Piano Teacher.* In Elfriede Jelinek's novel, he's just an idiot. I tried to make him more complex because idiots don't interest me—not in theatre, nor cinema.

The distinctive production design is by Christoph Kanter, who you discovered while filming Benny's Video. *Beyond the historical reconstruction, there is a sense of stylisation.*

We still aimed for authenticity. The story isn't that old; it takes place at the end of World War I, so we mostly adapted interiors rather than build new structures. The courtyard of the building, for example, was just as you see it in the film. I only added the shack for the donkey. We didn't try to stylise, except, of course, for the ending, which we just discussed. The public restrooms where Andreas ends up were built in a studio.

The overall visual tone is one of great whiteness.

That was to counterbalance the effects of colour. In general, with colour, it's harder to see what's essential. The whiteness allowed us to isolate key elements, like the donkey, or to highlight specific details.

It also enhances the Kafkaesque atmosphere of the film.

I don't find the story Kafkaesque. It's too gentle, and Kafka is never gentle. If it's minus twenty degrees and an iron bar falls on your hand—that's Kafkaesque. There is absolute despair and very aggressive humour in Kafka. In Joseph Roth, there is great sadness, but it's never depressing.

Andreas' donkey recalls Bresson's in Au hasard Balthazar. *Was that intentional?*

Of course.

It feels like your Balthazar embodies all the tenderness Andreas longs for, even if it's hopeless.

Yes, just like in Bresson's film, which is anything but optimistic. But there is also a tenderness in death. The shot of Balthazar lying dead, surrounded by sheep, with Schubert's music playing—it's heartbreaking.

There are several shots in your film that feel straight out of Bresson, as if you wanted to pay tribute to him.

That's most obvious in the shot of the window in the prison cell which forms a cross like in *A Man Escaped* and at the end of *Diary of a Country Priest*, during the passage about the birds I mentioned earlier. But if you look closely, there are at least two other shots that are direct references: the one showing the prisoners lined up in

The Rebellion.

the corridor, and then the one of them emptying their buckets into the courtyard. The first is nearly identical to Bresson's.

And like Bresson, you also use a piece by Schubert.

String Quintet in C Major. Its sadness fit the situation perfectly. No other composer captures the Austrian melancholy we talked about better than Schubert. The same atmosphere that runs through Joseph Roth's novels is there in Schubert's music, so using it in this film felt absolutely necessary.

Beyond the melancholy, the film also conveys a profound sense of individual helplessness in the face of the monstrous entity that society has become. This is a theme that recurs in several of your films, from Lemminge *to* Caché, *and your adaptation of* The Castle. *Before working on* The Castle, *you were involved in the hugely popular crime series* Tatort. *The episode you're credited with writing, back in 1993, is called* Kesseltreiben [Witch Hunt]. *Can you tell us a bit about it? We haven't seen it.*

You can forget about it because the film has nothing to do with the script I wrote. It was produced, like *Fräulein*, by Saarländischer

The Rebellion.

Rundfunk, but with a new script editor who had offered me the chance to write a script. I accepted, but the origins of this script go back further. It was originally commissioned by another broadcaster, Westdeutscher Rundfunk. To understand properly, it's important to recall that *Tatort* is not a traditional series with a recurring hero but rather a collection of standalone crime films. Nine regional broadcasters contribute to it, and each is required to highlight its local character, so there are as many different detectives as there are German federal states, each one featuring in its own region's episodes. I had written a script for Westdeutscher Rundfunk, set in North Rhine-Westphalia, in which I brought up the issue of nuclear power. At the time, I had the chance to meet a research physicist working at a university on the dangers specific to that field. He provided me with very alarming information about aging power plants that could become hazardous, and even gave me a tour of a modern, high-security facility. I did quite a bit of research, which I then used to write a crime thriller, but after reading my script, Westdeutscher Rundfunk refused to produce it.

For political reasons?

They never admitted it, but it was obvious. That's when the script editor at Saarländischer Rundfunk stepped in. With some modifications to the main character—turning him into a detective from Saarland—he took interest in my project. But just as we were about to start pre-production, he told me that the planned seven-week shoot had suddenly been reduced to four. For me, that was impossible. Then he gave me a choice: either we abandon the project altogether or I sell them my script so that someone else can direct it. I figured it was better to be paid for my work, so I opted for the second option, but when I saw the finished film, I realised it was a complete disaster, bearing no resemblance to my script. They had removed all the disturbing revelations about nuclear power and replaced them with clichés. For example, in my script, the nuclear plant workers are honest people, but in the final version they were all turned into villains, which stripped the film of any complexity or seriousness. I had my name removed from the credits and replaced it with "Richard Binder," a pseudonym I invented. That hasn't stopped some networks from rebroadcasting the film under the tagline "Screenplay by Haneke."

The Castle (1997)

The land surveyor K., newly appointed, arrives at night in the village where he is to take up his post. He finds lodging at an inn while waiting to be summoned to begin his work. The region appears to be governed by an administration based in a feared and near-inaccessible location known as The Castle, whose officials are almost impossible to reach. Shortly after his arrival, K. is saddled with two assistants who are undisciplined, mocking and, above all, of no help in his attempts to reach his superiors. He then meets Barnabas, a messenger from the castle who provides him with little useful information, and Frieda, a woman who works at another inn and claims to be the mistress of Klamm, the very man K. must meet to gain access to the castle. K. soon becomes Frieda's lover, hoping that she will help him achieve his goal, but from encounter to encounter, from closed doors to ones that open but to no purpose, K. is left wandering, powerless before the invisibility of power, never truly knowing what is expected of him.

Before discussing the origins of your adaptation of Kafka's The Castle, *which you directed in 1996 after* 71 Fragments of a Chronology of Chance, *we would like to ask why you returned to television after having started making films for the cinema.*

Simply because I was offered the opportunity. At a time when it was still difficult for me to make one feature film after another, it was gratifying to have someone ask what I wanted to do next. That's how I managed to push through *The Castle*, despite the network's lack of enthusiasm. I figured that if I was going to go back to television, I might as well take on something ambitious, and this adaptation felt like the ultimate challenge. What drew me to Kafka is his way of depicting reality that isn't quite real, and the challenge of finding a cinematic equivalent for that. At the same time, I would never have taken on a project like this for cinema because, as I've said before, the film is the finished *work*. I had seen Rudolf Noelte's 1968 adaptation with Maximilian Schell and disliked it. Noelte was a great theatre director but he knew nothing about cinema, and he made numerous errors with his adaptation, like showing the castle. Nothing in his film really works, and I thought I could at least try to do better.

Was it just a coincidence that you adapted this unfinished, frag-mented text right after making your own 71 Fragments?

Actually, it felt as if Kafka's text gave me permission to speak, in my own way, about fragments. I've always believed it's no accident that his novel is fragmented. Even if Kafka had lived longer, *The Castle* would have remained unfinished. It's like *The Man Without Qualities*, which Robert Musil spent decades writing without ever completing because a novel like that resists completion. I think there came a point in the history of literature and culture when it was no longer possible to pretend you could gather the whole world into a single book, which means this kind of approach can only ever be fragmentary. *The Castle* is probably the best-known example of that. For me, adapting it felt like a kind of necessity, almost like following a kind of roadmap.

What challenges did adapting the book pose?

It's always the same problem when you adapt a novel. Reading it takes several days, then you have to turn it into a two-hour film. If you manage to get even 20 percent of its richness onto the screen, you're doing well. The real difficulty is in making choices: what absolutely has to stay, what can be cut? You have to pare the story down to its essence. But with Kafka, where everything feels essential, that becomes even harder, and writing the script was a real struggle. Every time I cut something, it felt like I was committing a crime. I did the best I could, but it took a long time.

As in The Seventh Continent *and* 71 Fragments, *you inserted black frames between sequences.*

To reinforce the idea of fragmentation.

It also feels like a kind of breathing space, a musical pause.

Exactly. What I like is that it serves both as a way to structure the narrative and as something purely musical. In *The Seventh Continent*, every black frame lasted exactly two seconds, and in *71 Fragments*, their duration depended on the length and weight of the preceding scene, but I had no such rule for *The Castle*.

As in your other television films, you used voiceover, but in The Castle *it seems to create a sense of distance from the story.*

You're right. The voiceover isn't used here the way it was in *Drei Wege zum See* or *The Rebellion*, where the narrator's voice coexists with scenes of dialogue. In *The Castle*, it is the narrator who dictates the rhythm and structures the dialogue. He describes the situation, then gives way to the characters. That's hard to pull off in a film. We didn't record the voiceover before the shoot. Instead, I recorded myself reading the text so I could time it precisely, down to the second, so that the actors would know exactly when to begin speaking. They didn't particularly like doing that, but it was the best way I could find to stay as faithful as possible to Kafka. In *Drei Wege zum See*, I remember that in the scene where the photographer lists, in voiceover, all the famous people she has met, I made a point of *not* matching the images on screen to the names mentioned. At the time, that seemed like an elegant choice, but now I think it was a mistake. I've come to prefer a kind of simplicity, where you can test the truth of the image against the spoken text. That made filming *The Castle* more complicated, but I really enjoyed experimenting with voiceover in that way.

The uneven pacing makes it hard for the viewer to identify with the protagonist, and instead encourages them to reflect.

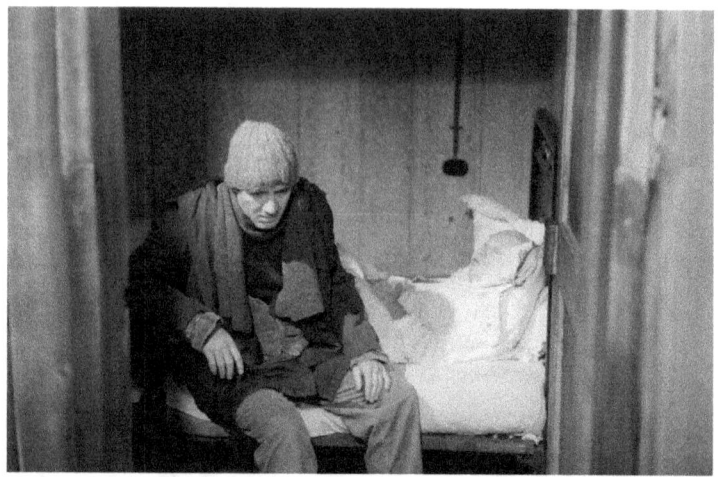

Ulrich Mühe and Norbert Schwientek in *The Castle*.

Yes, the rhythm is kind of offbeat, and you end up turning your focus back on yourself.

This sense of detachment is also brilliantly reinforced by Ulrich Mühe's restrained performance. He is the perfect embodiment of K.

K. is you and me. And Ulrich Mühe really was the ideal embodiment of that because he was the kind of person you wouldn't notice if you passed him on the street. No matter what situation you put him in, he was always credible—not as a character but as a kind of screen onto which you could project yourself. He was the complete opposite of Branko Samarovski, who played Andreas Plum in *The Rebellion*. Samarovski, with his expressive face, instantly *is* a character, but *The Castle* is not the story of *a* character, it is the story of all of us, which is why Mühe was perfect for the part. He is, in general, my ideal actor because my characters are always more than just characters. They have a universal dimension that speaks directly to something in us.

You stayed true to the comic element in the novel by giving some weight to K.'s two assistants. But like Ulrich Mühe, Frank Giering and Felix Eitner play their parts with a certain restraint.

The challenge was finding actors who could be funny without overplaying. I was very happy with their work. And they looked a bit alike, which enhanced their strangeness. That's something Noelte missed completely in his adaptation. He cast twins who weren't even actors. The crucial point in the scenes with the two assistants is to make the audience lose track of who is who. As in life, you're no longer sure who you're dealing with.

And to top it off, Susanne Lothar is extraordinary. Was this your first time working with her?

Yes, and we clicked right away. She's incredibly brave and likes taking risks and pushing things to the extreme, like Isabelle Huppert.

How did you meet her? Did you seek her out?

Susanne was a famous theatre actress, but I actually met her through Mühe, who was married to her at the time. Similarly, I met Benoît Magimel when I got in touch with Juliette Binoche, since they were a couple at the time. There's always an element of chance in these kinds of encounters.

Did acting together create any issues for the Mühe and Lothar?

Actors who are couples often say that working together is an advantage because they can continue rehearsing at home. I had actually previously directed an actor couple twice before and swore I would never do it again because I found everything more complicated. But with Ulrich and Susanne, it was different. They told me they never discussed work at home. Even when they had scenes together, they prepared separately because their approaches were different. Ulrich was a highly intellectual actor; he analysed every detail and knew exactly how to execute what he had prepared. Susanne, on the other hand, would learn her lines and immediately throw herself into the scene. I mentioned Isabelle Huppert earlier. She's like Ulrich and knows exactly what she's going to do. I can ask her to start crying on a specific word at a precise moment and she'll do it. Susanne works from pure emotion, which means that if she doesn't feel her character, her performance is off. She doesn't have it in her to fake it. When we were shooting the intense scenes in *Funny Games*, both Ulrich and Susanne were excellent, but we had to reshoot several of the early scenes because Susanne wasn't yet in the right mindset. She hadn't tapped into the emotional undercurrent she needs to really shine. It's a very delicate process.

Haneke directing Susanne Lothar
nd Ulrich Mühe in *The Castle*.

Every actor is different, and you have to adapt. That's very much one of the pleasures of this profession.

Watching the film, we were struck by the frequent use of lateral tracking shots. You constantly follow K. this way.

Yes, because he's always moving forward, on a path that never ends. The film concludes, like the novel, in the middle of a sentence, at a moment when he's still moving forward, as we're all doing. Even if we're not entirely sure what it is we're heading toward, we're always on the way.

Another major stylistic element is the lighting. You don't really play with shadows, but you do light scenes so that we're more aware of what's behind the characters, for example at the beginning, when K. enters the inn.

That wasn't intended as an effect. I simply wanted to reproduce normal human vision. When I look at you, I see only your face, and everything else is blurred. I've often worked this way. Nowadays, with digital technology, you end up seeing every last detail whether you want to or not.

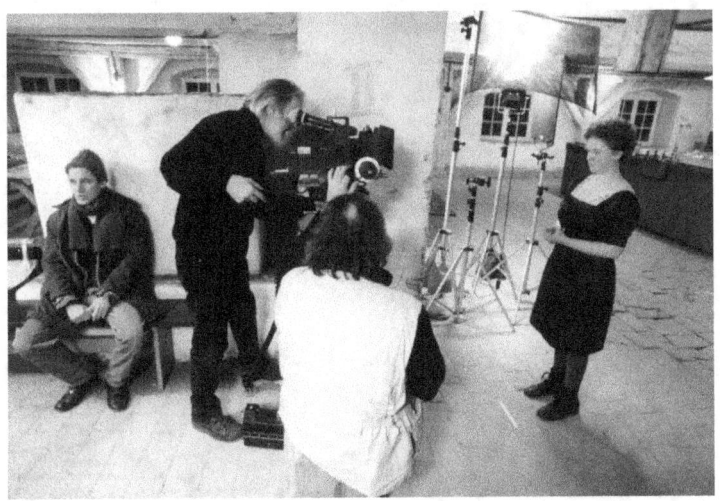

Haneke directing *The Castle*.

This lack of depth of field reinforces the sense of suffocation. The camera stays constantly on K., and when people in the background move, they are difficult to make out.

We have to stay with him because he's our stand-in. If you take that logic to the extreme, we could have shot the whole thing in subjective camera, but that wouldn't have made any sense.

Ending the film abruptly, like the novel, right in the middle of the story, is quite disorienting.

The producers certainly weren't thrilled, but it's simply a way of staying faithful to the text. I remember attending a Kafka film retrospective in Hamburg where they screened a Russian version of *The Castle*. It stuck to the novel for the first third, then just made up the rest. It had beautiful imagery, grand sets and lots of snow, but it was so bad I couldn't understand how anyone had thought it was a good idea.

Your version creates a strong sense of timelessness.

That's exactly what I was aiming for. Right from the start, you're not quite sure where or when it's taking place. That ambiguity is important, because if you pin the setting down too precisely, you end up stripping away some of the novel's complexity. We tried to

Haneke directs Birgit Linauer in *The Castle.*

choose everyday objects you might still find in a village fifty years from now. The only thing that inevitably fixes the story in time is the mode of transport. We debated whether to use a car, but I didn't like that idea, so we stuck to horses and sleighs—but subtly. I wasn't hugely enthusiastic about them either, but in some important scenes the characters needed some way of getting around, and those kinds of sleighs do still exist in some places, so we figured it could work.

Another striking feature is the absence of music. All that remains is silence, perhaps the silence of God, or of God's absence.

I've said it before: Kafka *with* music is unimaginable.

Seven

My beginnings in cinema — The fake Australian beach in *The Seventh Continent* — I'm no tormentor of children — Bach chorales in a scrapyard — *Benny's Video* and the weight of the media — The girl, the three pigs, and the fake snow — My meeting with Ulrich Mühe — *71 Fragments of a Chronology of Chance* as a choral film — The thorny question of emigration — The cross and the mikado — The violence of ping-pong

Let's now turn to your early work in cinema, starting with your trilogy: The Seventh Continent, Benny's Video *and* 71 Fragments of a Chronology of Chance. *Did you write all three screenplays in one go?*

I wrote the script for *The Seventh Continent* for television. Radio Bremen, a German station, had asked me to work on a project with them, and I pitched the story, inspired by an article published ten years earlier in *Stern* about a family that, before committing suicide, destroyed all their belongings. The article offered various psychological and social explanations, but what interested me was the idea of obliterating the material world that had, in a way, crushed you—before turning on yourself. The people at Radio Bremen weren't enthusiastic about the project, but when I told them I had no other ideas, they gave me an advance to write the script, and once they read it, they ended up backing out. Public opinion at the time was still reeling from a widely reported case of a man suffering from depression who took his own life after watching a TV programme. Around then I started getting offers to work in film, so I thought the script might be a good opportunity to try out what, for me, was still a new language. The first attempt fell apart after I teamed up with a producer who was so hopeless that I dropped the whole thing right away. Then I got in touch with

Haneke and Veit Heiduschka
at the Cannes Film Festival in 1989.

Veit Heiduschka at Wega-Film. He was very interested and managed
to secure funding relatively easily.

*Was the funding strictly for cinema, or was it in partnership with
television?*

As a purely Austrian production, *The Seventh Continent* bene-
fited from three funding sources: the state, the City of Vienna,
and Austria's public television, through a fund dedicated to films
produced for the big screen.

Why did you choose to approach Veit Heiduschka?

Because he was well known. At the time, there weren't many film
producers in Austria. If they wanted state funding, they couldn't
submit more than one project at a time, meaning they rarely
produced more than one film a year. To survive, most of them
co-produced with television—but not Heiduschka. He started off
by producing small films and had a major success in 1985 with
Müllers Büro, a musical crime comedy.

*You have been loyal to him. His name is attached to all your later
films, except* Code Unknown *and the U.S. version of* Funny Games.

It's less about Heiduschka himself and more about his production director, Michael Katz, who is quite brilliant. Without him, I probably wouldn't have made *The White Ribbon*, because it was such a complicated project, and he was the only one I trusted to ensure everything ran smoothly. He's a film fanatic and a real pro who always understands exactly what I'm after. We argued a lot at first because his tastes are so different from mine. He loves action films and comedies, which are basically the exact opposite of what I do, but he quickly saw the point of my films and gave his all. He recently produced the first feature film of one of my students and was present at every step of the way to help.

The Seventh Continent (1989)

Linz, 1987. A couple, Georg and Anna, and their young daughter, Eva. A clear picture of socio-professional success. A high-tech family environment. Yet, beneath the routine of daily life, an undefined malaise begins to surface. A recurring image of an Australian beach appears, an elusive call toward an equally undefined elsewhere.

1988. An increasingly mechanical existence, superimposed onto what is supposed to be a living reality. The sight of a fatal car accident provokes no emotional reaction, only the emergence of an idea.

1989. Georg suggests to Anna that they cancel their newspaper subscription. He resigns from his job. She transfers ownership of her shop to her brother. The couple withdraws all their money from the bank. Georg buys an axe, a hammer and an electric drill. Eva is to stop attending school. Georg sells the family car. He rips out the telephone line. Anna tears up their clothes. Eva destroys her books. Georg saws apart the furniture, smashes the aquarium and flushes banknotes down the toilet. Eva drinks a mixture prepared by her parents, Anna swallows pills, Georg fills a syringe. The television remains on, but no programmes are being broadcast.

The bodies are discovered on October 17, 1990. Georg's parents do not believe it was a suicide and filed a complaint for murder. The case is closed without further action.

Did you immediately find the structure for your story?

No, at first I wanted to tell the story in flashback, starting with the suicide and working backwards. I spent a lot of time developing this approach on the Greek island where I had gone to write, but I couldn't come up with any flashbacks that didn't feel like explanations of the family's behaviour. I was stuck for three weeks. Then, suddenly, it hit me: the film shouldn't rely on flashbacks at all. I needed to write it as a chronicle, taking one day in these people's lives, then another a year later, and so on, juxtaposing the scenes. That way, it would be up to the viewer to connect the dots. Moreover, it was a kind of storytelling that I had never tried before.

One of the great innovations in The Seventh Continent *is fragmentation, both narratively and aesthetically—fragmentation in the timeline and in the way the shots are tightly framed, all of which creates intense tension.*

Yes, it's very claustrophobic. What I wanted to show is what, in German, we call *Die Verdinglichung des Lebens*, which you could translate as "the reification of life," or in other words, how our day-to-day existence becomes routine and how we end up glued to objects. That's why the editing is so rhythmic and why I use tight framing on objects that have lost their original meaning and have come to define our existence.

Is this a way of denouncing how people become alienated through material things?

Yes, and that's why this family ends up destroying everything they own. But what's tragic is that they do it without truly achieving liberation. They destroy their belongings the same way they have lived: mechanically. That, to me, is the saddest part of the film. They could have made a radical break and liberated themselves from all the rubbish that poisons their lives, in a sort of ecstatic suicide, but that's something they can't even begin to imagine. In the end, man ceases to exist because he is merely the sum of his habits, and even after destroying everything, nothing has changed. Their material world has consumed their inner life, which is why they have nothing left to do but commit suicide, even if it serves no purpose.

And that act is misunderstood, since Georg's parents are convinced it was murder.

In truth, they don't *want* to understand. They refuse to accept that their son took his own life. That's a perfectly normal reaction; it saves them from feeling guilty. Even if they can understand it intellectually, they can't accept it emotionally because that would mean they're in the same position as he was.

In a similar vein, there's a strange moment early in the film when Eva, the couple's daughter, pretends to be blind at school. Is that a metaphor?

You could see it as a metaphor, but also as slightly neurotic behaviour caused by the oppressive environment she lives in. Children in such situations sometimes invent stories in which they are persecuted. It's a way of crying out for help. But I don't want to impose my own interpretation. That's one way of looking at it. There are plenty of others.

The young actress you chose for the role, Leni Tanzer, is incredibly expressive, with her beautiful face and heavy eyelids.

It's difficult to play someone pretending to be blind, and she pulled it off beautifully.

How did you choose her?

As always, by auditioning dozens and dozens of children. She came in, and I immediately knew she was the one. It was the same with the boy in *Benny's Video*.

Do you send an assistant around the country to find children for these roles?

For the initial selection, the casting director takes photos and conducts interviews. I review everything and pick who I want to meet, then I talk to them a little to gauge their level of shyness. If their look and personality seem right, I have them do a screen test, always the most difficult scenes in the script. That way, I can immediately see if the child is right for the role. It's the same with adult actors. I always tell my students that casting is half their job. The other half is preparation. Casting isn't just about choosing a good actor; it's about choosing the *right* actor for a particular role.

Leni Tanzer in *The Seventh Continent*.

There have been times when I had a very talented actor who just didn't work in the role I gave him. That was my fault, of course. The same applies to children.

Eva marks the start of a long series of children in your films who fall victim to the alienated world of adults.

I swear I'm not a child torturer! But that's the reality of the world, and, of course, it's also a dramatic device that has a powerful impact on audiences. The same applies to animals, who suffer a lot in my films. Like children, they can't defend themselves, making the effects of violence all the more palpable. You could almost say the same about women. I always give them more rewarding roles than men. Being a victim is actually more rewarding for an actor. Playing a hero? That's just Charlton Heston nonsense. It's really boring.

Earlier we were talking about all the slaps scattered through your films. Part of your strength as a filmmaker is the way you calibrate violence.

I try to avoid extremes because they immediately feel false. In daily life, disagreements are usually moderate, and even the slightest act of violence affects us deeply. When I directed *Who's Afraid of*

Virginia Woolf? in Berlin, the actors wanted to start by slapping each other or throwing whiskey in each other's faces in the first act. I explained that such an outburst was already out of the ordinary, and if they began like that, by the third act they would have no choice but to murder each other.

Did you feel that by working in cinema, you could explore things in greater complexity?

For me, moving into cinema was primarily a different way of writing my scripts, more than just directing, since in my case the direction always follows the screenplay. Most of my television films were adaptations of literary works, and as I've said before, my goal was to encourage viewers to read the books after watching the adaptations. In German, there's a word for this: *Bildungsauftrag*—a kind of mission to educate or inform the public. That fits well with television. But in cinema, there is no such obligation. A novel adapted for the screen is simply raw material for the filmmaker, which is why literary adaptations in cinema are rarely successful. They either illustrate the book in a flat, literal way, or they completely betray it in order to make a good film.

When you write your scripts, have you already planned out the shot-by-shot structure?

Everything is written and planned in detail. I can't imagine working any other way. *Code Unknown*, for example, would have been impossible to shoot in long takes if everything hadn't already been fully mapped out in the script. You need to be able to visualise the layout of the space in order to follow a character with a camera.

Do you ever make adjustments to what you originally planned?

It depends on the style of the film. In *The Seventh Continent* and *Code Unknown*, everything was written and filmed exactly as I had planned. With *The White Ribbon*, some scenes were shot differently than originally conceived. The first draft of the script had been written ten years earlier, and back then, I wouldn't have dared to shoot the film in long takes. In the original script, for example, the scene where Martin is punished took place on screen, but when I reread it I found it weak, and after much thought I designed a studio set that allowed me to stage the punishment indirectly, entirely off screen.

The Seventh Continent.

Was structuring The Seventh Continent, *your first feature film, into three clearly defined time periods, each with precise actions, a way of giving yourself more control?*

What you're describing isn't unique to a first film; it's something we always try to achieve when constructing the structure of a film: finding the right form to express what we want to say, an aesthetic that works for both the imagery and the storytelling. It requires great rigour. Let me give you an example. The other day, a student presented his script to me. In the middle of the story, he had inserted a brief montage to indicate the passage of time, the only one in the entire screenplay. I told him it didn't work because, until that point, his story had been told linearly, and suddenly, time was supposed to speed up. That would only be acceptable if he structured the entire film that way; otherwise, it felt like an artificial trick to escape a narrative dead-end. A screenplay must have a well-thought-out, aesthetically coherent structure, almost like a musical composition. Of all the art forms, cinema is undoubtedly closest to music.

This musical structure in The Seventh Continent *is evident in your use of recurring visual motifs, like the garage door closing or the Australia travel ad, and also in your use of Bach's chorales, which return like a refrain.*

Some members of the audience might recognise the Bach chorales, which I also used in *71 Fragments*. In the scene in *71 Fragments*

The Seventh Continent.

near the end, the main character is standing outside a bank, and next to it is a travel agency. When the door opens, you hear a pop version of a Bach chorale playing inside. I like that kind of small detail. It's a wink to anyone who notices. If the audience picks up on it, great; if not, it doesn't matter. The first award I ever received for a film was at the Ghent Festival, for my use of Alban Berg's Violin Concerto in the junkyard scene in *The Seventh Continent*. In its second movement, there's a reference to a Bach chorale, *Es ist genug* [It is enough]. If you recognise it, that's an added pleasure. It's not essential to the plot, but it deepens the film's atmosphere.

How did you shoot that scene?

In the script, it was written that the father and daughter were in a car junkyard while a boat passed by, but during filming we cheated. The junkyard and the boat scene were filmed in different locations. We brought two old cars onto a dock by the Danube, near a railing, to make the shots match.

Why did you feel the need to have that white boat passing near the junkyard?

It felt real. That's what the little girl sees at that moment. My challenge was to show her doing something in this strange place while her father was getting rid of the car.

For us as viewers, the passing boat recalls the Australia travel ad.

Exactly. It's the last glimmer of hope at that point in the film. But we don't know if it's something that's really happening or just something Eva imagines.

And Alban Berg's music?

Purely because of the Bach chorale I mentioned. "Es ist genug, Herr, wenn es dir gefällt, so spanne mich doch aus." ["It is enough, Lord; if it pleases You, release me from this world."]

Following this same paradoxical juxtaposition of the boat and the junkyard, you also contrast the fancy dinner the woman orders from the caterer with the tools, including the axe, that the man buys.

That contrast is there to build tension, to make the viewer uneasy, until they start to grasp what's coming. For me, it's not really a contradiction. The champagne and the axe both serve the same purpose.

Why did you choose Australia for the poster that appears five times?

First, because it's far away, and also because of the alliteration between Australia and Austria. More importantly, during the 1970s and 1980s, many Germans and Austrians emigrated to Australia. My brother-in-law, Susie's brother, moved there to work as a chef. Much like America in earlier times, Australia had become a land of desire, a dream destination for a fresh start.

Did you hesitate about when the poster should start coming to life?

No. When writing the script, I wasn't sure exactly what the final version of the poster would look like, but I had already decided that, from its second appearance, the ocean in the image would begin to move. In reality, we couldn't find the exact landscape we wanted for the poster, so we had to create a visual effect, combining footage of the sea and the surrounding land, which were filmed in separate locations. This gave the image a slightly unreal quality, which adds to the oppressive atmosphere. When you first see the poster, you don't immediately understand it. It makes you stop and wonder.

How did you come up with the title The Seventh Continent?

It wasn't mine. It was suggested by the wife of the lead actor, Dieter Berner, because I had no idea what to call the film. As soon as I heard it, I thought it was a good idea. If you count Antarctica, that gives you six continents, so the seventh suggests another place entirely, a land of longing, a kind of *Sehnsucht* — that deep, aching longing for something else.

Why did you choose a variety show as the last television programme the family watches before they die?

Because it was neutral. When you use radio or TV in a scene, you have to be careful the programme doesn't carry too much meaning because it might end up commenting on the scene in a way you don't want. That's why, in my films, you mostly hear weather reports or traffic updates, things that don't steer audiences in any particular direction. In *71 Fragments*, the television news clips were meant to provide context for the action without influencing it. To avoid any risk of distortion or manipulation, we stuck to actual reports from the dates referenced in the script, even though, from day to day, the news is always more or less always the same. For the final night in *The Seventh Continent*, I wanted something that was pure entertainment, and a variety show was a good fit.

It's interesting that The Seventh Continent *ends with a shot of a television screen broadcasting nothing at all, watched by a dying man, while in your next film,* Nachruf für einen Mörder, *which was made for television and which we have already discussed, you explore a massacre carried out by a young man, and you examine everything that was broadcast on Austrian TV that day.*

That really was a coincidence, although it's true that this was around the time when I started getting very interested in the media, and once you're immersed in a particular theme or subject, you tend to stick with it. It's like when your wife is pregnant, and suddenly, everywhere you go, you notice pregnant women for the first time. That's what Cassavetes has his character say in *A Woman Under the Influence*.

People often talk about how prominent television screens are in your films, but what also stands out is how often you frame characters behind or near windows. Why is that?

It's often just a practical necessity, for example the bank scene, where the camera is inside the booth with the clerk, who is on one side of the glass, while the couple is on the other. But the prevalence of windows in my films also comes from a natural behaviour I have observed in real life, which is that during arguments, people tend to look away, staring into the distance through the nearest window to avoid making direct eye contact with their interlocutor. It's like part of a visual reflex, a spatial pattern that repeats itself. And it works really well on screen.

These recurring objects and setups are interesting, because unlike some directors who feel the need to constantly reinvent themselves, you seem more inclined to revisit the same themes and visual language in order to go deeper with them.

That's simply because I can only tell stories about things I feel I know, whether I'm right or not. For example, I could never make a comedy. I wouldn't know how to do it. Not that I don't like the genre; I really enjoy watching comedies when they're well done, but it's just not something I can do. I wouldn't even be much help to the actors. I like directing them in dramatic scenes or arguments, but comedy? That would be impossible for me. Remember what I told you about my disastrous experience in the theatre, trying to stage that Labiche farce.

In The Seventh Continent, *the black frames between sequences vary in length. How did you decide how long they should be?*

It was really a question of rhythm, or musicality. If a scene conveyed something very simple, the black screen would be short, but if it required more effort from the viewer, more time to process what they had just seen, it would last longer. I eventually gave up using this technique after *71 Fragments* because projectionists tended to cut the black screens, especially if they fell at the start or end of a reel.

After the scene where the father rips out the phone cord, there are thirteen seconds of black. Why so long?

To make it clear that everything is over.

The film is divided into three parts of very unequal length. It becomes clearer why the third feels so heavy when you realise that it's longer than the first two combined.

The Seventh Continent.

The third part is the longest because it's the sum of everything I didn't show in the first two. It marks a radical shift. In contrast, the second part is the shortest because it only shows the small changes in routine compared to what we saw in the first.

Why, in the first part, does the mother wear a yellow bathrobe, then a white one in the second, and by the third she is dressed only in black or khaki?

That gradual loss of colour is emotional. It mirrors the changes in how the character is feeling.

Similarly, in the dinner scene with the brother-in-law, played by Udo Samel, we notice that in the shots of the couple, the background is grey, but in the reverse shots of the depressed brother-in-law, it's noticeably darker.

Yes, but that wasn't intentional. It was because of the layout of the set we built in the studio. Since it was night time, the brother-in-law had his back to the window, whereas the couple was positioned in front of the fish tank. I had no choice but to shoot it that way, using realistic lighting in the studio, because of the later scene where the father destroys the fish tank. That was actually the trickiest scene to shoot. After that, the set started to stink because everything was soaked. We still had several days of filming left.

In the sequence where household possessions are destroyed, there is a particularly provocative shot: the banknotes being flushed down the toilet.

I knew that would shock people; I even warned my producer. He thought the most disturbing moment would be the shots of the fish dying. I should mention that we saved all of them except one… The first screening in Cannes, at the Directors' Fortnight proved me right: a few dozen left the theatre at the moment the money was destroyed. That was predictable because money remains one of the last great taboos, more than the suffering of animals, more than the death of a child. You can show anything, except that. It's as unacceptable today as spitting on a crucifix was in the Middle Ages.

Pierre-Henri Deleau selected the film for the Directors' Fortnight at Cannes. Do you remember where he first saw it?

He was searching for films all over the world and went to the Austrian Film Commission—the equivalent of your Unifrance—where they screened several films for him, including mine. He liked it and selected it. Naturally, he then wanted to see my subsequent films, *Benny's Video* and *71 Fragments of a Chronology of Chance*, which he also screened at the Directors' Fortnight. I owe him a great deal. I was especially happy about *The Seventh Continent* because it was the first time an Austrian film had been selected for the Directors' Fortnight. To be precise, Deleau also selected another Austrian feature that year, Michael Schottenberg's *Caracas*. Additionally, another Austrian film, Michael Synek's *Die Toten Fische*, was shown at the Critics Week. Synek is very talented, but he never made another feature because he spent twenty years paying off the debts he incurred making that film.

Let's move on to Benny's Video. *You may have noticed that we haven't yet mentioned the term "emotional glaciation," which annoys you a bit, even though it perfectly describes your relentless style.*

I try to find a form that perfectly matches the content. When dealing with a serious subject, there's an obligation to ensure the form is convincing and serious as well. I always advise my students not to tackle subjects like the Holocaust for their first film, not just because of financial constraints but because they lack the maturity to find the right form. It's better for them to make a film about their grandmother. As I often say, only Alain Resnais, with *Night and Fog*, and, of course, Claude Lanzmann, with *Shoah*, managed to handle that subject. But those are documentaries. Spielberg's *Schindler's List* was a disaster. But that's another story…

Formal rigour allows for a form of sublimation, even transcendence. While your trilogy may seem emotionally cold at first, its beauty quickly dispels that impression.

I hope so. It's the same criticism people made about Bresson, calling his cinema "cold," although personally, I find it deeply moving. It's the kind of cinema that is more serious and less simplistic or emotionally manipulative than a television film or a mainstream production.

Compared with your later feature films, your trilogy has a different aesthetic, where the concept of media plays a crucial role. In these three films, the individual is crushed by media, by television and video.

In *Caché*, and in a different way in *Code Unknown*, media also play a recurring role. In fact, I have tried to give all my films a self-reflexive dimension. This connects them to German literature after the Second World War. Since the Nazis had proven themselves such masters of media manipulation—outdoing even Eisenstein in terms of propaganda—intellectuals became acutely aware of how literature and cinema could be used for manipulation. That, in my view, is why major German-language writers turned toward self-reflexive literature, a literature that, as Adorno pointed out, reflected its own means of expression, mirrored itself, and thus made readers aware that they were engaging with a work of art, not reality. That's the tradition my films belong to. I can't work any other way. When I write a script, I feel compelled to build in a certain distance; otherwise, I feel uncomfortable. Even in *The White Ribbon*, where the action is linear, it still passes through the filter of a narrator who expresses his doubts about the truth of what is being shown.

Is that connected to something you often say, that we're no longer in the 19th century, when it was still possible to create the illusion of reality?

Yes, exactly. In the 19th century, literature sought to reaffirm the bourgeoisie's place in society, even when it was critical of it. That's no longer possible. Today, we're forced to take a stand, to be forever denouncing what's wrong, both in form and content.

Benny's Video, *which was screened at Cannes in 1992, is an especially emblematic film because it shows how a teenager is alienated through his relationship with video technology and how people can no longer perceive reality except through a screen. How did you come up with the story?*

I came across several news reports about young people who had committed murder and, when asked why, simply answered: "I wanted to know what it felt like." That deeply disturbed me, and I began thinking about the issue.

Benny's Video (1992)

Benny, a teenager, is obsessed with video and violence. The former allows him to record the latter and watch it endlessly. He is particularly captivated by footage of a pig being slaughtered on a farm. In a video rental store, he notices a girl his own age. Shortly thereafter, he invites her to his home and shows her his audiovisual setup, along with the film of the pig. As always, his video camera is running and records the entire scene. Benny then shows the girl the bolt pistol he has stolen from the farmhouse. When she refuses to pull the trigger and instead dares him to do it, he shoots her, seriously wounding her, then finishing her off. Some time later, Benny shows the recording of the "accidental" killing to his parents, who have just returned home. Shocked by what they see and intent on protecting their son, they decide to dispose of the body. While the father cuts the corpse into pieces, the mother travels to Egypt with her son. Upon their return, everything appears to be in order. Benny resumes his activities at school and in his choir. Soon afterward, Benny is seen at the police station, where he plays back the recording of his parents' conversation, in which they discuss eliminating all traces of the "accident." The mother and father are arrested. Benny watches them. "Excuse me," he says politely.

According to Marshall McLuhan, television is a cool medium. The faces of your three main characters all display a cold, detached gaze.

Exactly. That kind of behaviour doesn't come out of a warm family environment. Psychologists have written plenty about this. There are people who aren't necessarily perverse, but who simply lack a sense of compassion. Like Benny, they can kill without feeling the slightest bit of remorse. If you look into their backgrounds, you almost always find they were raised in emotionally cold households. The lack of compassion they experienced makes it hard for them to feel pity in return.

The world of video—the "global village" so dear to McLuhan— acts like a screen between people and the real world, distorting how we perceive reality and turning other human beings into objects.

Which leads to acts of extreme violence, the kind we constantly see in the media. I often say, if television were my only source of information about the world, I would have killed myself by now. The news is nothing but disasters, violence and suffering. Fiction films pile it on with even more spectacle, pushing us further away from a real sense of what's true. If you haven't had direct experience of physical violence—and fortunately, most people in Europe haven't—and you're a child, you can easily mistake this kind of violence-as-spectacle for reality. Even if someone tells a kid, "You're not supposed to hit people," it's hard for them to believe that when all they see on TV is people hitting each other. On top of that, it's made to look fun, even entertaining. It warps the way we see things. If your life is fairly normal, you can work around it and eventually figure these things out, but if you're under emotional or social pressure, it can get hard to tell the difference between fiction and reality. You can already see this in school playgrounds. When I was a kid, if we got into a fight at school, hitting someone in the face was absolutely off-limits. These days, it's not unusual to see kids kicking each other in the face. Where does that shift come from? People often say it's society's fault, that things have just gotten more violent. But that's only part of the story. The horrors of the Second World War didn't immediately make everyday life more violent. I'm not saying it's all down to the media either; that would be silly. But I do think it's clear that the media play a role in how violence has evolved in our daily lives.

Arno Frisch and Ingrid Stassner in *Benny's Video*.

The media have contributed to a kind of "de-realisation of the world." We no longer perceive reality directly; we only see it through its representation.

And there's also the issue of repetition in how violence is shown. In everyday life, you see people honking their horns or being rude on the subway, but you rarely see someone actually hitting someone else. On TV, though, it never stops.

There's a particularly chilling moment in your film, when right after Benny kills the girl, he walks calmly to the fridge and takes out a yogurt.

I don't actually find that behaviour chilling. When you're in shock, you're capable of doing totally unexpected things. In German, there's a word for it: *Übersprungshandlung*, which basically means jumping over the situation emotionally and doing some kind of substitute action. He could have turned on the TV, sat down, then stood up again. In moments like that, you do things without realising it. The brain shuts down rational thought as a way to protect itself from the trauma.

You don't show the murder itself. Instead, we just hear the sound of the bolt pistol Benny uses. Was that your way of making it more effective?

Absolutely. All the best thrillers and horror films work that way. It's always more powerful to let the audience imagine something than to force an image on them, because the image is almost always less powerful. Sometimes banality can be effective too, but in this case, if you show Benny finishing her off, it just falls flat on a technical level. You're asking two teenagers to act out a death scene, which is unlikely to be very convincing. I've rarely seen any actor do it well, with the exception of Oskar Werner in *Ship of Fools*. I have no idea how he did it, but the moment he has the heart attack, it's like his whole body just stops. It's astonishing. He was one of the great actors of the 20th century. Generally speaking, I don't think you should show a character dying; it almost always rings false. That's the technical reason. The purely cinematic reason is that our imagination provides more than any image ever could.

But we do see the scene on Benny's video monitor.

That's meant to make the audience stop and think. You're watching one medium—video—framed by another: cinema. It's like that Magritte painting, the one with the man looking into a mirror and seeing the back of his own head.

It even feels like, in that image-within-the-image, Benny is literally pushing the girl out of frame. After the first shot, she falls. He tells her he's going to help her, then comes back to reload the gun and pushes her out of frame again each time he fires.

Because he doesn't want her to leave the room. And since the camera is fixed, there's no way to pan.

In other words, you arrange things so that the character's motivations align with your staging?

Exactly. That's why we chose that particular camera angle. Without the door in the frame, we wouldn't have been able to get that effect.

Then you make us live through it again, when Benny shows the footage to his parents. This time, there's an added level of horror, because now we're seeing the parents' reactions.

I've noticed that audiences are often more disturbed the second time than the first. The first time, it's so shocking you're kind of numb to it, but the second time, you identify with the parents, and that hits much harder emotionally.

Also, when you see it again, you remember how long the scene lasts, and you dread having to sit through the whole thing again.

Yes, that works well.

Meanwhile, the mother watches the evening news with total detachment, even though it's covering a xenophobic attack and the war in Yugoslavia.

She's no different from the rest of us... I remember how shocked we all were when the massacres in Yugoslavia first started. But after two years of war, with those images leading the nightly news almost every day, we became what the Germans call *abgestumpft*: numb, jaded, desensitised. We stopped paying attention. To me, the most disturbing moment is when the girl watches the video of the pig being slaughtered and says, "Oh look, it's snowing!" That's when it gets really perverse.

This is the first film where you really tackle the idea of covering up serious wrongdoing, a theme you push even further in Caché. *Here, the parents, faced with their child's crime, do everything they can to erase the evidence. Would you say this impulse to avoid responsibility and guilt is part of a broader moral and emotional numbness in Western society today?*

Absolutely. That's exactly what it is. You can even read the film politically. The way the parents act—pretending to care about their son's future when really they're just protecting themselves—is no different from how Austria has dealt with its own recent history.

It's an idea that you generalise in Caché.

Yes, but we could just as easily have set that story somewhere other than France. This kind of behaviour exists everywhere. Every country has shameful chapters that it has swept under the rug of history.

But here the critique feels more material. You're mostly going after self-centred materialism.

The real shame doesn't lie with the people who commit evil acts; it lies with those who look away. The ones who dare to do harm are actually pretty rare, and in a way, they're brave. They know they'll probably have to face the consequences one day. Most people

Arno Frisch in *Benny's Video*.

prefer to think of themselves as innocent by simply not seeing what's happening. I do the same thing. At best, I can say I step slightly outside that general indifference by confronting it head-on in my work, but the truth is that we often look away because we feel powerless. Take how we deal with the Third World. We're all guilty. But where's the solution? We donate a little money after an earthquake or for some good cause, then we wash our hands of it.

But in Benny's Video, *you also explore the ambiguity of evil. Benny didn't lure the girl over to kill her; it was a chain of events that turned him into a murderer.*

I made sure to stage it in a way where you're never quite sure if it was an accident or something deliberate. He seems annoyed when she falls. I wanted to retain that ambiguity.

That's why there is this kind of game between them, where they call each other cowards and dare one another. On the other hand, the parents' reaction is cold-blooded, as they organise the disposal of the body in the most meticulous detail.

It's not that simple. Imagine you have a teenage son who killed someone—whether it was premeditated or not—and you realise that it will be nearly impossible to prove it was an accident. What do you do? Go straight to the police? I'm not excusing their actions; I just want to show how hard and complicated the situation is for the parents. That's what interests me, not judging them.

When we saw Benny cleaning blood off the floor of his room, we couldn't help but think of Norman Bates in the shower scene in Psycho. *Did that cross your mind when you were writing it?*

No, because the situations are really quite different. As with Hitchcock, the idea was to show that getting rid of all that blood isn't as easy as it looks, but what mattered more in this scene was that he couldn't stop the body from leaving marks as he dragged it. What really mattered to me was him pulling the girl's skirt back down over her legs.

And he has to film it to realise the skirt isn't in the right position

Yes, because his gaze is more focused that way. When you're looking through a camera's viewfinder, you see with a different kind of intensity. In real life, you might see everything, but you don't really look. When I frame a shot, I pay attention to everything I want to include. It's a different way of seeing. If you want a film reference—not one that's in the movie, but one that applies—it would be Michael Powell's *Peeping Tom*, which links the need to look with the need to film.

It's also interesting that both times Benny sees the girl at the video store, it's through the glass, as if she is framed in a kind of television screen.

Exactly.

The scene of the girl's murder is also sexually charged. There's the moment when Benny's camera, on its tripod, isolates the two young people's waists in the frame, as if suggesting the promise of intercourse. Then, after the murder, there's Benny's almost masturbatory act of smearing part of his naked body with his victim's blood. Is this meant to convey his sexual impotence?

I'm open to all interpretations, but I didn't film it as a sign of impotence. Given that they are both 15 years old, Benny and the girl are too young to have a sexual relationship. For me, it's clear that they are both still virgins. But there is obviously a kind of physical attraction between them. You could even argue that Benny's physical aggression is his clumsy way of trying to get closer to her. That

Arno Frisch and Ingrid Stassner in *Benny's Video*.

said, I agree with you about the masturbatory aspect of the gesture with the blood, and I can confirm that the pelvic framing was a very deliberate "accident."

What is striking and at the same time unsettling is that Benny only communicates with his parents through the images he has filmed. He does the same with the police, bringing his tapes to the station to get his parents convicted. And at the very end of your film, there is yet another film: he sees his parents at the police station through a surveillance screen.

This puts the audience in the same position as when they were watching the murder on Benny's monitor at the beginning.

From the spectator's perspective, this is a powerful moment of manipulation. When the parents discuss how to cover up the crime, the camera is positioned in Benny's room, aligned with the slightly open door, and we can barely hear what the parents are saying. Later, we see the same scene again, but with clearer sound, as Benny presents it to the police. That's when we realise Benny had secretly recorded from his room, his parents' scheme to exonerate him.

Actually, if you watched the film in a cinema, you would clearly hear the key words spoken by Benny's parents that he recorded, although on the DVD the dialogue is inaudible. That undermines what I was trying to do in terms of manipulating the audience while still maintaining a sense of realism. And the picture quality on the DVDs of my first three theatrical films is so bad that I can't watch them. We're trying to remaster them, but it's expensive.

Benny's Video also owes a lot to the quality of its three actors. Can you tell us how you chose them?

My wife Susie knew Arno Frisch because his brother went to school with my stepson. She kept telling me to audition him because he was really eager to act, but I didn't want to bother with neighbours' kids, so I searched everywhere in German-speaking countries, but couldn't find anyone. After Susie insisted again, "Just meet Arno, it won't cost you anything!" I gave in. I met with him, and it was immediately clear that he had to play Benny. He fit the character perfectly. In real life, he's just as you see him on screen, with the kind of arrogance that would work wonderfully in *Funny Games*.

Casting Ulrich Mühe as the father must have been a more straightforward process.

Not at all. It was our first collaboration, and I made a serious mistake. I initially thought of him, but for some reason, I cast another actor, whose name I would rather not mention, and we started shooting the farm scene at the beginning, where the pig has to be slaughtered. All he had to say to his son is, "*Lass das!*" ["Stop that!"] because he doesn't want to be filmed. And he was terrible. This was a major theatre star… I told myself we could redo the sound later, that it was just his first day of shooting, but after forty takes, he was still just as bad. The following week, I shot scenes without him, then he returned for the scene where the father enters the room where the young people are partying, slightly irritated. He only had to say, "Hello, everyone!" and again he was terrible. After a few more days of filming without him, he showed up for the scene where the father walks into Benny's room and asks him to open the window. He couldn't even open the door properly. I filmed anyway, thinking maybe it was my fault, that I was being too hostile toward him and that we would get a better sense of his performance when reviewing the rushes. Everyone on the production team was supposed to see the footage. As it happened, we had to screen it somewhere other than our usual viewing room, and the projection was terrible; the image kept shaking, so we changed venues. This time, the picture was stable and everyone was relieved—except me. I was so horrified by the actor's performance that I stood up and said we either recast the father or shut down production. Everyone was shocked because this theatre star was very expensive, but I insisted and got my way, then contacted Ulrich Mühe's agent, Erna Baumbauer, who I knew well. She was the best in the business, representing all the top German-speaking actors. She scolded me a little, but kindly as always, and reminded me that she had warned me from the start that I had picked the wrong actor. I asked if I could reach out to Ulrich Mühe, and in her strong Bavarian accent she told me to just call him, so I did. I explained the situation, and he immediately agreed. He joined us on set a few days later. Of course, we still had to pay the full salary of the first actor and reshoot the scene with the pig. With a different animal, of course. In fact, we had to slaughter a third pig because the wind was so strong that day that the fake snow—which I really wanted—didn't fall within the frame the first time!

Did you cast Angela Winkler because of her performance in Volker Schlöndorff's The Lost Honour of Katharina Blum?

No, not because of that, or any of her films, actually, where I often found her a bit irritating. I hired her because of her outstanding work on stage. She was incredible in Peter Zadek's productions. I think she's the greatest German actress of her generation. But in 1970s cinema, she somehow became this icon of the perpetually depressed German woman.

Benny's Video *is also the first time you worked with production designer Christoph Kanter, with whom you would go on to collaborate on eight of your next ten films.*

That happened more or less by chance. I wasn't too happy with the production design on *The Seventh Continent*, and for *Benny's Video* someone suggested Kanter. Things went really well with him, and we've tried to work together ever since. We get along very well, even though we hardly ever see each other outside of work. It's not some kind of rule; I do have a lot of friends from the professional world, but they rarely end up being my close collaborators. As for Kanter, he's someone who, like me, really loves the

Ulrich Mühe in *Benny's Video.*

prep work. He hates improvising on set. We start talking about the film very early on, and the final result always matches what I had in mind. He's extremely smart, very skilled with computers, and a master at building sets.

Had you seen his set designs in other films?

I think so, but I don't really remember. He's younger than me. He's German and started out in theatre. I don't know how he ended up in Austria, but he became the best production designer in the country. We obviously plan to keep working together.

This film also gave you the chance to work for the first time with Christian Berger, who would go on to become one of your regular cinematographers.

As I've said before, working with the same people is convenient because you know their strengths and weaknesses. It's like me as a writer. I know myself, and when I write a script, I avoid scenes that I would struggle to shoot. Another advantage of working with the same team is that I know they'll have the patience to put up with me... I'm difficult to work with because I'm very impatient and I've been known to yell on set. People who know me know that when I blow up, it's never personal—it's all about the work. That's why they're willing to keep working with me, even if I make them suffer a bit now and then, especially the cinematographer and the production designer, which are key roles on set. My editor is just as important, but we've never argued because post-production is calmer. There's no shooting stress. On set, I'm always at 100 percent, which isn't always pleasant for the people around me.

Do you check on people's availability while you're still writing?

Yes. For instance, while I was writing Amour, I brought on Darius Khondji, who had already shot the *Funny Games* remake. I had actually wanted him for *Time of the Wolf*, but he wasn't available.

What films of his had you noticed?

Se7en. I was especially struck by the camerawork and lighting in that film. At the time, it felt like the only film where the blacks were truly deep, which isn't easy to achieve. Darius is a fantastic cinematographer, just like Christian Berger and Jürgen Jürges, with whom I did three films: *Funny Games, Code Unknown* and *Time of the Wolf*. The issue with Jürgen is that he's slow, and that throws off my rhythm, but he's such a likeable guy that I can never bring myself to yell at him. He might take half an hour to light a close-up, and then, even when everything's already perfect, he'll want to tweak little things for each of the twenty takes. When I start to lose my temper, he'll calmly say, with a slight stutter, "There's always room for improvement." It's endearing, but also quite exhausting. Darius is a bit faster, probably because he's used to working in the American system. Even though, in Hollywood, he still gets more time to set up his lighting than we do in Europe. Since *The Piano Teacher* and especially *Caché*, Christian Berger has been saving a lot of setup time thanks to a new lighting system invented by an engineer from Tyrol. It uses powerful parallel light beams that can be redirected like sunlight. Christian figured out how to adapt it for cinema. It's very practical. What he does is rig a few big lights above or outside the set, then place small mirrors around to bounce the light exactly where it's needed. It makes lighting a scene much faster. There's one main light source, then you fill in where necessary. I think this technology has a bright future. Christian has even made commercials promoting it to Americans. But he's not much of a businessman.

Does he have exclusive rights to that lighting system?

No, but no one really dares get into it, because people are reluctant to change how they work. And the lighting equipment companies aren't thrilled either, since this invention makes most of their inventory obsolete.

Going back to Benny's Video, *there are a few references to the Second World War. The scene where Benny cleans up the blood, and especially the moment when his father sees his shaved head and mentions the deportees, evoke the concentration camps. Why these references?*

When Benny shaves his head, it's ambiguous. It can be interpreted in different ways. It's a kind of what we call *Buße* in German: an act of penitence. He's trying to atone for what he did. But it's also a cry for help to his parents, because looking like that, he's bound to shock his family and social circle. And yes, the image might bring the camps to mind, especially since his father mentions them, but he brings them up because he doesn't understand what his son is doing. Or more likely, he doesn't want to understand.

As a filmmaker, did you feel compelled to bring up that part of history?

Compelled? I don't know. I feel the need to talk about it because, as I've said before, it's a subject too often swept under the rug, and it's the artist's duty to bring hidden things to light.

A lot of young filmmakers in the New German Cinema of the 1960s and '70s—Schlöndorff, Wenders, Fassbinder—seemed to feel that same need. Did you have any kind of relationship with them?

None. I wasn't in Germany at the time, and I'm not very familiar with their films. I've already mentioned that I didn't like Fassbinder. Too melodramatic for my taste, and I didn't like his casting choices. He mixed good actors, like Karl-Heinz Böhm and Klaus Löwitsch, with bad ones, including members of his Munich theatre crowd. The result felt completely artificial, especially in the way they spoke. People interpreted this as a form of distancing and anti-realism, but honestly, it mostly came down to the fact that a lot of his actors just weren't very good. Toward the end of his life, he started working with great actors, though he kept giving the smaller parts to his friends, which led to an odd clash of voices and styles that didn't mesh. That said, I always admired his drive and how he could churn out film after film. He really was remarkable, even if his stuff wasn't my thing. I did like Wim Wenders'

Angela Winkler in *Benny's Video*.

early films—*Kings of the Road* in particular—and a few others I've managed to see. I also liked Herzog's *The Enigma of Kaspar Hauser*, and I found Hans-Jürgen Syberberg's films interesting, even though they were the total opposite of mine. Back then, like a lot of people, I was especially into Italian and French cinema.

The filmmaker you were most compared to at the time of Benny's Video *was Atom Egoyan.*

Yes, because of the use of video.

Had you seen his Family Viewing?

I met Egoyan at the Toronto Film Festival, where I was showing *The Seventh Continent*. I was walking down the street when this young guy came up and said, "Excuse me, are you Mr. Haneke? My name's Atom Egoyan. I don't know if you've heard of me, but I thought your film was amazing. What you're doing is exactly what I'm aiming for, even if I haven't quite managed it yet." I was flattered, and asked if he had a film in the festival too. It was *Family Viewing*, which I went to see and really liked. We met again later in Paris, then at Cannes. He's a lovely guy. Unfortunately, I haven't had the chance to see all his films.

In the video store scene, Benny rents a copy of The Toxic Avenger, *a horror film that's a cult favourite. Why that film?*

I actually didn't know the film. I asked Michael Katz to bring me clips from cheap horror films, and he showed me about twenty. I picked that one, just based on one over-the-top scene. I didn't even watch the whole thing. I just needed a striking moment.

When Benny goes to the cinema, we don't see the film he's watching, but when he comes out there's a poster for Catherine Breillat's 36 Fillette.

We just used the posters that were up at that cinema when we shot the scene. Nothing was faked. At most, I chose to highlight a specific title among the various films playing there. I did the same kind of thing later in *Caché*.

Caché *features posters for Almodóvar's* Bad Education *and Annaud's* Two Brothers. *It feels like the whole film is summed up in those two. Surely you chose those titles on purpose?*

Yes, in that case we had more options. But you can check... They were really showing in French cinemas at the time.

What about Annie Hall, *the Woody Allen film that the husband goes to see at the end of* Variation. *Did you choose that for a specific reason?*

We specifically went out and got that poster because the German title is an ironic little wink at our characters, especially the husband. In German the film is called *Der Stadtneurotiker*, which you could translate as "the neurotic city-dweller."

Benny and his mother escape the reality of the murder by travelling to Egypt. Is this a biblical reference?

I really don't remember. Now that you mention it, I probably had that in mind, but I can't say for certain.

If not for that reason, why Egypt?

Because of a scene involving an eclipse, which I ended up cutting. We had imagined this scene as a reference to the Egyptian sun cult. For them, if the sun were to disappear, it signified the end of the world.

Why did you cut that scene?

Haneke directing *Benny's Video.*
Cinematographer Christian Berger behind the camera.

The effect we had created for the eclipse wasn't bad, but the scene dragged, and I had to cut it to maintain the tension.

It appears as a bonus on the DVD edition of the film. It's the only deleted scene from your films that we know of.

I also cut several scenes from *Code Unknown*. More precisely, these were written scenes that I never shot because the producer, Marin Karmitz, couldn't finance them. They were set in Romania, Africa, even Paris, amounting to about twenty minutes in total. In the end, it's probably for the best that they weren't filmed because otherwise the film would have been too long. There are scenes from *Time of the Wolf* that I had to discard because of my poor casting choices. I made a few mistakes on that film—some of which are still visible—but they were even more glaring in the scenes I cut. It's a shame really, because on paper, the script was much more complex than what made it into the final cut.

Let's move on to the third part of your trilogy, 71 Fragments of a Chronology of Chance, *released in 1994. Was it after* Benny's Video *that you decided to make a trilogy?*

No, I think it was after *The Seventh Continent.*

Did you already have a clear idea of what the third part would be?

Honestly, I don't remember. What I do know is that the films naturally followed one another. After the trilogy, I felt that I hadn't explored the theme of violence deeply enough, so I wrote *Funny Games*.

71 Fragments of a Chronology of Chance (1994)

Vienna, December 23, 1993. A title card informs us that a student has shot three people in a bank before taking his own life.

October 12: The news on television: war rages in Somalia... A boy leaves Bucharest and illegally immigrates to Austria, then wanders through the streets and subway of the capital. A security guard mistreats his wife. Students play pick-up sticks. A couple adopts a very wary little girl. An elderly man struggles to communicate with his daughter, who works at the bank he frequents. A young man trains at ping-pong against an automated machine.

October 26: The day's news: riots in Ulster, strikes in France, an attack in Turkey... The ping-pong player acquires a firearm. The boy begs, steals and evades the police.

October 30: The boy turns himself in to the police and recounts his experiences on television. The adoptive parents have failed with the difficult little girl.

November 17: War in the Middle East, ethnic cleansing in former Yugoslavia... The couple adopts the boy from Bucharest.

December 23: Christmas on TV. Fighting continues in Sarajevo. Michael Jackson is accused of abusing a minor... The adoptive mother takes the boy into town for shopping. The security guard enters a bank. The adoptive mother leaves the boy in the car to go into the same bank. The ping-pong player struggles to pay for his petrol. The bank employee's father also ends up in the same bank. Unable to get change, the ping-pong player heads there too. Frustrated, he goes directly to the counter, ignoring the queue. A customer calls him out on it, they fight, and the player is knocked down. Back in his car, he hides, then gets into an argument with another driver who is angry that he is blocking traffic. Enraged, he returns to the bank, pulls out his gun, and fires randomly at customers, killing the security guard and the adoptive mother. He walks back to his car, still shooting, then kills himself. The boy waits alone in the car. On television, it is reported that the triple murder had no apparent motive. In Bosnia, Christmas is spent under shelling. Meanwhile, Michael Jackson declares himself innocent.

A common theme across the three films is the destruction of a group caused by the disintegration of society. In the first two films, you depict a family. In the third, you expand the scope, intertwining the stories of multiple characters, including a young man who suddenly starts shooting people.

My initial idea was to create a series of characters, one of whom would become the others' killer by the end. In other words, any one of them could have turned out to be the shooter. Once again, the media and the constant flood of information they drenched us with played a big role. I included five blocks of television news throughout the film.

The 1990s saw the rise of the ensemble film, which interweaves the parallel stories of multiple characters. Robert Altman is often credited with pioneering the genre with Nashville *in 1975. Just before your film, in 1993, he made Short Cuts.*

Which is a masterpiece.

Did these films inspire you?

I hadn't seen *Nashville* at the time, but *71 Fragments* wasn't my first ensemble film. That was *Lemminge*. I actually think writing an ensemble film is easier than writing a story with just two or three characters. When you have five storylines, five lives, you're forced to cut to the chase and keep only the best bits. With a straightforward chronological narrative, it's harder to build something that keeps the tension going. In an ensemble film, the real challenge is getting the structure right. But if you do, it's usually more rewarding.

As in the first two films of the trilogy, you don't provide any psychological or sociological explanations that might reduce the film's impact. At the same time, everything you show subtly shapes the characters' behaviour. Do you make a point of not saying too much?

Of course. There's always the danger of over-explaining, of being too heavy-handed. When I start a film like *71 Fragments*, I quickly accumulate a lot of ideas and notes, but by the time the final structure is in place, two-thirds of that material has been scrapped. It's a slow process. The real challenge in writing a screenplay isn't writing the scenes; that part is quick and enjoyable. It's building the overall structure. The real work is asking: if I leave this character here, when do I go back to them? Are the links between those two scenes strong enough? The main goal is to create tension from the very start and sustain it until the end, otherwise you lose the audience.

Was the number 71 in the title set from the beginning, or was it decided later in editing?

It was pure chance. If I had ended up with 73, the title would have been *73 Fragments of a Chronology of Chance*. The number has no symbolic meaning for me.

The second part of the title is strange because chance, by definition, doesn't follow a chronology.

That's meant to be ironic, to express something that can't really be put into words. Take the old man, for example. If he happens to be in the bank at the same time as the murderer, it's pure chance. But it's also the result of a chronology in his life. If he didn't have a daughter working at that bank, he might have gone to a different one. That's how chance works. From one person to another, it doesn't carry the same weight or come from the same place. For some, it's God's will; for others, it's fate. It all depends on one's beliefs. For me, chance is the least significant factor because it's neutral, but for those who see it as divine will or destiny, it immediately takes on a more dramatic and meaningful weight. The irony was already present in the title of Bresson's film *Au hasard Balthazar*, where, of course, nothing happens by chance, and anyone can project onto the donkey whatever they want or whatever they believe.

Branko Samarovski in *71 Fragments of a Chronology of Chance.*

But in your film, you're God. As in Caché, *you always have the answers.*

Naturally. But something great flows through me. A book, a film or a painting is the work of its creator, but if that work is bad, it isn't because the creator is an idiot; it's because they are less gifted than someone else in picking up on what's in the air at that particular moment. Talent is about knowing how to observe, about being tuned in to your era, and being able to filter reality through your own sensibility. The artistic value of a work always depends more on the creator's sensitivity than on their intelligence.

Regarding the news segments that punctuate the narrative, you said you didn't manipulate the dates. But how did you choose them?

I chose them by interweaving the characters' storylines. Take the example of the Romanian boy who illegally enters Austria. I assumed he would stay there for three months. If he arrived on April 20, his story would end around July 20. The news excerpts correspond to that time frame. Only once did I slightly alter the chronology, using news from the day before or after what I had originally planned, because it was too striking to ignore. I was still surprised by how closely reality aligned with my expectations.

Every day's news broadcast contained the same mix of trivialities and significant events, whether political or otherwise.

That's how you allow small personal stories to intersect with larger historical ones. A French critic remarked that your film shows how a student shooter could coexist with Michael Jackson.

That worked out perfectly, because I couldn't have predicted I would put Michael Jackson in a film. I wanted a piece of entertainment news — there's always one at the end of a news broadcast — and I was fortunate that Jackson happened to be in the headlines at that time. I included him twice: at the beginning and at the end of the last day. That repetition was essential to show how, by the end of the day, the story I have told has now become part of the news.

The film revisits several of your favourite themes, such as the representation of society through the media and the difficulty of communication within couples. But you also introduce the theme of immigration, which reappears in Code Unknown *and* Caché.

It was a subject that was becoming increasingly relevant. In Austria, no one used to worry about immigration, but little by little, the media started talking about it more and more.

From a humanistic perspective, do you think this mixing of races and cultures will improve communication between people, or will it be undermined by the way the media portray it?

That's a difficult question. If we focus on Austria, we've had a highly mixed population for a long time. Just flipping through the Vienna telephone directory, you'll see that more than half the names are of Czech or Yugoslav origin. I think this cultural blending has played a crucial role in my country's artistic landscape. German-language literature, for example, has far more Austrian writers than German ones, so this mixing of cultures has been beneficial. But I also have reservations about the religious militancy of contemporary waves of immigration. This borders on racism — which is not where I personally stand — but I must admit that the rise of Islamist movements and the behaviour of some of their adherents, who come here and make no effort to integrate, concerns me. This doesn't apply to people who understand what it means to live among others with respect and tolerance, but the poorest and least educated often have only one reference point:

71 Fragments of a Chronology of Chance.

their traditions. Being in a foreign country, they feel surrounded by enemies and cling to their language and culture, which is where the real communication barriers begin. When we witness events like the recent incident in Austria, where, on the orders of the Interior Minister, police stormed a school to seize two children for deportation, it becomes clear that such actions are intolerable. What is the correct position on these issues? I confess I'm a bit lost. I'm naturally in favour of tolerance, but how do you remain tolerant of something that is becoming difficult to live with? There is certainly guilt involved here. I would never say that Africans should stay in their own countries, but it's also naive to say, "We have to welcome everyone!" It's a real problem, and it will become Europe's biggest challenge in this new century.

With the Romanian child and the adoptive parents in 71 *Fragments, the issue of Islamism isn't relevant.*

No. Immigration is framed differently there, and I am entirely in favour of it in the case of the boy because I will always defend people who are persecuted for political or other reasons in their home countries. They must be granted asylum; that's self-evident. The adoptive couple, however, seems ambiguous, because when the little girl doesn't meet their expectations, they opt for another child, one who seems easier to handle.

There's even a consumerist aspect to their behaviour. They want the little Romanian boy because they saw him on TV.

They're a frustrated couple who think that acquiring a child will somehow give their lives a new direction. You can see this in how they treat the little girl. Speaking of which, last year in a pastry shop in Vienna, I was surprised to be served by a young woman who turned out to be the little girl from the film! I was amazed because she had grown into a wonderful young woman. She no longer had that withdrawn, almost vacant look she'd had during the shoot.

And the Romanian boy?

He wasn't some poor child. We held a casting session in Romania and he came with his mother. He immediately stood out; he was very handsome and talented, but filming wasn't easy for him. He hated shooting the scene where he begged on the street. He performed it very seriously, but he felt very uncomfortable because he was so proud.

What the child steals in the film is linked to images: comic books, a camera. It's as if his desire to integrate into society is expressed through images.

That was intentional, of course. He takes photos of people he sees, even though there's no film in the camera. What he enjoys is the act of "shooting." It's his way of protecting himself against the gaze of others.

Why pick-up sticks?

At one point, the film's title was *Pick-Up Sticks*, but it was already taken, for a Japanese film, I think. Otherwise, it wouldn't have been a bad title.

Because it serves as a metaphor?

Yes, somewhat. Chance—how the sticks fall at the start—plays a big part. After that, each stick is dependent on the others.

The second game played in the film, the one where you have to reassemble a cross, echoes Pascal's Wager and the security guard's prayer. Does this suggest a struggle with religion?

Gabriel Cosmin Urdes in *71 Fragments of a Chronology of Chance.*

Absolutely. I've been grappling with religion since I was a teenager. As I've mentioned before, before wanting to become a pianist, I considered becoming a pastor. Fortunately, that calling didn't last long... Today, I'm not a believer in the way the Church defines it. You can't simply explain existential problems through religion. There will always be in life something extra, something science can never fully explain. In the film, the religious dimension is tied to Christianity, but it could have been any other religion and the core issue would be the same.

Your films seem to present three recurring questions without providing clear answers, about religion, awareness of Western materialism, and art as a means of escape.

No—for me, art isn't an escape from reality. Quite the opposite; it's a way to get closer to that extra element I just mentioned. Art provides for us a richness of expression that surpasses everyday life and allows us to move toward the eye of the storm. You can't see anything when you're caught in a cyclone, but once you reach its eye, everything becomes calm and perhaps even clear.

That's one of the hallmarks of your films: not providing answers.

We're always trying to find answers; that's the entire history of philosophy and art. Humanity tries to solve its existential problems by seeking definitive answers, even while knowing they don't exist. The simple act of continuing to search is what gives meaning to life.

Does the ping-pong sequence symbolise the endless back-and-forth of questions and answers?

For me, it was a strong image because, in that situation, the young man is fighting against a machine. In other words, he is playing against himself and getting nowhere. I also knew—just as with the money being flushed down the toilet in *The Seventh Continent*— that it would frustrate audiences.

Except that, in this case, it's the very nature of the shot that's disturbing, whereas in The Seventh Continent, *it was the situation itself.*

Yes, but also because in both cases these are static shots that convey a certain violence. A critic wrote that the most violent scene shown at the Cannes Film Festival that year was the ping-pong scene in *71 Fragments*. I liked that idea. The violence here hits harder because it's left to the imagination, unlike in Hollywood action films, where it's all spectacle. To make his performance more authentic, the actor asked if he could practice with the ball machine. While we were setting up the lights, he played for two hours straight without a break, so by the time we filmed, he was genuinely exhausted. You can see that in the shot.

Did you choose an actor who knew how to play ping-pong?

He could play at about the level I was at when I was 18. I played a lot but not at a competitive level. As soon as he got the role, he trained every day.

We very much like film's opening sequence, after the first news segment, where we think we're looking at stars, only to realise it's a river. We believe we're looking up when, in fact, we're being pulled downward. The overhead shot is a technique you had already used in your television films.

Those are always risky shots because they prompt the question: Who is watching? I always advise my students to stick to more conventional angles. As soon as you tilt the camera up or down, it's immediately perceived as theatrical or, at the very least, artificial.

Lukas Milo in *71 Fragments of a Chronology of Chance.*

Here, though, I had good reason. The only way to shoot the scene was to fix the camera to a bridge, tracking the boy's movement from above. We could have filmed him at eye level, but since it's the beginning of the film, I wanted to give the scene a sense of scale. The artificiality of it is intentional; it's like putting quotation marks around the shot. We return to that same angle at the end, following the shooter as he walks between the cars, crosses the street, and returns to his vehicle to take his own life. Both times, the character is moving toward a final destination. The idea was to link those two movements through the mise-en-scène.

Those shots make us wonder: Who is watching?

Maybe it's Racine's God, who sees earthly life as nothing more than a spectacle.

Eight

Back to the Lumière cinematograph — *The Moor's Head* is too heavy — The provocations of *Funny Games* — Horror and farce at the push of a remote — Beckett or Chekhov? — A long take to avoid the obscene — The sound of race cars — Susanne Lothar versus Naomi Watts — A shot-for-shot remake — A cigarette and an unruly dog — Underwear or wetsuit — My mixing-room pleasures

In 1995, on the occasion of the hundredth anniversary of the invention of the cinematograph, you participated in the collective film Lumière et Compagnie.

I accepted the invitation because I found the idea amusing. Then I wondered what I could come up with that would tie into the idea of the media reflecting on itself, and hit on the idea of filming a television news broadcast on the anniversary of the first film shoot, March 19, 1995.

It's hard not to think of Nachruf für einen Mörder, *into which you incorporated real television programmes. Did you do the same kind of calculations for* Lumière et Compagnie *regarding the length of each news clip from that day?*

I don't remember. I know that we started by recording the news, then I edited the excerpts to fit the required length.

There were four constraints on every film made for Lumière et Compagnie: *a single 52-second take, no additional lighting, no synchronous sound, and no more than three takes. We see the news anchor, followed in succession by a rifle, images of war with UN trucks, a corpse being carried by two men, Queen Elizabeth II of England, sports—skiing, football and hockey—and the weather. Did you edit the footage?*

I edited the excerpts beforehand. Then with the Lumière camera, I filmed the pre-edited video playing on a television screen in a single take.

In the short documentary preceding your segment, you look genuinely delighted when handling the special film stock, inspecting the perforations and trying to understand how the camera works.

It's true that I was really into it. Part of the pleasure was using that gear, along with the freedom to shoot whatever I wanted.

Like every other director involved in the project, you were asked two questions. To the first— "Is cinema mortal?"—you answered: "Of course, like everything."

That was a spontaneous answer. And it's the truth.

Would you say the same thing today?

Of course. If you wanted to be mean about it, you could even say that a good part of cinema is already dead.

To the second question— "Why do you film?"—you answered with a quip: "You don't ask a centipede how it walks, or it will trip over its own feet!"

That's as silly an answer as the question itself. I don't know what else to say to such a question. "Why do you write? Because!"

Have you seen Lumière et Compagnie *in its entirety?*

There was a screening in Paris with almost all the directors, which I attended. Participating in the film wasn't particularly important to me. It was, above all, a fun experience and, let's not forget, the first film I shot in France.

That same year, Paulus Manker, who appeared in Wer war Edgar Allan?, *directed* The Head of the Moor, *based on a script you wrote. When did you write it, and why didn't you direct it yourself?*

I wrote it before making *The Seventh Continent*, for the German television channel Sender Freies Berlin, but, for reasons I can't recall, they didn't want to proceed with it. I then tried to get it produced as a theatrical film. Klaus Maria Brandauer agreed to star, but we couldn't secure the funding and I got frustrated and lost interest in the script—until Paulus read it and thought it was very good. He even asked me to sell it to him. I thought, why not? That's how it happened.

The Head of the Moor (1995)

A corrosive gas spreads through Vienna following a malfunction at a chemical plant. Georg, a researcher at the plant, returns to his office and believes he sees a severely burned man sitting in his chair. Regaining his senses, he begins to contemplate the inevitable ecological consequences of the impending disaster. This thought turns into anxiety, then into a full-blown obsession. His suffering wife, Anna, reproaches him. He slaps her, then apologises, and decides to take his family to a country house, far from the capital. Anna refuses and leaves on vacation with the children. Left alone, Georg begins covering the floor of his living room with a thick layer of soil, transforming the space into a gigantic greenhouse where he can grow food for survival. He builds a chicken coop and starts breeding rabbits. He rarely leaves his apartment and insists on wearing a face mask, attracting curiosity from those around him. Eventually, he isolates himself completely, cutting off all communication with his loved ones. On the television news, he learns that people have begun fleeing the city. When Anna returns from vacation, she finds her husband completely deranged. Their son injures his foot by stepping on a nail. Enraged, Anna strikes Georg. He retaliates by forcibly preventing his family from leaving. That night, he kills his wife with a glass ball and stabs his children, but the sound accompanying the massacre is that of frightened chickens. He places the kitchen knife in his wife's lifeless hand then walks to the bathroom and, seeing his blood-covered reflection in the mirror, takes the knife back and slashes his own face. Suddenly, Anna reappears, accompanied by paramedics and police officers. Their children watch as their father is carried away, restrained on a stretcher.

Paulus Manker assembled several of your past collaborators: the production company Wega-Film, editor Marie Homolková, Angela Winkler,

Leni Tanzer, the little girl from The Seventh Continent, *and cinematographer Walter Kindler, who had worked on* Lemminge, Variation *and* Fräulein.

Paulus, who had only directed one film before—*Schmutz*, with Kindler as his cinematographer—wanted to rely on a team he already knew. But in my opinion, it didn't help him. It reinforced his attempt to make a "Haneke film," whereas *Schmutz* had been more personal and much better. I had written the dialogue and helped with the narrative structure, but the story itself was entirely his, and since it was his idea, he was more at ease directing *Schmutz* than he was with *The Head of the Moor*. With this film, I don't know what went wrong. Maybe he felt intimidated, maybe he didn't feel free enough to make the script his own. In any case, he shot an enormous amount of footage, reshooting many scenes later while abandoning others in the editing process. I never visited the set; I didn't want to interfere with the production, but I know it was a difficult shoot for everyone involved.

Your idea was to give Manker complete creative freedom?

Absolutely. By selling him the script, I told him he could do whatever he wanted with it. But Paulus was too faithful to a text that I probably would have changed had I directed the film myself. In *Schmutz*, he had demonstrated a real flair for composing striking images. I'm the opposite; I aim for restraint. The result was an unfortunate blend of our two approaches. The worst part is the acting, which is ironic because Paulus is an excellent director of actors. He knew Angela Winkler well from working with her in theatre and Gert Voss, who plays Georg, is one of our greatest stage actors, but both of them overact as if they were still on stage. It's a real shame.

The script refers to a chemical disaster, but we learn almost nothing about it. This is an idea you would later revisit in Time of the Wolf. *At the time, was ecology one of your major concerns?*

It's what preoccupies the main character and triggers his neurotic fear, but it's like in Bergman's *Winter Light*, where Max von Sydow's character commits suicide because he is obsessed with the idea that the Chinese will take over the world. It's mostly a stand-in for a deeper psychological crisis. In this case, Georg fixates on an ecological threat, but what it really reflects is a much deeper

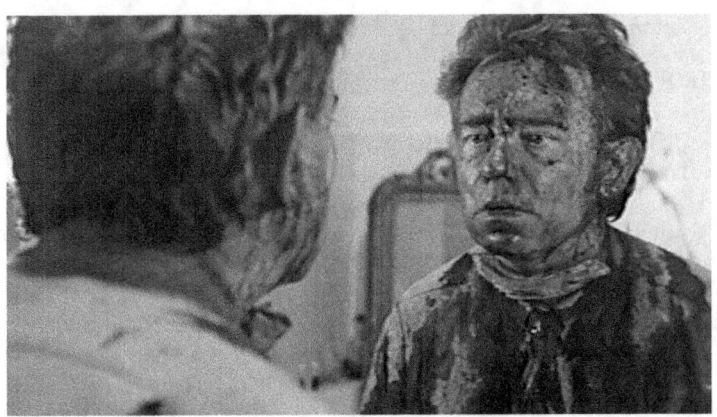

Gert Voss in *The Head of the Moor.*

unease. At the outset, everything he says is true, but his reaction—his sudden compulsion to buy a house in the countryside to protect his family, his decision to cut himself off from his work and the rest of the world—is excessive. I had read about a real-life story of a father who locked his family inside their home, forcing them to request permission in writing every time they wanted to go out. That gave me the idea for the script.

The night time scene of violence, with flashes of light, the panicked chickens, and Georg wreaking havoc in the apartment, is very striking.

Yes, but in his attempt to impress, Paulus overdid it. He's always aiming for some big spectacle, but he forgot that to pull that off, you need a big story, but a small one like mine. It's the age-old rule: the form has to match the content.

Along those lines, there's a rather spectacular shot at the beginning—of the burned man Georg discovers upon entering his office— that doesn't really work. We quickly understand that it's a hallucination, which foreshadows everything that follows, including the ending, where the massacre is all in Georg's head. That completely contradicts your usual refusal to reassure the audience.

Let's not forget that I wrote this script for television, and with television you have to play by different rules. That might be why I never felt the need to revisit and improve my script later on.

Why the title The Head of the Moor?

In Austria, there's a well-known image of a Moor's head, though it doesn't resemble the one painted on the wall in the film. It's the logo of the company Meinl, which sold coffee before becoming a large food chain and then disappearing completely. In Austria, when we say *Mohrenkopf* instead of *Der Kopf des Mohren*, people immediately think of a well-known pastry, so the image is very much part of Austrian popular culture. In the film, the one we see is an advertisement that gradually vanishes as a house is being built in front of it. It echoes the idea of the Moor as an outsider, someone pushed to the margins of society.

And why end with the quote from Gotthold Ephraim Lessing: "Glauben Sie mir: wer über gewisse Dinge den Verstand nicht verliert, der hat keinen zu verlieren" ["Believe me: he who does not lose his mind over certain things has no mind to lose"]?

It's an idea that has lost none of its relevance. It reminds us that in extreme situations, losing your mind is a human reaction. Georg is more sensitive than the people around him, so of course he goes mad. And maybe, in a way, more than anyone else, his response is the correct one.

Did your collaboration with Manker end there?

No, we stayed friends. In fact, I gave him a small role as the deranged killer in *Code Unknown*. Later, we had a falling out around the time of *The Piano Teacher*, which we can discuss later. I wasn't the one who was upset… He has a habit of suing everyone and losing a lot of money in the process. But we have since reconciled and regularly exchange emails.

Funny Games (1997)

Anna, Georg, their son Schorschi and their dog Rolfi arrive at their country house near a lake. Shortly after, Anna is visited by a young man, Peter, who, as a guest of their neighbours, asks for some eggs to help them out. He clumsily drops the eggs and immediately asks for four more, to Anna's surprise. A moment later, he accidentally knocks her phone into the sink. His friend Paul appears—also dressed entirely in white, gloves and all—and suavely backs up Peter's request, even as Anna starts to get annoyed. Georg steps in, trying to diffuse the situation, but the conversation escalates, and Paul violently strikes Georg with a golf club. The two young men then take the family hostage, killing the dog. Several times, Paul addresses the audience, making them complicit in the physical and psychological tortures inflicted on the family, for instance forcing Anna to undress in front of her helpless husband. Later, Schorschi manages to escape but is quickly caught by Paul. While Paul makes himself a sandwich in the kitchen, Peter shoots the child with a shotgun. After tying up the couple, the two assailants leave. Anna eventually frees herself, unties her husband, who is in severe pain from his injured leg, and sets out to find help, leaving him to try and repair their phone to call the police. A car stops in the night. Anna flags it town, only to discover that it is her two tormentors. The horrors resume in the house. Anna is forced to recite a prayer, forwards and backwards, to earn the right to choose who—herself or her husband—will be killed first, and with which weapon. Suddenly, luck is on her side. She manages to seize Peter's shotgun and shoots him. Paul grabs the gun, then takes the remote control and rewinds the film back to the moment Anna attempts to take the weapon. This time, she fails. Georg is shot dead, and Anna, bound and gagged, is thrown into the lake alive. The next morning, Paul arrives at a neighbour's house—a friend of the couple—and asks for eggs. He says Anna sent him, as unexpected guests have just arrived.

Let's talk about Funny Games *and its American remake, which you directed ten years later. How do you view the film now, considering it earned you a reputation as a filmmaker associated with violence?*

I'm still proud of the film. It worked exactly as I intended in terms of provocation in that it drove some people absolutely mad. In reality, those viewers should have been angry at themselves. I've always thought that anyone who sat through the whole film got exactly what they deserved. No one forced them to stay in their seat. My aim was to show what violence really is, and how easily the audience can become complicit with the torturers, while constantly reminding them that what they're watching is just a film. The people who cried scandal after watching the whole thing just make me laugh. After the first slap, they just sat there as things got worse and worse, even though they could have walked out at any time. But they didn't. They stayed glued to their seats because cinema is such a powerful tool of manipulation that, no matter how unpleasant the experience was, they still wanted to see how it ended. In that sense, I'm totally in line with Hitchcock, who said of *Psycho*: "I know exactly when and how people will react." *Funny Games* is, in its own way, an exposé, a critique, of how easily we can fall victim to manipulation. That was my goal, and I think I achieved it. The problem is that since then, there have been far worse films than mine, aimed at much younger audiences.

Which films are you referring to?

The *Saw* series, for example.

But for us, Saw *doesn't belong in the same category, and neither do the Hollywood slasher films of the 1980s*—Friday the 13th, A Nightmare on Elm Street, Halloween—*which glorify the killer figure preying on interchangeable, clueless victims. Those films are entirely unreal, and the pleasure comes from the sheer excess and gore. The moment the screening ends, you have a cup of coffee and move on.*

That's exactly what I wanted to avoid—and call out—with *Funny Games.*

And for that very reason, even though you make us complicit with the killers, you also place us on the side of the victims, the real characters whose suffering we feel. The audience you were targeting with Funny Games *definitely picked up on that. They didn't want to endure the horrors inflicted on the characters.*

That's exactly the problem. The audience I hoped to reach with *Funny Games* didn't really show up. That's why I did the American remake in Hollywood, with big-name actors. And the same thing happened. It was a bit frustrating because I honestly believe that even the most unsophisticated filmgoer could have understood what I was trying to do. But, of course, if there's no willingness to even try to understand, it's not going to work.

Susanne Lothar, Stefan Clapczynski and Ulrich Mühe in *Funny Games.*

Still, Funny Games *left a deep impression on those who did see it. No other film on this theme has really matched it since. For us,* Funny Games *had the same impact* Salò *did in its day.*

I take that as a compliment because, as I've said before, *Salò* is the film that affected me the most. I was so shaken by it that I genuinely struggled to recover. But it also opened my eyes.

One big difference between Funny Games *and* Salò *is your refusal to show graphic violence. That's what gives your film its power. We are constantly afraid we're about to see something horrific, but in the end we don't, even though it feels like we did.*

I've even read reviews where critics described things that aren't in the film. Similarly, I once read an Austrian article about *Benny's Video* that gave a detailed description of the young girl's murder, even though it happens entirely off-screen.

When did you come up with the idea for Funny Games?

It wasn't an idea that came to me all at once. It took a long time to develop. Back in 1970, when I was in Baden-Baden working as a television script editor, I wrote an early story in the hope of directing a film myself. From that, I developed a script I've already mentioned to you, *Wochenende*. It was inspired by a scene in

François Truffaut's *Shoot the Piano Player*, where the main character is forced to kill someone who threatens him and then has to go on the run. In my version, the fugitive hides out in a country house by a lake. He either breaks a window to get in or goes through the garage, I don't remember exactly. The next morning, the family who owns the house shows up for the weekend. The man holds them at gunpoint, and the tension keeps building until the wife manages to manipulate him into killing her husband, who she wanted to get rid of anyway. That way, she avoids any consequences, while the fugitive is arrested and sent to prison. As I told you, even though I got some funding for the project, I couldn't get it fully financed, but that core idea stayed with me. Later on—around 1986, I think—I was invited to revisit it as part of a television co-production between Germany and Georgia. The plan was to shoot in Tbilisi, but I arrived on the first day of a revolution and was stuck in my hotel room. At night, hearing gunfire in the streets outside, I started reworking the original story into what would become *Funny Games*. At that point, though, the reflexive structure—the self-reflexive distancing element—was still missing, and without that I wasn't interested in making just another thriller. It wasn't until much later, when I figured out how to incorporate that reflexive approach, that I started trying to get the film produced. You could say the gestation of *Funny Games* took about fifteen years.

Does this self-reflexive approach have anything to do with the impact the famous Albert Finney wink at the camera in Tom Jones *had on you as a young viewer? You have often cited it as a major cinematic shock.*

No, I didn't think of that when writing *Funny Games*. But it's true that *Tom Jones* was the first time I was confronted with a technique that questioned an art form from within.

We thought of it when we saw Arno Frisch turn toward us and wink.

When I decided to handle the story in a self-reflexive way, I started thinking about the tools I had to be able to do that. The first was having the actor speak directly to the camera. The second was the idea of rewinding the film at a certain point. I have to admit that I was pretty pleased with myself when I came up with that one.

Having a character rewind the film itself—not just a video, as in
Benny's Video *or* Caché—*was, as far as I know, an unprecedented
idea.*

And made possible by the advent of VCRs. Before that, it would
have been inconceivable.

*And beyond its distancing effect, the device also serves as a critique
of those who, obsessed with violence, can rewatch those kinds of
scenes endlessly, almost obsessively, in the privacy of their own
home. It's an idea hinted at in* Benny's Video.

Exactly. *Funny Games* was an opportunity for me to explore a
similar theme from another angle. Just as in Greek tragedy, where
every great tragedy had its counterpart in the form of farce, you
could say that *Funny Games* is *Benny's Video* played as farce.

*Except that it's hard to see it as farce. Even with the distancing
effects, we really feel for the characters.*

That's because the situations—and the acting—are so believable
that you end up buying into it. I told the two actors playing the
torturers to lean into comedy, and the ones playing the victims to
stay firmly in tragedy. That's what makes the dynamic between
them so unbearable. By acting like it's all a joke, the two killers
show a complete lack of compassion for their hostages, which
makes them completely unpredictable.

*Is it true that you originally offered the role of Anna, the mother,
to Isabelle Huppert?*

That's true. She turned it down, though. That was back when we
didn't yet know each other.

Did you write the role with her in mind?

No. It was only after finishing the script that I thought of Isabelle.
But I was very pleased with Susanne Lothar's performance. I had
just worked with her and her husband, Ulrich Mühe, on *The
Castle*, and I wanted to continue our collaboration.

Why did you name the two torturers Peter and Paul?

Naomi Watts and Tim Roth in the U.S. remake of *Funny Games*

On one hand, they're Fathers of the Church, and I liked the playful alliteration. But they also go by Tom and Jerry, or Beavis and Butt-Head.

Why does Paul suddenly call Peter "Tom"?

What a crazy scene that is! Paul gives his sidekick three different names just to mess with him for being so uptight and serious. It throws off the victims, but it also throws off the audience. I thought it was very funny.

So it's not a symbolic way of addressing potential American viewers?

No, but from the very beginning, I had American audiences in mind. The hallway of the country house, with that staircase, is proof. It was built on a soundstage in an American style. You don't find hallways like that in Austria. Still, I couldn't get American audiences on board. I thought it was because of the language; foreign films in their original versions with English subtitles are only shown in art house cinemas in America. But then the same thing happened with the American version. When it was released, it felt like the American critics were out to get me. Most of them tore the film apart. They thought it was ridiculous: "We know this already! It's naive to point it out to us…" They just didn't want to hear a critique of their own cinema, and instead of actually talking about the film, they kept harping on about the fact that it was a shot-for-shot remake and accused me of making the same film twice. If you read a review saying a film is bad and you've already seen it, it doesn't exactly make you want to go see it. But the truth is that it was mostly the critics, not the general public, who had seen the Austrian version.

How would you describe your relationship with film criticism?

I'm fairly relaxed about it these days. I only read articles in major newspapers and a few magazines I respect. Criticism is still important for the box office, but the stakes aren't as high as when I was starting out. When you're a young filmmaker making "difficult" films, you're very vulnerable. I can't complain; I was well supported by critics, starting with *Benny's Video*, especially abroad. In Austria, I made an impact with *The Seventh Continent* because it was selected for the Directors' Fortnight at Cannes, then with *Funny Games*, again at Cannes, since it had been a long time since an Austrian film had been in the official competition at a major festival. But it took success abroad for Austrian critics to finally support me. I think it's tied to Austria's inferiority complex, particularly in cinema, where we don't have a particularly strong tradition. If they wanted to be taken seriously, Austrian critics couldn't possibly praise an Austrian film. More broadly, I find that criticism is too factional and that judgments vary according to which group you belong to. And too often critics don't really discuss the film they saw; they have a vague idea of how the story or theme should have been treated. It's like blaming an apple for not being a pear. Of course, criticism can be insightful, but since I already know my films' strengths and weaknesses, reading reviews doesn't really help me. In fact, when I make a mistake, I hope it goes unnoticed. It's unfortunate for me if a critic spots it and calls it out, though that is their job. The only kind of criticism that really annoys me is the personal attack, when the critic goes after the filmmaker rather than the film.

Before comparing the two versions of Funny Games, *let's go back to the Austrian version. The theme of self-reflexivity reaches its peak in the second-to-last scene. After throwing Susanne Lothar into the water, Paul tells Peter: "The fiction is real, isn't it? You can see it in the film." This underlines the idea that whether you film reality or fiction, cinema is always a representation.*

Exactly. That's the point.

Frank Giering and Arno Frisch in *Funny Games*.

In that scene, the dialogue turns the two boys—especially the one played by Arno Frisch—into Nietzschean supermen. Were you trying to show that modern society has completely lost its humanist grip on reality?

That's what people say all the time nowadays, but fortunately there are still people with a humanist sensibility who are actively working to improve things. Because of the way human relationships are mediated—where everyone seems to know everything about everyone—it can feel as if the world is falling apart. But I don't think that's true. Of course, the political situation, corporate conglomerates, and globalization are catastrophic, but if there's going to be a real catastrophe, it won't happen for another hundred years. Historically, humanity has always existed on the edge of the abyss; it just manifests differently in each era. Honestly, unless I were a prince, I wouldn't have wanted to live a hundred or two hundred years ago. And even then, better to have a toothache today than two centuries ago. People forget that, on the whole, we live better lives than our ancestors. My films are made as a reaction against mainstream cinema, which lies by pretending that everything's fine, so I have to push in the opposite direction to counterbalance that. But not for a second do I believe that all people are like the two boys in *Funny Games*.

Paul and Peter, compared to Benny, seem like extreme characters.

They aren't real characters. They're gleeful embodiments of evil. They're abstractions. *Funny Games* isn't a realistic film. It may seem realistic in terms of acting and situations, but if you look closely, it's actually about pitting a textbook bourgeois family against two purely fictional figures, which is an idea I had already explored in *The Seventh Continent*, where the family was just a model, a pretext to demonstrate something. It was only when I started working in France that my films became increasingly realistic.

Is Funny Games *the conclusion of your first period, the so-called trilogy?*

In part, yes. My early films were based on models and archetypes. I only returned to that with *Caché*, though the characters in that one are much more realistic, even if they're not particularly complex. From the start, they're clearly defined in their behaviours, and they never deviate from their predetermined paths. In *Caché*, everything is stripped down. It's very Beckett-like. Not that I'm comparing myself to him, but I mention Beckett in contrast to the existential complexity of Chekhov's characters. As I grow older, I feel increasingly drawn to Chekhov's world. It's always easy to justify your work in hindsight, whereas at the time, a lot of things happen by chance. It's true that at different stages of my life I've been drawn to different concerns, which has shaped the way I work, but I can't be fully aware of that in the moment.

Before writing the script for Funny Games, *were you aware of the notorious crime that shocked Chicago in the 1920s, the murder of teenager Bobby Franks by two wealthy young men, Nathan Leopold and Richard Loeb, who had a sadomasochistic homosexual relationship? Hitchcock and Richard Fleischer drew inspiration on the story for their respective films* Rope *and* Compulsion.

I wasn't aware of either the case or those two films and I didn't base the script on any real-life events. But there was something in the air at the time. I particularly remember an article in *Der Spiegel* about a case in Spain where two young men had lured a homeless person to a secluded place to torture him. They put on surgical gloves and ripped out his tongue. They were discovered because they enjoyed it so much that they wanted to do it again and invited a friend to join them. That friend told a priest, who called the police. They were caught because of a box of those surgical gloves, which the police found at one of their homes. One of the young men, who was clearly very intelligent, wrote an essay in prison explaining why he had the right to act as he did, citing Nietzsche and others. It's a very wild story.

We assumed you were familiar with Rope *because Hitchcock shot the entire film in long takes, which are one of your specialties. There is one in* Funny Games *that shocked audiences at Cannes, the one in the living room which is more than ten minutes long, where the two parents are tied up next to their murdered child, at the foot of a blood-splattered TV screen. Do you remember how you came up with that scene?*

I first described the situation, then asked myself how it could be filmed. You can't show a child whose head has been bashed in because it comes off as either ridiculous or just plain disgusting. Likewise, the emotions the parents are feeling at that moment can't be acted out. The only way to handle it was to keep the camera as far away as possible, avoiding close-ups of their faces. What we see is limited to the mother trying to find a knife to free herself, then her husband, before attempting to escape. That was the only part of the scene that could be shown. It's also a scene where you hear more than you see. If it had been shot more conventionally, there would have been no tension. The long take seemed perfectly suited to the situation. In general, I always follow the same principle: whenever I have to show something horrible, I film it from a distance. Close-ups of suffering feel obscene to me.

Are there other things that shouldn't be filmed?

All suffering and death. I find close-ups of massacre victims unbearable, especially in documentaries. I just don't want to see that. It's a matter of taste.

Taste or ethics?

In German, *Geschmack* [taste] means that if someone has good taste, it also implies a certain ethics. Taste isn't just about aesthetics; it implies respect—in this case, respect for the suffering of others.

One striking element in the scene is the car race playing on the television.

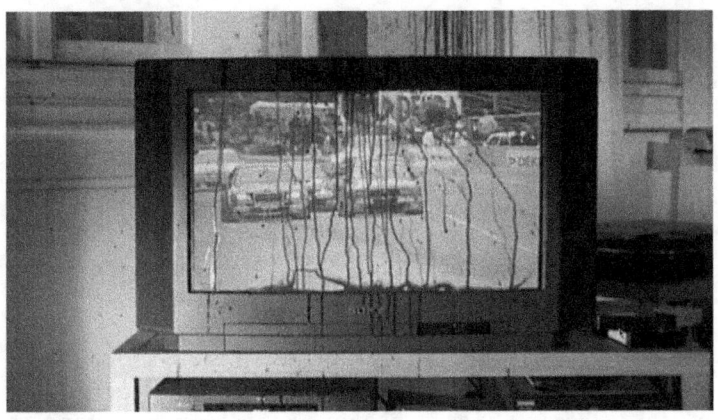

Funny Games.

I thought for a long time about what to put on that screen. A programme with dialogue would have destroyed the tension, and something idyllic would have added an ironic dimension. The car race had the advantage of providing an infernal noise while feeling anonymous and realistic. We used a real broadcast with its original commentary. I had no other ideas. I think it works.

Did you consider the obsessive nature of car racing, endlessly going in circles on a track?

I think that adds something to the scene, but I was primarily interested in the noise of the race.

Can we draw a connection between that deafening noise and the jarring shift from opera to John Zorn in the opening sequence?

Yes, both are violent sounds. John Zorn was actually my editor's idea. Before that, I had an experimental track—edgy, but not edgy enough. And John Zorn isn't just straight-up heavy metal; it's more of a commentary on the genre, just as *Funny Games* is a commentary on the thriller.

How did you direct Susanne Lothar in that long take? Did you give her precise timing for her movements?

I remember exactly how we did it. Susanne and Ulrich were in their dressing rooms, and I went to see them to explain what they should feel at each key moment and how that would translate into movement. Then we went to the set and I walked them through the blocking in detail, step by step, while also revisiting their characters' emotional arcs. After that, I told them to take their time getting ready in their dressing rooms. The whole crew was already in position, waiting silently. When Susanne and Ulrich came out, they got into place and nailed it on the first go, except for one small thing that bugged me, so I asked for another take. They agreed, but I stopped it after a minute because it didn't feel right, so I asked for a third take, and that one was spot on. They finished the scene exactly as the film reel ran out. Nothing was timed; when I wrote the scene, I just had a sense it would take up about one full reel of film. I'm tempted to say that they couldn't have done a fourth take because it was so exhausting, but then again, take the prayer scene, which we did twenty-eight takes of because Susanne couldn't get it quite right. At that point, you can't give up; you have to keep going until it works. It was tough on everyone, but especially Susanne, but in the end the fatigue worked in her favour. Before that, I could hear in her sobs that something wasn't quite right; the tension wasn't fully there. I always tell my students: your best asset is a good ear. You hear a scene's truth way before you see it. In a wide shot, you can't really judge anything while the camera's rolling. Sound is what tells you if it's working or not.

There's a staggering scene where Susanne Lothar, gagged, has her face completely distorted by crying and terror. How did she manage to reach that kind of emotional peak?

She arrived on set in that state. She had been crying in her dressing room for half an hour so her eyes would look swollen. She was also made up, but she insisted on crying beforehand for a long time. She must have a bit of a masochistic streak because she actually enjoys filming these kinds of scenes. She likes playing extreme situations; that's her strength. Dialogue scenes, on the other hand, don't always come as naturally to her, so she really shines in the second half of *Funny Games*, whereas in the first part she's not as strong as Naomi Watts in the American remake, who brings more charm and an extraordinary lightness to those early scenes. Conversely, Naomi is weaker than Susanne in the second half of the American version. Overall, I find both of their performances in the two films remarkable.

There's one directorial choice at the beginning of the film that didn't quite convince us, the shifting focus, sometimes on Lothar,

Susanne Lothar and Stefan Clapczynski in *Funny Games*.

sometimes on Mühe, when they're sitting in the car wondering about their neighbours' strange behaviour.

I don't like it much either, but it seemed unavoidable. If we had broken up the scene more, its flow would have been broken. I wanted to shoot it as simply as possible. It's the end of a long drive, they're tired, and I stuck to a single camera position, one that shows them together at a certain distance because there's no reason to get any closer. That's why I changed focus between them while maintaining the same angle. I don't love that technique, and I only use it when I can't find a better option.

In the remake, those focus shifts are gone. Was that a way of correcting your direction?

No, the set-up was exactly the same. It just comes across better in the remake because the focus puller handled the transitions more delicately than the one in Austria.

Let's go back to sound for a moment. After the death of Karl Schlifelner, the sound engineer you collaborated with for the trilogy, you brought in Walter Amann for Funny Games. *He did an equally meticulous job, for example the subtle sound of the automatic closing of the metal gate at the beginning of the film.*

That's a mixing trick; my specialty! I love adding little details like those. I was very happy when *The White Ribbon*, which is actually a fairly quiet film, won a sound award in Germany because we paid

The German poster for *Funny Games*.

The American poster for the U.S. remake of *Funny Games*

close attention to the subtlest of noises. It's the accumulation of small sounds that anchors a film in reality. It's hard to get right, but I love working with my French sound team, Jean-Pierre Laforce and Guillaume Sciama.

You explained why you made an American version of Funny Games, *but you haven't told us who initiated the project.*

The English producer Chris Coen, who had a small American production company. He came to see me at Cannes in 2005 to propose the project. I said yes because at the top of the list of actors he had in mind was Naomi Watts. Since I had always thought she would be the ideal actress for a remake, I felt that, at the very least, this producer and I shared a common vision.

How did you assemble your American crew?

That was a big headache. The only positive aspect was having cinematographer Darius Khondji and his team on board. They were fantastic, even though they cost two or three times more than the crew the producers had originally budgeted for. For all the other departments, I was stuck with very cheap hires instead of the people I had suggested, especially for costumes and set design.

Were these people whose work you had admired in other films?

Yes, but the production refused to hire them, claiming they weren't available. I suspect they didn't even try to reach out because they knew those people were too expensive. With Khondji's team, the film went way over budget. A few weeks into the shoot, the insurance company stepped in, fired the production manager and his team, and replaced them with a guy whose only job was to watch the schedule and remind me I was falling behind. I would tell him I was doing my best and that breathing down my neck wasn't going to help. Then I chased him off the set. He wasn't doing anything except hanging around looking miserable, like it was his money we were spending. It was a mess, especially without a proper production manager. My only saving grace was a clause in my contract that guaranteed a shot-for-shot remake, which meant they couldn't ask me to cut scenes to save time. I had insisted on that clause because anything goes in America. Some idiot could decide to recut the film however they liked, or even shoot a new ending, but this way they were stuck. They had to let me film everything.

Still, by the end, it was a nightmare. On the last day, we shot the scene where the little boy tries to escape at night. The poor kid had a fever, and we filmed from 9 a.m. straight through to 3 a.m. the next morning because we absolutely had to wrap that day. The insurance company refused to approve even one extra day. It was all very unpleasant. I can honestly say it was my worst filming experience.

Given how expensive he was, how did you manage to get Darius Khondji on board?

Because I mentioned him right from the start, and because he's well-known and respected in the industry, especially in America. I had actually wanted to work with him on *Time of the Wolf*, but he wasn't available back then.

Besides Naomi Watts, how did you cast the rest of the actors?

Through a standard casting process. Tim Roth wasn't my first choice; I would have preferred Philip Seymour Hoffman but he declined because, at that stage in his career—after *Capote*—it wouldn't have been good for him to play that role. I understood his reasoning because it's the most thankless role in the film. In the American mindset, he comes off as a coward who doesn't protect his family.

Wouldn't casting Hoffman have been awkward, given how much he physically resembles Michael Pitt?

Maybe, but that would have been amusing too.

A bit of added unease.

Another layer of confusion, yes. Anyway, the role went to Tim Roth. He's a good actor, but we didn't really get along. Normally I have a good relationship with actors, but with him it was tough. He didn't want anything explained to him and just wanted to do things his own way, which led to tension on set. On top of that, Michael Pitt has major issues with authority. I would put up with him losing his temper and trying to provoke me because I knew he was doing it partly to assert himself, but mostly to improve his performance. We're actually good friends now, and I really admire him. I think he's fantastic in the film. So is Brady Corbet, who plays his partner in crime. Naomi also had a hard time on set because she wasn't comfortable with how meticulous I am. She even broke down and cried once, early on, during the kitchen scene, which we shot at least ten times. She was struggling to remember all the little gestures I was asking for: cut this, open the fridge, pick up the phone... I told her to take a breath, that we had time. She thought I was being so strict because it was a remake, but then we went out to dinner and I showed her the original script, and she saw that it had already been written that way, that all the gestures were part of the first film too. She realised that she had no choice but to adapt to that constraint. There are exceptions, of course, but generally speaking American directors don't work closely with actors. They block the scene, do a rehearsal, then keep their eyes glued to the monitor, occasionally emerging to shout a few notes through a megaphone before the next take. I'm on set the whole time, always working with the actors, repeating to the actors what I'm looking for until I get it. They weren't used to that, and it really got on their nerves that I insisted a glass be placed precisely here, not there.

Did the actors start to push back because of that lack of freedom?

Yes. At one point Naomi even said, "I'm not a puppet!" That's when I showed her the storyboard from the original film, so she could see this was just how I work, remake or not. Normally, when an actor struggles, you try to adjust things so they don't get stuck, but since this was a remake, we couldn't really change too much. I wanted to stick as closely as possible to the original shots and framing. I did, however, have to make a few compromises when it came to Michael Pitt's positioning in some of the shots.

Did you show the Austrian version to the crew?

No, but everyone had seen it already just to get a sense of it. I asked the cast and crew not to rewatch it during the shoot, though; I didn't want it to influence or inhibit them. I told them to just trust my direction.

But you had the original on hand during the shoot?

Of course. I even had drawings and photos of every shot from the first film. That way, if a scene got tricky, I could check it with Darius. I had also built a storyboard from stills taken directly from the Austrian version.

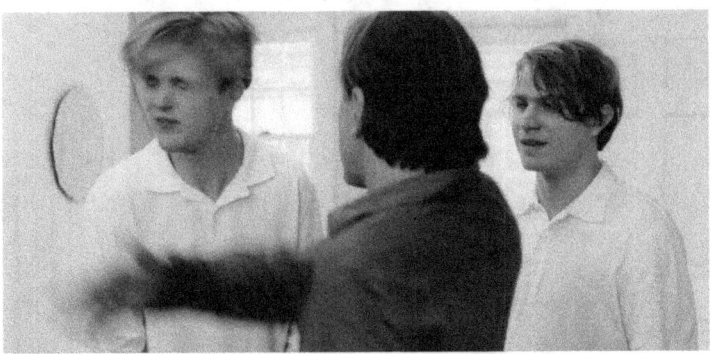

Michael Pitt, Tim Roth and Brady Corbet
in the U.S. remake of *Funny Games*

The original screenplay was translated into English. Were there any modifications in the American version?

Very few. For the opening sequence, I had a discussion with Tim Roth, who told me that in America, people would listen to different music than the opera in the original. I told him that this type of people—urban, cultured, bourgeois—exist everywhere, so that wasn't really an issue. The only real change we had to make was in the scene where they talk about calling the police. In the German version, the characters ask each other what the number is, which wouldn't make sense in America, where everyone knows it's 9-1-1, so I tweaked the dialogue accordingly.

The two torturers use trendy slang, like the word "awesome," which originally meant "terrifying," but now has the opposite meaning.

We worked with several translators: a traditional translator, then a dubbing specialist, and finally a writer-director—whose name I've forgotten—who helped me go over the idiomatic expressions.

Despite your limited command of English, you wanted to have as much control as possible over the translation of the original dialogue?

Yes. It's because I don't have a strong command of the language that I wanted several opinions, so I could be sure of the final result.

There was a rumour that you requested the original house be transported to the United States.

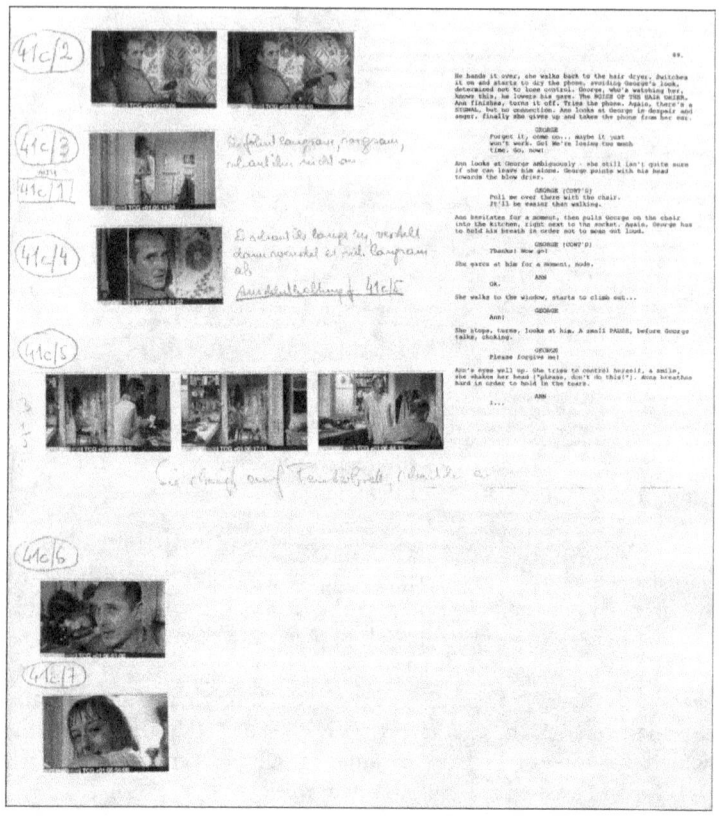

Shot breakdown of a sequence, with frames from the first version, featured on the left-hand script page of the U.S. remake of *Funny Games*

That's not true. But since the Austrian house had already been built in a sort of American style, I just reused the blueprints so it could be rebuilt identically. The furniture and curtains are different, but the dimensions were copied so I could keep my blocking intact. Finding the right exteriors was more difficult. Normally, you scout locations, then build your shots around them, but here it was the other way around: we had to find locations that matched the existing shot list. We did manage it, but sometimes had to adapt the locations to the shots, like the bridge leading to the lake, which we had to build, and which cost a fortune. For the scene where Naomi is looking for the dog, we were able to keep the same right-to-left camera movement, but the geography was flipped compared to the original.

89

(41c/2)

Aber er hält es ihr schon hin, sie geht damit zurück zum Föhn, den sie eingeschaltet auf die Arbeitsplatte gelegt hat und beginnt, das Handy im heißen Luftstrom zu trocknen. Dabei meidet sie Georgs Blick, um ihre Fassung behalten zu können. Georg, der sie anschaut, spürt das, senkt den Blick. Das FÖHNGERÄUSCH. Schließlich schaltet Anna den Föhn aus und probiert erneut die Funktion des Handys. Wieder gibt es ein SIGNAL von sich, aber eine Verbindung scheint nicht zustandezukommen, denn Anna schaut Georg mit einem verzweifelt wütenden Blick an, während sie das Gerät vom Ohr nimmt.

(41c/3) (41c/4) (41c/5)

GEORG:

    Laß es, komm...vielleicht geht es überhaupt nicht
    mehr. Geh Du! Wir verlieren viel zu viel Zeit. Laß
    mich das machen. Geh jetzt!

(während dessen spielt sie weiter am handy rum, das Signal spielt)

Anna, die sich wegen des Handys wütend halb weggewandt hat, schaut Georg fragend an - sie ist noch immer nicht sicher, ob sie ihn allein lassen kann. Georg deutet mit dem Kopf auf den Föhn:

    Zieh mich bitte mit dem Sessel dorthin. Das ist, glaub
    ich, leichter als gehen.

Anna zögert noch einen Moment, dann geht sie zu Georg und zieht ihn mit dem Sessel in die Küche herein, neben den Stromanschluß des Föhns. Wieder muß Georg während dieser Aktion die Luft anhalten, um nicht vor Schmerzen aufzuschrein.

    Danke. Und jetzt lauf.

Er löst Feuchmelter verschleben fühlt schließlich, einer Idee gleichfalls, einer muscle.

Sie schaut ihn einen Moment lang an, dann nickt sie.

ANNA:

    O.K.

Sie geht zum Fenster, setzt an, rauszusteigen, da sagt

GEORG:

    Anna!

(41c/6)

Sie hält inne, dreht sich zu ihm, schaut ihn an. Eine kurze PAUSE bevor Georg mit erstickter Stimme sagt:

    Bitte verzeih mir!

(41c/7)

Anna schießen die Tränen in die Augen. Sie will die Fassung bewahren, versucht ein Lächeln und schüttelt den Kopf ("Tu das nicht, bitte!"), zieht tief den Atem ein, um die Tränen zurückzudrängen:

ANNA:

    Es...

...and, on the right-hand page, the original shot breakdown.

One of the only visible differences between the two versions is the colour of the tarp covering the family's boat. It's blue in the Austrian version and white in the American one. Did that have any symbolic meaning for you?

No. That was the prop master not following my instructions. In general, I struggled with the lack of professionalism on set; it sometimes ended up being very costly, like that early shot of the car driving past, seen from the lake. In Austria, we mounted the

Ulrich Mühe and Susanne Lothar in *Funny Games.*

camera on a little boat and got it in two takes. In America, this massive crew showed up, but we had to do it three times because they couldn't get the boat to move at the same speed as the car. Every morning when I arrived on set, I was blocked by a whole convoy of cars. Every department head had their own driver. It's certainly a way of making films, but only if you have three times the budget and schedule.

Another difference between the two versions is the breed of the dog: a German shepherd in the Austrian version, a golden retriever in the American one.

A German shepherd made sense for the Austrian version. That's the breed families usually get when they want a guard dog. But in America, people tend to go for golden retrievers because they're friendly and make for the quintessential family dog. Ours was beautiful and gentle, but no one warned me that the breed isn't in the least bit aggressive. On top of that, it wasn't well trained, so it couldn't do anything I needed it to do.

The way the dead dog is discovered differs between versions. In Austria, it falls from the driver's seat; in America, from the trunk.

I actually prefer the American version. They showed up with a dead dog prop that was stiff as a brick, so I asked them to take just the skin and stuff it with rice. That way, the fall looked more realistic. A lot of people asked me what I did to the dog...

Tim Roth and Naomi Watts in the U.S. remake of *Funny Games*

The mother's outfit also changes when she is tied up and trying to free herself. In the Austrian version, Susanne Lothar wears a slip dress; in the American version, Naomi Watts is in underwear.

That was a practical decision. Susanne's dress wasn't really suited for the countryside; it looked more like something for the city, but the upside was that it allowed for wearing a full slip underneath. For Naomi, I wanted a simple summer dress, the kind a young woman might wear in that setting, but you don't wear a slip under a dress like that, so I gave her the choice: we could have a custom dress made that would work with a slip, even if it didn't quite look right, or... She immediately said she didn't mind doing the scene in just her underwear. She mostly wanted to feel comfortable in the dress and then in the difficult scene that followed. It wasn't about showing off her body. We gave her very plain, no-frills underwear; anything else would have felt obscene. I wanted her to appear childlike in that scene.

In the German dialogue, Arno Frisch wonders if the mother has love handles, while in the English version, Michael Pitt asks if her breasts sag.

That change was made for the sake of rhyme. At that point, the two torturers are improvising rhymed lines, and I wanted to preserve the rhythmic flow. It's the same thing with the line "*Das Kind ist blind, die Mamma zieht sich aus geschwind*," meaning: "The child is blind, and the mama undresses quickly." We had to find an equivalent in English, something that rhymed as well. In other

Tim Roth in the U.S. remake of *Funny Games*

places, there were wordplays that were hard to translate, and as for the prayer Anna is forced to say, we adapted that for each version, using real prayers that children actually say in each language.

The long take we talked about is actually one minute shorter in the American remake of Funny Games, *and the timing of the two actresses is completely different. Susanne Lothar stays frozen for a long time, while Naomi Watts moves almost immediately, trying to get up. Then, amazingly, they both turn off the TV at exactly the same moment, but in the end, there is still a full minute of difference. The Austrian version stretches things out.*

Further proof that the second half of the Austrian version is better than the American version. I didn't discuss this difference in performance with Naomi, but it's true that I was less meticulous in preparing this shot with the actors in the American version. Watts and Roth felt so constrained by the remake that I gave them more freedom, especially in the way they paced their actions during this long take. The problem is that, unlike Lothar and Mühe, they don't really play the scene together. Mühe is much more moving and authentic than Roth, who is excellent in other scenes — just not this one.

Naomi Watts in the U.S. remake of *Funny Games*

How many takes did you do for the long shot in the American version?

I don't remember exactly, but it wasn't many. We did a few more than in the Austrian version because I could tell I wasn't going to get the same result, and I wanted something more truthful.

On the television screen, we see a clip from Howard Hawks' Bringing Up Baby, *with Cary Grant and Katharine Hepburn. Why that film?*

I chose it from a list of films for which we didn't have to pay licensing fees. Another reason was the rhythm of the dialogue in that scene. And a little burst of comedy felt welcome in such a grim film.

We don't know of any other films that have been remade shot for shot, and even more remarkably, by their own director.

Neither do I. There was Gus Van Sant's *Psycho* remake, but that was more of a formal exercise, a study of Hitchcock's original, which is a different thing entirely.

Moreover, Van Sant didn't stick rigidly to the original's shot structure. He added some scenes and visualised Norman Bates' inner world.

For me, there were two questions when it came to doing a remake. The first one you already know the answer to: why do it? And second: how do I do it? Do I have anything new to add? The answer to that is: no… Everything I wanted to say is in the first film. My goal, therefore, was to reach the audience I hadn't reached with the Austrian film. I stuck with the same approach, which was a fascinating way of proceeding, because it turned out to be extremely difficult to remake the exact same film under completely different conditions. It felt like a kind of athletic challenge. And I managed to overcome all the obstacles! That gave me a real sense of satisfaction, especially since on set I was constantly worried that each shot might not be as good as the original. And because of the premise of the remake, I knew I wouldn't be able to cut anything that didn't work.

How do you feel about these twin films?

I'm glad to see I wasn't completely misguided in doing the remake. I think I even improved certain things with some of the actors. Arno Frisch is extraordinary, but Michael Pitt is even better. Arno wasn't really acting; he's just naturally arrogant, and that quality fit the character perfectly. Michael, on the other hand, is a trained Hollywood actor. He plays the part, adding all sorts of subtle details, which suited the idea of Americanising the story to reach a broader audience. Brady Corbet is very good too, but Frank Giering was better; he came across as less threatening, more comical, and ultimately more frightening. In the end, it was a tough experience. I underestimated the difficulties, but since I achieved what I set out to do, I'm very happy with the result.

Ron Howard planned to remake Caché. *Do you have any thoughts about that?*

He has already dropped the idea. But I had no problem with it. Americans can remake my films however they like, as long as they pay me well. I would actually be curious to compare their version to mine.

If the Americans asked you to direct the remake of Caché *yourself, would you?*

No. They did actually offer it to me while I was remaking *Funny Games.* There was already a budget and some actors lined up, but I wasn't interested. It would be absurd for me to direct a second remake of one of my own films.

Nine

Code Unknown and the struggle to communicate —
Bourdieu, Black people, Romanians, and Juliette Binoche
— In Marin Karmitz's kingdom — My best reviews — The
secrets of the deaf and mute — A choral film in long takes
— Memories of my father — The long gestation of *The
Piano Teacher* — Isabelle Huppert can do anything —
Filming the obscene — Annie Girardot's tears — A body
double for Benoît Magimel — Schubert and Schober —
Dubbing is the destruction of a film

Before discussing the origins of Code Unknown, *could you tell us
about its rarely mentioned subtitle: "Incomplete Account of Various Journeys"?*

It's directly tied to the content of the film.

*Yes, but this subtitle inevitably brings to mind the title of your
earlier ensemble film, which also played with the idea of an incomplete narrative:* 71 Fragments of a Chronology of Chance.

You could say that *Code Unknown*, which weaves together several
storylines drawn from everyday French life, is like a French
remake of *71 Fragments*. Actually, it's the only film I have made
where I had to do some research, because I didn't know anything
about the African and Romanian communities living in France.
The husband of my French publicist, Matilde Incerti, is Romanian, and he introduced me to some of his fellow countrymen
in Paris. He's also a university professor, and he put me in touch
with a number of African students. I spent about three months
observing these communities before I wrote a single line. What
I'm proudest of with this film is that, after a screening, one of the
students I had interviewed told me he would never have thought a
white man could describe the black community so accurately. That
meant a lot to me, especially since I had taken a rare risk: writing

about a world I didn't really know, at least not before I started digging into it. The farm storyline was inspired by Pierre Bourdieu's *The Weight of the World*, where he talks about the despair of farmers forced to slaughter their own livestock. The only story in the film that comes from a world I actually know is the one about the actress, played by Juliette Binoche, which connects to my own job. The photographs in the film are by Luc Delahaye, who had a role in *Paris*, Raymond Depardon's film.

Is the photographer character inspired by Depardon, who often spoke of his guilt about abandoning his family's farm to become a photographer?

He's a mix of influences. I borrowed a lot from a treatment Depardon had written with a journalist, about a war photographer who struggles to readjust after coming home. Depardon had decided not to make that film, and he gave me the script and let me use it however I wanted.

There are echoes of the war photographer in Drei Wege zum See, *particularly in his questioning of the usefulness of his profession.*

Exactly. In fact, I reused fragments of dialogue from *Drei Wege zum See* in *Code Unknown*.

Did you also do research on what it means to be deaf and mute?

I already had the idea of including deaf and mute characters, but the scene with the drums came about by chance. I was doing some background research one day when I heard drumming in a park. I went over and saw a group led by a young black conductor; he's the man you see at the end of the film next to Amadou. He's also the one who trained the real deaf and mute people to act alongside the rest of the cast. As you can see, *Code Unknown* required a lot of groundwork. I do think it's a fair and accurate film, not just something an outsider dreamt up, as some French critics claimed when it was released. I was quite shocked and hurt by the negative reviews, especially since French critics had generally been supportive of my earlier films. Ironically, *Code Unknown* got the best reviews of my career everywhere else in the world.

Code Unknown (2000)

One morning in Paris, Anne, an actress, leaves her home and crosses paths with Jean, the younger brother of her partner, Georges, a war photographer on assignment in Kosovo. Jean, having fled his father's farm, finds himself homeless. Anne gives him her keys and the access code to her building. Relieved, the boy eats a pastry and casually throws the crumpled wrapper onto a Romanian beggar, Maria, sitting outside the bakery. Amadou, a young Black musician, is outraged. A confrontation ensues and a crowd gathers. The police arrest Amadou and Maria to check their identification.

Anne rehearses at the theatre and does voiceover work for her first film. At home, her reunion with Georges is strained, and she worries about the mistreatment of a child by her neighbours. Maria is deported to Romania, where she brings money for her daughter's wedding. She hides her life as a beggar from her family but wants to return to France. Amadou, who teaches music to deaf children, sees his mother struggling with the contradictions between French culture and their African roots, while his taxi driver father returns to their homeland in search of a new wife.

Back in Paris, Maria resumes begging. In the subway, Anne is harassed by an immigrant teenager. Another man, also of North African descent, comes to her defence, prompting the boy to spit on Anne before leaving. Georges returns to see Anne but cannot enter the building because the access code has been changed.

Is it true that this film came about because Juliette Binoche wanted to work with you?

That's true. She called me one day after a conversation with Matilde Incerti. Matilde has been the publicist on all my films since *Funny Games*, and she also works a lot with Juliette. She gave her DVDs of my trilogy, and after Juliette had watched the three films, she gave me a call. I remember I was in a taxi in Spain heading to a festival when I suddenly heard, "Hello, this is Juliette Binoche. I saw your films and I'd love for us to work together." I told her that was great idea, that I didn't have any ideas just yet, but I

would think about it. At the time, Marin Karmitz had just turned
down my script for *Time of the Wolf*, telling me he thought it was
interesting but didn't think it would make any money, adding that
that if I ever had another script, I should feel free to show it to
him. After Juliette's call, I thought maybe having both our names
attached might pique his interest—and it did. Karmitz gave me the
green light for a film set in Paris, with Juliette at the centre of a
web of intersecting stories. I rented a little apartment in Paris and
stayed there for three months to do my research, then went back
to Vienna to write the script. I gave the script to Karmitz, who
immediately said yes. Then I gave it to Juliette, and after she read
it, she said, "I'd love to be your editor on this film!" I asked if she
was joking, since there wasn't really going to be anything to edit; it
was all designed as long takes. I think she hesitated a bit—maybe,
though I'm not sure—because she was slightly disappointed not
to have a more central role. But she eventually said yes, and everything went very smoothly. Working with her is a joy.

*When you told Karmitz that Juliette Binoche had agreed to the film
and that it was a mix of interwoven stories, did you tell him what
it would be about?*

I don't remember exactly what I said, but I already had the immigration theme in mind—the Romanian storyline—since I had
touched on that in *71 Fragments*. And because this was set in
France, I knew I would also have to include something about the
black community, though I didn't yet know how. That's why I did
all the research myself, out of my own pocket.

*Did you know from the start that the film would be shot entirely
in long takes?*

Yes, because I hadn't been able to do that in *71 Fragments*, and
I saw this as a new challenge, just as happened later, when I had
to stick rigidly to the original shot breakdown for the American
remake of *Funny Games*.

*Are those kinds of constraints a way for you to push yourself aes-
thetically?*

I'm not sure. In *Code Unknown*, it was more about staying true
to the idea of fragmentation. Each fragment had to be a self-con-
tained moment, so it made sense to do them as long takes. But

I don't want to make long takes into some kind of rule. In *The White Ribbon*, for instance, there are lots of long takes, but most of the scenes actually worked better when they were broken down into shot/reverse-shot setups. I don't think I'll ever do another film entirely in long takes.

Before we get into the most powerful long takes in Code Unknown, *can you say something about the opening scene, where deaf children try to guess what a little girl is miming?*

I gave the girl the word she had to mime, but I didn't tell the others what it was. And I'm not telling you either!

So the children's varied reactions weren't scripted?

They were, because otherwise it would have taken too long. The suggested answers were all predetermined. If the girl mimed the given word as accurately as possible, she could only elicit those specific responses.

Many of these responses seem to reflect themes from your work: "alone," "hiding place," "gangster," "bad conscience," "sadness," "locked in." Like the overture of an opera, was this a way of announcing the themes that would unfold in the film?

Yes, but put more simply, I would describe the sequence as being like a sentence that ends with a colon, with the rest of the film developing what has just been introduced. And then, at the end, we come back to the group of children, with the boy trying to explain something really beautiful, only this time, you have to figure it out on your own, since there is no shot of the group's reactions.

A relatively optimistic ending, for once.

It's my least sad film.

Thanks to the deaf and mute children... In this film, they are the only ones who know how to communicate, and they soften the underlying discomfort we feel from the title alone: Code Unknown, *the idea of exclusion through ignorance.*

I chose that title because of something I had noticed in France that didn't exist in Austria at the time. Now we're starting to get digital entry systems on buildings too, but back then, we only had

Ona Lu Yenke, Luminita Gheorghiu and
Alexandre Hamidi in *Code Unknown.*

doorbells. While I was researching the script in Paris, every person
I met gave me a code to get in. It really struck me. I thought it
worked perfectly as a metaphor for the breakdown in modern
communication.

*As usual, you wrap things up by circling back to the beginning. The
last sequence mirrors the first.*

That's how most musical structures work. When I write scripts,
I draw a lot from musical techniques: ellipses, repetitions, counterpoint—especially in ensemble films, where the structure is inher-
ently more complex. In some ways it's easier because you can just
focus each scene on the essentials, but it's also trickier because you
have to make sure the audience can follow and engage with each
storyline. A scene that goes on too long kills the tension, and when
you pick a story back up, you have to introduce an unexpected
situation to reignite interest.

*How did you shoot the second long take on the pavement, with
Binoche and her partner's younger brother, who causes a scene after
humiliating a beggar? The way it is staged makes it the most striking scene in the film.*

It was huge amount of work. First, we had to find a street where
we could actually pull off the scene as written. For a long time, we
came up empty. Then when we finally chose a location, we had
to adapt it to match the script. The spot where the young man

plays his instrument was originally just a passageway leading to an empty courtyard. We had to build the back of a supermarket there, since that kind of place is popular with beggars because there's so much foot traffic. The bakery didn't exist either. There was a carpet store there, which we had to completely convert. As for the movements, everything was timed down to the second. One bit of dialogue, for instance, lasted five seconds and had to be spoken while the character took exactly seven steps in a specific spot. The camera movements had to be just as precise. We spent a full day rehearsing with the camera and the actors. Then a second day with the camera, the actors, and the extras. We didn't actually shoot the scene until the third day. I think we did twenty-eight takes, and the one we ended up using was the very last one. In every other take, either an actor flubbed their lines or one of the two hundred extras looked into the camera. One small mistake would set off another. It was like trying to wrangle a bag of fleas. But when everything finally clicked, it was incredibly satisfying.

Would you have attempted something like that without the help of video playback?

No, because it's impossible to monitor everything in such a shot, even if I were to stand close to the camera and study the frame. I can't keep track of forty people at once; I have to focus on the essentials. Thanks to the video monitor, I can review everything carefully. I can catch an extra who, for the third time, is looking directly into the lens or notice that Juliette has forgotten a line because she's exhausted.

Wouldn't it have been cheaper to shoot it in a studio?

Out of the question. We would have had to build an entire section of the street, the shops, the passage leading to the supermarket, and also simulate traffic and reflections of the buildings on the opposite side of the street. To make it look real, we would have needed Hollywood-level resources. In a studio, this single sequence would have swallowed the entire film's budget. Altering the real storefronts, compensating the shop owners, and setting up the camera tracks was more cost effective, though it was still the most expensive shot in the film. Another long take—the one in the café—actually required even more attempts. It's less spectacular but just as complex in terms of timing: the conversation at the table, Juliette's departure, the young couple at the next table, Juliette's return. In

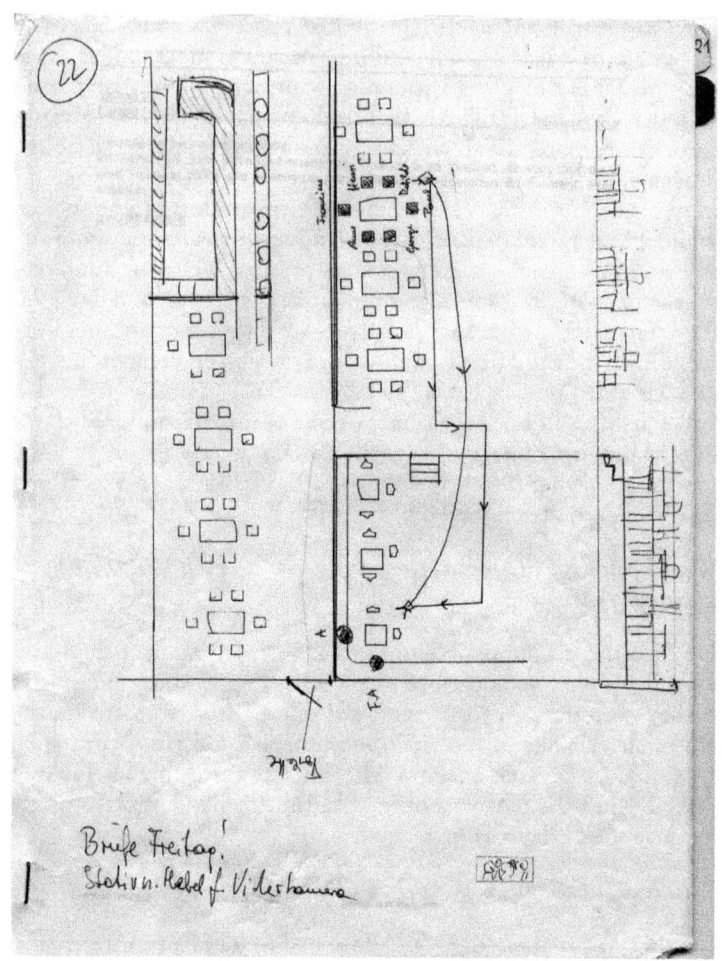

The storyboard of the café long take.

every take, someone made a mistake. We shot it more than thirty times.

What's striking about that shot is that the camera moves away from Juliette at the table and frames the young couple, then suddenly she reappears from the restroom behind them without us having seen her leave. It's only on a second viewing that we realise why we missed her first departure: at that precise moment, you draw our attention to the couple arguing.

That was the trick. I designed it to create a surprise effect. It was all meticulously choreographed. We had to know who was doing what and when. Juliette waited for my signal to get up and leave. Then, at the right moment, I signalled an assistant to send her back to the table.

Some people have said you can be seen in that scene. But we didn't spot you...

That's news to me... I finally have a cameo in one of my films! It might be true, but I haven't noticed myself in the frame. On a related note, I can tell you a less amusing story. At the end of the Austrian *Funny Games*, the two torturers were supposed to throw Susanne Lothar into the lake. We wanted to do just one take because Susanne was dreading being tossed into the freezing water while bound. The key was to ensure that her body didn't surface too quickly. To help with that, I planned for the boat to make a sharp turn as soon as she was thrown in, to shift the focus. Since we didn't have video playback, I used a small handheld camera to check the framing. I saw that she didn't resurface. Perfect! She's "dead." We don't need a second take. Later, in the editing room, I trimmed the shot to the right length, no problem. But when we screened it in the sound studio, where I saw it on a large screen for the first time—disaster! Susanne's head suddenly appeared. Today, we could easily erase her digitally, but at the time, it was impossible. The shot had to be sent to Germany, where they painstakingly removed her frame by frame. It cost a fortune. It just goes to show: mistakes happen, even when you think you've planned for everything. Even with video playback, we might have missed it. On a small screen, you don't always catch these details, which can lead to nasty surprises.

Another scene that stood out to us was the one in the subway, filmed with a single static shot.

That one really worried me because the fixed shot was an additional constraint. On top of that, the RATP only allowed us to shoot from 2 a.m. to 5 a.m. The idea of shooting this scene in just three hours made me nervous. Of course, I had rehearsed extensively with the two boys beforehand because it was difficult, especially for the one who had to laugh provocatively at the other's jokes. It's always easier to cry on cue than to laugh convincingly over and over. A professional actor can cry as many times as needed,

Maurice Bénichou, Walid Afkir and Juliette Binoche in *Code Unknown*.

but laughter immediately sounds fake if it isn't real. We did an extensive casting search among non-professionals to find someone who could pull off a believable laugh.

How many takes did you do?

Not many, because we just didn't have time. Juliette and Maurice Bénichou nailed it every time. The tricky part was working with the extras. They had to react to the behaviour of the two boys—and with extras, you never know what to expect.

The shot reminds us of the one featuring the banker's father in 71 Fragments, *which was also remarkable.*

That was a shot we had to redo over and over because the actor was an elderly man—a former music-hall performer, now deceased—who kept forgetting his lines. When someone blanks after seven minutes of filming, it isn't easy to start over again. Apart from these memory slips, he was excellent. Memorising such a long monologue and performing it with that much intensity each time, while trying not to trip up in the same places as before, is very hard.

Besides the advantages we have already discussed, long takes also seem to help you get closer to the truth of a character. Take the director's off-screen line during the audition scene, spoken to Juliette Binoche's character in the film within the film: "Show me your real face!"

Yes, absolutely, that's part of it. That particular scene is very ambiguous because you don't know if it's just acting or if Juliette's character is actually about to be gassed. We understand she's come in for a casting, but you can't help wondering if she's walked into a trap. I get a lot of pleasure out of creating those kinds of doubts. It's only later, in the café, that she explains the film she was auditioning for is about a real estate agent who lures people into his villa, locks them up, and watches them die. I had actually wanted to make a film based on that premise myself, but one day, while I was talking about it, someone mentioned that there was already an English-language novel with a similar storyline: *The Collector* by John Fowles.

Which was adapted for the screen under the same title by William Wyler, starring Terence Stamp.

So I dropped the idea and folded it into *Code Unknown* instead. But since then, reality has caught up with fiction in Austria, with the case of Natascha Kampusch, the girl who was abducted and held captive for eight years before she managed to escape.

From a structural point of view, Code Unknown *differs from the traditional ensemble film because, after intertwining all these destinies, you don't bring them all together at the end.*

That was a real challenge: how to bring them together at the end. I ultimately reunited three of them: Juliette, the Romanian woman, and the war photographer. In most ensemble films, there's usually a situation or event that either brings all the characters together in the same place or lets them react in parallel. In *Short Cuts*, it's an earthquake. In *Magnolia*, it's the raining frogs. That film also features a song playing on television that all the characters end up singing along to. It's very celebratory, but not exactly believable in a realistic film.

In Code Unknown, *the event that creates a partial reunion is the drum concert by the deaf and mute children, who are the only characters who establish any real communication in the film.*

Yes, and at the same time it's unsettling because there's a certain aggressiveness in the way the drums are played. It's also a form of protest, even if, for the children, it's mostly a joyful experience.

In a film where you constantly depict a kind of return to barbarism, this drumming sequence seems to mark a brief moment of euphoria.

It's not euphoria. Let's just say I try to observe the world as clearly as I can, without letting it erode my optimism.

Even the title, Code Unknown, *evokes the difficulty of communication. We all function with codes that others don't have access to.*

That's the Babel myth, which leads to people being cut off from one another. We never truly communicate because, from one person to another, gestures and words don't carry the same meaning. We might have the illusion of communicating when we fall in love and believe that the other person feels the same as we do, but after a while, reality sets in. The only areas where one can truly be in sync with another person are through sex and music. Of course, even in those areas there can be deception, but the intensity of the connection surpasses anything that can be conveyed through verbal communication, where every word is a potential source of misunderstanding.

That struggle to communicate really comes through in the scenes between Georges, the photographer, and his father, the farmer.

Farmers generally don't talk much.

Here again we find one of your recurring themes: a lack of communication with the father.

It's a theme that appears in different ways across several of my films although as I've told you, it doesn't correspond to any personal experience. In fact, when my father saw *Lemminge*, he asked me, "Why this terrible image of the father in your film?" Just as I'm telling you now, all I could say was: "I don't know."

Your father was an actor and director, but you didn't have much of a relationship with him.

I only really got to know him when I directed him in the theatre, which was a lot of fun. He was very elegant and was always meticulously dressed. Once, on television, he played Thomas Mann, but his refined acting style made him particularly brilliant in classical comedy. He was very funny, especially in a production of Eugène Scribe's *Le Verre d'eau.* In private, while he was very stubborn—

Juliette Binoche in *Code Unknown.*

like me—he was also quite charming and had a better sense of humour than I do. He loved making jokes.

What was his name?

Fritz, which is my middle name. Fritz is the diminutive of Friedrich, which was the name of my grandfather and great-grandfather on my father's side. My father even insisted that my son David have Friedrich as his third name.

Do you remember the play in which you directed him?

A somewhat forgotten work by Dieter Forte called *Martin Luther und Thomas Münzer oder die Einführung der Buchhaltung* [*Martin Luther and Thomas Münzer or the Introduction of Book-Keeping*]. It originally lasted eight hours, but I cut it down to four and a half. My father played Fugger, the first great merchant in German-speaking history. It's not exactly a comedy, but it was quite funny.

You never directed your father in any of your films?

No, by the time I started working in cinema, he had already passed away. And I didn't have any roles for him in my television films.

Was casting him in your theatre production a way of getting to know him better?

No, it was because, in Baden-Baden, when I was starting out in theatre, we lacked good actors, and I thought he could raise the level. I had met him several times before, but only for a weekend or very briefly. It was through working together that we truly got to know each other. I remember that since the play was very long, I kept cutting parts of it, and one day my father said to me, "If you cut one more line, I'm walking out!" Then he added, "My son is taking revenge for the authority I never had over him." That was typical of his humour. Always tinged with irony.

When you say you grew up without a father, does that mean you never saw him as a child?

I saw him only once when I was four or five years old. It was just after the war, around 1946 or '47. Austria and Germany were divided into zones occupied by the four Allied powers. We were in Salzburg and my father was in Germany, where he had started a new life. There was a no man's land between the two, and I was with my mother and grandmother on the side occupied by the British and Americans. I wasn't allowed to go to Germany to see my father and he couldn't come to Austria, but we were permitted to meet between the two border checkpoints. I still remember him walking toward me. My mother was with me. We said hello to each other. It all felt a bit awkward.

Was it an arranged meeting?

Yes, but I'm not exactly sure by who. It felt very staged. I saw him again later when I was twelve, while my mother was performing at the Burgtheate. She had gone to the Bregenz Festival, where she had a role in *Hamlet*. My father happened to be on the shores of Lake Constance and we spent two days together. To be honest, I felt more like I was with an uncle than with a father. It was only later, when I lived in Baden-Baden and he was in Mainz, just an hour and a half away by car, that we started seeing each other regularly. That's when I cast him in my production. It was a lot of fun.

And proof that biography doesn't explain works of art.

The only things in my films that relate to personal experiences are my rejection and fear of violence in its various forms, as well as a deep mistrust of anything related to communication.

Listening to you, one gets the sense that Code Unknown *is the favourite of your films.*

I think that's fair to say. And I know many people who think the same. They say it's my richest, most balanced film. But *Caché* isn't bad either.

There's a strong human dimension in Code Unknown. *It seems to reflect on how Western society is inevitably becoming multi-ethnic, while still struggling with true intercultural exchange.*

That's your interpretation. Others will see it differently. As always, my concern when making the film was to allow for as many interpretations as possible, to invite the viewer to bring their own thoughts to what I present. It's especially crucial that the ending doesn't lock itself into the director's point of view but instead encourages audiences to engage with their own convictions. That's the only way, I think, to stay truly connected to them.

Which makes the subtitle particularly relevant: "An incomplete account"—since you have to limit yourself in the telling—"of various journeys," allowing the viewer to follow you, or not, as they wish.

Exactly. As I said, the meaning of the film is right there in a subtitle.

How did you come to direct The Piano Teacher? *Is it true that Paulus Manker was originally meant to direct it? We have also read that you had been thinking about the project for fifteen years.*

Correct on both counts. When I read the novel, shortly after it was published, I immediately thought it would make a great film. In fact, I even thought it might be the perfect choice for my first feature, so I asked Elfriede Jelinek for the rights. She told me she had already written her own adaptation with feminist filmmaker Valie Export, a specialist in video installations and experimental films. The project had fallen through for financial reasons, and Jelinek had decided to give up on cinema altogether. She refused to sell the rights to *The Piano Teacher*. As it happens, Paulus Manker had acted in a rather successful adaptation of Jelinek's previous novel, *Die Ausgesperrten* [*The Excluded*], and had developed a bit of a rapport with her, so when he asked for the rights to *The Piano Teacher*, she gave them to him. Paulus then asked me to write the screenplay for him. I suggested that it was a little odd to hand me that job given that I had previously tried to acquire the rights to the book myself, even though, in fact, by that point I had other projects in hand and no longer wanted to direct *The Piano Teacher*. I told him that I would do it if I was well paid. He agreed, and I wrote his screenplay. He wanted to make the film with Kathleen Turner, which I thought was a bad idea because she was too old for the role. He went to America to meet her, but she turned him down. He then turned to Helen Mirren, which was a better idea. She was also a bit too old to play Erika, but I know she could have captured the complexities. Mirren also said no. She felt that she'd had her fill of perversion after Peter Greenaway's *The Cook, the Thief, His Wife & Her Lover*. I had told Paulus from the start that Isabelle Huppert was perfect for the part, but he didn't want to hear it. He didn't speak French and couldn't imagine shooting a film in that language, so he kept searching. After almost ten years, he still hadn't found his actress. Veit Heiduschka, who was set to produce the film, had gone to school with Jelinek and knew her well. He eventually asked if she would be okay with me directing, and since she was frustrated that Paulus' version wasn't going anywhere, she agreed. Heiduschka then offered me the job. I told him I had to talk to Paulus first, since I had written the adaptation for him, and that if I were to direct, I would write a new version. I met with Paulus, who said he wanted to talk to Jelinek first—and then vanished for several months. I left him messages saying it was totally fine if he didn't want me to do it, but he should just say so. Meanwhile, the project kept moving forward, and Heiduschka was pressuring me to decide. I finally agreed, on two conditions: that Jelinek confirmed her approval, and that Huppert played the lead role.

Did Jelinek read your version of the screenplay?

I don't remember, but I'm sure that the notoriety I had gained in the meantime with my films encouraged her to give her approval. She didn't get involved in the screenplay at all, not in my new version or the one I had written for Paulus. From the outset, she told us that we could use her text as we liked.

Was she happy with the film?

Happy? I don't know. Her novel is autobiographical; she had quite a perverse relationship with her mother, who died during the film's production so she was afraid of seeing it. To buck herself up, she

Thomas Weinhappel, Susanne Haneke, Michael Haneke
and Elfriede Jelinek.

came to a screening with a friend, and afterwards she told us it was
a good film. Later, she always spoke positively about it, but she's
such a polite woman that you never know what she really thinks.
Since it was a theatrical film, I took some liberties with the novel,
starting with changing the structure significantly, including dras-
tically reducing the sections devoted to the mother-daughter relationship, which occupied more than half the text. I also removed
all the flashbacks of Erika's youth. Instead, I created a mother for
Anna—the student Erika is jealous of—who isn't even in the novel.
I used that other mother-daughter pair to evoke Erika's childhood
in a more indirect way.

The Piano Teacher (2001)

Vienna, present day. Erika Kohut, a music professor at
the conservatory, lives with her overbearing and domi-
neering mother, who is deeply traumatised by the death
of her husband, who went mad, and obsessed with her
unfulfilled dream of an illustrious career for her daughter. Erika is a demanding teacher, sometimes cruel to her
students. Privately frustrated, she indulges in voyeurism
and self-harm, regularly mutilating her genitals. After
meeting her at a private concert, the young Walter Klem-

mer becomes fixated on her. He decides to gain admission to her class and seduce her. She treats him harshly but is forced to acknowledge both his talent as a performer and her physical attraction to him. Perverse games bring them closer. Erika becomes possessive, and upon seeing Walter showing kindness to Anna, her sensitive and fragile student, she injures the girl by slipping shards of glass into her coat pocket. Walter realises the gravity of this act and confronts Erika more directly on an overtly sexual level, but Erika can only ensure and prolong their encounters by imposing a series of sadomasochistic rules. Upon seeing Erika's mother, Walter grasps Erika's devastating complexity and forces a particularly violent sexual encounter on her, bringing their relationship to an end. At a concert where Erika is set to replace the recovering Anna, she sees Walter arrive with a female companion. He greets her. She withdraws, takes the knife she had slipped into her bag, stabs herself in the chest, then walks out, controlling her pain.

The rights to the novel were acquired by Wega-Film. Was it after Huppert came on board that MK2 became involved?

As soon as we knew Isabelle would be in the film, we had to look abroad. With Isabelle's salary and those of the other French actors, the budget exceeded Wega-Film's means, so we absolutely needed a French partner. I went to see Marin Karmitz, who had already produced *Code Unknown*. He hadn't behaved too well during that shoot because he tried to meddle in everything, but I respect him. He knows cinema, has produced a lot of great films, and is good at looking after his own interests. As I once said: "He's a king in his kingdom and I'm a king in mine. But two kings in one kingdom? That doesn't work." He keeps a very tight grip on anything to do with money, which can be frustrating for people working with him on the creative side, and since he didn't treat Wega-Film very well either, I stopped working with him after *The Piano Teacher*. I was very happy collaborating with Margaret Menegoz at Les Films du Losange. She let me do what I wanted, while still keeping a close eye on the finances. With her, it was simple: I told her what I want to do and she set the boundaries. We talked it through and either found a solution—or we didn't. In fact, we always found one. Neither of us ever felt frustrated.

Did you have a similar relationship with Veit Heiduschka?

That's different. You can't really compare. Austrian producers aren't real producers because they don't have capital, they don't know how to sell a film, and they rely on Austria's Film Federation, from which they receive subsidies, out of which they take their salaries. If I hadn't found foreign distributors myself, I would still be working in Vienna, completely unknown. That said, Heiduschka remained loyal to me and made sure that Michael Katz, the production manager I really click with, stayed on board. He lets me work with total freedom. Karmitz, on the other hand, would never have allowed me to replace an actor once we had started filming *Benny's Video*'s.

Jelinek's novel creates distancing effects by alternating between "I" and "she" when referring to the protagonist. Did you try to translate this literary technique into cinematic terms?

If I had written the first adaptation for myself, maybe I would have, but in my second version, I opted for a factual style very different from my other films. In a way, both the script and the directing style are closer to what I used to do for television. That probably explains why *The Piano Teacher* was my biggest box-office success. In terms of form, it was my most accessible film.

It felt like you transposed that distancing effect into Huppert's performance. In the audition scene with Walter, for example, there's a long take where we can see on her face, especially in her eyes, that she is losing control, overwhelmed by her physical desire.

If that's how it came across, I'm glad, though I don't remember making that choice consciously.

One of the most significant changes from the novel is the development of Walter's character.

In the novel, Walter is an idiot, but if you have an idiot in a drama on screen, the whole film falls apart because the audience won't care about him. In a novel, it can work because of the writing style. Throughout her book, Jelinek denounces herself, spits out her self-hatred, and extends it to all the other characters. With cinema, where you have this supposed objectivity of the camera—casting the same gaze on everyone—you can't have a major character who's completely uninteresting. To create real tension between Erika

Isabelle Huppert in *The Piano Teacher.*

and Walter, I absolutely had to give him some appealing qualities, otherwise it wouldn't make sense why she's so obsessed with him.

Did you change Walter's sport, from canoeing in the novel to ice hockey in the film, for budgetary reasons?

No. It was because the ice rink was right next to the conservatory. Seeing that well-known building gave me the idea to have him play hockey instead, which saved me from including the long chase through the city which is described in the novel. Moreover, this change offered me a beautiful metaphor: Erika as an ice princess. If I remember correctly, that idea actually came from Paulus Manker.

Why did you change the peep-show scene? In the novel, Erika watches a live show where a young woman performs, but in your version, she isolates herself in a video booth.

I could say that the projection of images aligns better with my medium of expression, but the real reason is that I visited a peep-show during location scouting and I found it so dull, so completely unerotic, that visually it just wasn't unusable.

This also allows you to be more explicit in your depiction, show-ing penetrative sex rather than mere caresses, as in the novel. We assume you didn't shoot those pornographic images yourself.

No, of course not. As usual, I was given a list of available films, from which I made my selection.

You also changed the Prater Park sequence. In the novel, Erika observes an older woman having sex in the park with a Turkish man. In the film, it's a younger, more conventional couple in a drive-in theatre.

I changed the location for a simple reason: at night, the Prater is too dark to film a realistic scene. I needed a better-lit place where she could plausibly spy on a couple's sexual activity. The open-air cinema met those conditions while also being reminiscent of the sex shop's video booth. Sticking to the same medium—film—seemed more powerful to me. Plus I found the scene with the Turkish man too much of a caricature.

Making The Piano Teacher *involved you shooting sex scenes yourself. What limits did you set?*

I wanted to capture the obscenity of the book without ever being pornographic. It's a matter of taste, knowing what you can and can't do. For me, anything goes, as long as the actor's dignity isn't compromised. When filming the scene where Benoît Magimel, who plays Walter, lowers his pants to throw himself on Isabelle, for example, there was one take where his rear ended up fully in frame, and I immediately stopped it.

Did you discuss these sex scenes with your actors before filming?

Yes. I promised them that I would protect them as much as possible. And I kept that promise.

Did you agree not to show their genitals?

Yes, but it went further than that. In the bathroom scene, where Walter starts masturbating, she tells him to stop touching his erect penis but insists he let her watch. In the novel, she watches him lose his erection, which is exactly what I wanted to film. When I told Benoît we were going to film it just as it was in the script, he flat-out refused. When I decided to hire a body double, Benoît wanted to choose him himself. My line producer then held a kind of "erect penis casting," with porn actors, and Benoît picked one. The problem was that once on set, the guy, who was gay, couldn't get it up. I told him to take his time and get comfortable, but two or three hours later, still nothing. He asked if he could come back with his boyfriend, because with him there, he was sure it would work, so they showed up... with a pump. It was wild. But even then, no luck. We were all laughing. Eventually they told us the reason it wasn't working was because my cameraman and I were intimidating them, so we stepped out and let them do whatever they needed to do. We even showed the boyfriend how to press the button to roll the camera, but we still had to wait ages before they finally emerged. Mission finally accomplished! That night, I had guests over for dinner and showed up two hours late. When I explained why, you can imagine the laughs. At least we had a usable take, and I went ahead and edited it in. That's when I realised there was a lighting issue. One of the crew, thinking he was being helpful, had taken two lamps and swapped them for different ones, with a different colour temperature, which meant the shot no longer matched the rest of the scene. I kept it anyway; I had worked too hard for that damn shot. At the first screenings, there were some strong reactions, especially from Karmitz's wife. I stood my ground and insisted the shot would stay, until we got to the colour grading stage, when I had to admit it just didn't work. The lighting was off and it would never match, so I cut it. I regretted it because in the script I had planned to go all the way, to show the penis losing its erection.

With today's digital tools, would you consider reintegrating it?

No. It's done. Watching the film today, that shot isn't missed.

It's always tricky to use porn actors in mainstream films.

In Bruno Dumont's *The Life of Jesus* a shot like that makes a very strong impact.

Except there's a big issue with hair colour. Dumont's actress is blonde, while her porn double, whose genitals are shown, is a red head!

Speaking of which, I have a funny story about *The White Ribbon*. In the scene where the dead woman's body is shown, her genitals are visible. The actress who played the living woman absolutely refused to do nudity, so we asked the Romanian extras if any of them would be willing to play the corpse for extra pay. One woman agreed, on the condition that her husband wouldn't be able to recognise her when he saw the film, so at her request we dyed her pubic hair.

You include a powerful self-mutilation scene in the bathtub. But the novel has more, including one where Erika sticks pins into her chest.

We shot that, but in combination with the bathtub scene, it didn't work. There had to be just one self-mutilation scene; any more and it started to feel repetitive. In the novel, there are several, but what works in literature doesn't always translate to the screen.

Before accepting the project, did Huppert have any concerns about those scenes?

She had found *Funny Games* too harsh. When I offered *The Piano Teacher* to her, I asked her not to read the novel. In a recent interview, she said that she followed my advice, but also said that she hadn't even read my script before accepting the role. Apparently she first looked at it on the plane to Vienna and was shocked. But maybe she was joking.

How do you explain your desire to work with her?

Because she's the best actress I know—not just in France—for this kind of role.

Which films of hers had you seen that impressed you?

She didn't really move me in her early films. In *The Lacemaker*, for example, she was good, but not extraordinary. But as she aged, she became more beautiful and reached a level of acting that few performers can achieve. Perhaps only Helen Mirren or Meryl Streep come close.

How did you come to cast Benoît Magimel?

That was pure chance. I met him during the filming of *Code Unknown*, at a dinner hosted by Juliette Binoche, who was his partner at the time. That's when I learned he was an actor. Since he was a handsome young man, I thought of him for the role of Walter. I had him do an audition and immediately knew he was right for the role.

Was Annie Girardot your first choice for Erika's mother?

No. I first thought of Jeanne Moreau. We met, and she was absolutely charming. She said she was interested and wanted to do the film. I then started discussing her costumes and hairstyle for the film, but she replied that there was no rush. Later, when I tried to bring it up again, her tone completely changed and she insisted on using her own hairdresser and that she only wore one specific colour and certain kinds of clothing. Annette Beaufays, our costume designer, and I tried to accommodate everything she asked for and brought her a selection. She tried them on, somewhat reluctantly, but when we left her place, Annette, who is usually not overly emotional, actually burst into tears because of how condescending Jeanne had been toward her. We went to a café, and not ten minutes later, Marin Karmitz called to say Jeanne had phoned him too, complaining about the costumes, saying she wouldn't wear them, and that I needed to speak to her. That's when I made my decision: I wasn't going to move forward with her. She would have wanted to control everything, and I don't work that way. I never called her back. We started thinking about who else could play the part, and I thought of Annie Girardot, even though she already had a reputation for struggling to remember her lines. I decided to give it a try anyway and brought her in for a test. It wasn't easy, but I thought she was a brilliant actress, so I figured we would make it work. The shoot was tough for her because she was in the early stage of Alzheimer's. She had a coach with her on set at all times, constantly drilling her lines to help her remember them. I later cast her again as Daniel Auteuil's mother in *Caché*. That was much easier; it was just one scene, shot in shot/reverse-shot, and the dialogue was shorter. More importantly, we worked around her memory issues by giving her an earpiece that was invisible on camera. An assistant sat in the next room feeding her the lines, and Annie delivered the performance flawlessly.

A rumour circulated suggesting that certain scenes showing Huppert and Girardot in situations deemed too violent were cut from the film.

Not true. That rumour may have come from an interview Annie gave, where she said Isabelle didn't exactly have a gentle touch. It's true that Isabelle actually slapped her in a scene, which must not have been pleasant, as Annie herself mentioned in her autobiography. What's odd is that right after the shoot, she kept saying, "A thousand thanks to Michael for giving me this opportunity to act again!" But then, after the awards ceremony in Cannes, where

Annie Girardot and Isabelle Huppert in *The Piano Teacher.*

Karmitz had only invited Isabelle and Benoît, Annie was upset with us all and started talking less kindly about the experience. Of course, this was all due to her illness. It was heartbreaking on the set of *Caché* to hear her ask Daniel Auteuil, after half a day of filming with him, what role he was playing in the movie. Sad, but also very moving to see her extraordinary talent still come through, even as her illness prevented her from understanding what was happening around her. We were all shaken by the suffering she was going through. I remember, at the end of one scene, when Daniel leaves the room, Annie was supposed to follow him with her eyes, but she couldn't do it. We did take after take trying to get that look, but it just didn't happen. Realising she couldn't manage it, Annie started crying and tried hard to hold back the tears. I kept that take in the final cut because it was so moving in the context of her role. You think she is crying because of the loneliness she will be plunged into once her son leaves, but really it was Annie Girardot crying, feeling betrayed and humiliated by her failing mind. Her death, which happened during the filming of *Amour*, hit me hard.

One of the most powerful moments in The Piano Teacher *is when, at the end, Erika stabs herself in the chest. Huppert makes a little grimace of pain; subtle but incredibly effective. How did you direct her?*

That grimace is described precisely in the novel. I remember the line: "Sie bleckt die Zähne wie ein geiferndes Pferd" ["She bares her teeth like a frothing horse"], which I included in the script. My great pleasure in writing the adaptation was to do it in Jelinek's style, even though that wasn't strictly necessary. Isabelle did wonder how to act it out. She wasn't very comfortable with the description because she was afraid of looking ridiculous. I encouraged her to go for it, reminding her that the situation itself was ridiculous, that the character was making a gesture verging on madness, and in the end what she did was incredibly powerful.

Did you do multiple takes?

Yes, and I don't remember which one we used. From a technical standpoint, there was also the issue of the special effect. We placed a metal plate under her blouse to prevent any injury, and the blood appearing gradually was added digitally, but her movement also had to be anatomically correct. The arm motion had to be light but firm enough to create the illusion of the blade piercing the flesh.

How did you shoot the self-harming scene in the bathtub?

We came up with a whole system. Our props master, standing off-camera, pumped fake blood through a small tube attached near Isabelle's groin. In the low-angle shot where she sits on the edge of the tub, mirror in hand, beginning to mutilate herself, her robe was arranged to hide both the tubing and her body.

When you show blood in your films, it always looks real. What do you actually use?

For *The Piano Teacher*, we did numerous tests. The ones with real animal blood weren't convincing, so we went with fake blood, though I don't remember exactly what. I didn't want it too liquid or too bright red; it had to be something darker and heavier. It took a lot of trial and error before we got it right.

Did you stay true to Jelinek's musical choices?

I respected her choices: Schoenberg for the audition scene, and the two Bach pieces during the concert. But I also added some pieces, like the Rachmaninoff. *The Winterreise* [*Winter Journey*] lieder were in the novel, including one of the most famous texts, *Der Wegweiser* [*The Signpost*]: "Was vermeid' ich denn die Wege,/Wo die ander'n Wand'rer geh'n?/Habe ja doch nichts begangen,/Daß ich Menschen sollte scheu'n," which means: "Why do I avoid the paths/that other travellers take?/I have done nothing wrong/that should make me shun mankind." It's a key text quoted by Thomas Mann in *Doctor Faustus*, when the narrator recounts how his friend, the composer, once mentioned it and was moved to tears, because it speaks to the heart of his problem: feeling guilty even though he isn't; he just sees the world more clearly than most. If I recall correctly, Jelinek quotes it in the novel as a standalone fragment, disconnected from its musical setting. In several passages, she plays with language, quoting lines from Schubert lieder without identifying them, and also mentions pieces without giving any specifics, including some that Walter rehearses. At one point, Erika insists: "Leave the Schubert…" without saying which piece she means. I was the one who selected almost all of those pieces.

We liked your use of the famous Andante from Schubert's Trio No. 2, Opus 100. *It begins conventionally, played by Erika and her musician friends, but then continues over scenes of Erika walking through the streets, follows her into the shopping mall and the peep show, and only fades out once the images of porn start.*

I'm glad you noticed that. There are several moments where I overlapped the music in this way, to guide us into the following scene. Schubert's music already has something unsettling about it, and paired with those visuals, that feeling is amplified. It's the same thing at the end of the peep show scene, when we start to hear the second verse of a Schubert lied we had heard earlier: "Ich bin zu Ende mit allen Träumen,/Was will ich unter den Schläfern säumen?" ["I am done with all dreams,/Why linger among the sleepers?"] There are plenty of other examples I could point to.

Was this relationship between music and image your way of replicating the sudden shifts in the novel that reflect Erika's instability?

That's exactly what I was aiming for. I really believe that you can be cultured and perverse. Culture doesn't protect us from the darker parts of life.

Regarding Schubert's Trio, *did you take into account its use in other films?*

I knew that Kubrick had used it in *Barry Lyndon*, but I didn't care. The Mendelssohn *Octet*, which is heard during the rehearsal in the concert hall, was also used by Louis Malle in *Les Amants*. I used the *Quintet in C Major* in *The Rebellion*. Who cares if it's been

Benoît Magimel in *The Piano Teacher.*

used in lots of films; it's so moving. There is enough music in *The Piano Teacher* that has never been heard in a film before that I felt I could afford to include the Schubert Trio too. Anyway, when you're working with Schubert, it's hard to avoid certain pieces.

One striking thing about Huppert and Magimel's performances is that they actually play the piano themselves in the film. Did they have any prior experience before being cast?

Isabelle played a little; some very simple pieces. She learned to read music as a child, but it was clear that her hands weren't ready for the kind of repertoire she had to play in the film. She didn't have a lot to do, but it still took a lot of rehearsal. She had to play the pieces flawlessly, at the exact tempo we had pre-recorded and timed down to the second. It was even tougher for Benoît, especially with the Schoenberg, which is rhythmically very complex. When I cast him, he told me he didn't know a thing about the piano. He started taking lessons in France with a teacher, but when he first came to show me what he had learned, I was convinced we were in a lot of trouble because he really wasn't very good. But he stuck with it, practising for hours every day, and by the time we shot the audition scene, right at the end of the shoot to give him as much prep time as possible, he was playing on a live piano, totally in sync with the playback of the recording. Everyone was impressed, especially his piano teacher.

How long did Magimel train before he had to play those scenes?

A few months. When he arrived at the beginning of the shoot, he wasn't ready because the teacher he had started with in France wasn't very good. Fortunately, in Vienna, we had an excellent piano teacher who helped him make fast progress.

During Walter and Erika's discussion about Schumann and the decline of the mind, we noticed your personal touch with the addition of an Adorno quote. But what stood out most was the boldness of the staging. Instead of a standard shot-reverse shot, you keep the camera entirely on Erika.

From a strictly dramatic point of view, it didn't make sense to cut between them. Even when Walter speaks, it's really about her. The whole conversation—about losing oneself, about Schumann's decline—is a reflection of her story, so it was essential to stay on her. But I'm fully aware that with a less talented actress than Isabelle, this approach wouldn't have worked, or, at least, it would have lost much of its impact.

Schober, the last name you created for Anna's mother—

—is a well-known name, as Schober was a friend of Schubert. But in the film, of course, it's just a private joke.

Did you cast Susanne Lothar as Madame Schober out of friendship?

No. She was simply the best actress for the role. I never make professional decisions based on friendship, only in my private life.

How did you handle the language barrier between the French-speaking and German-speaking actors?

It was complicated. On one hand, the film's action takes place entirely in Vienna, and I needed to recreate that Viennese atmosphere. On the other hand, I couldn't ask Isabelle Huppert to perform in both languages, as it would have disrupted the emotional flow, so I cast French actors for the three main roles and Austrian or German actors for all the others. The German-speaking characters talk a lot among themselves but very little with the French-speaking trio. The only exceptions were the two scenes, in the street and in a classroom, between Isabelle and Susanne, where they discuss young Anna. Each actress spoke in her own language, and we had to dub one of them in both versions, the French and the German.

Did the language barrier affect their performances?

Yes, especially in the classroom scene, which is quite long and intense. But each actress knew the meaning of the lines spoken in the other's language, and everything went smoothly because they genuinely liked each other. Isabelle had loved Susanne's work in *Lulu*, which was directed by Peter Zadek, and Susanne had always admired Isabelle, so it wasn't a battle between two stars but rather a moment of real connection.

Which version of the film do you consider the best in terms of sound?

The French version, because the majority of the dialogue is in French. But among all my films dubbed in German, this is by far the best. I found two excellent actresses and an actor, and we took three times longer than planned for the dubbing. For my other French films dubbed in German, even the ones where I oversaw the dubbing myself, the results were disappointing. You never quite reach the same level of performance with voice actors. Not to mention the actor I had for the lead role in *Caché*, who was downright bad, and since I had already replaced the original actor, I had to make do. Starting with *The White Ribbon*, I decided not to direct the dubbing myself. For the Austrian *Funny Games*, I supervised the French version with Hervé Icovic, a friend who is a dubbing director. I personally directed the actors, but I wasn't happy with the result. It might be fair to say that dubbing really is the systematic destruction of a film because the essence of the atmosphere created between characters evaporates. You can't compare the performance of an actor playing with a partner in front of a camera to that of someone working in front of a screen and a microphone.

What language did you write The Piano Teacher *script in?*

German, of course.

Then why, in the German edition of the screenplay, are the story-boarded pages illustrated with dialogue in French?

Once the German screenplay was finished, it was translated into French for the French-speaking actors. During filming, I had both versions in front of me, with the French dialogue on the left-hand page of my German script. That way, if I had any doubts, I could cross-check between the two versions.

Haneke on the set of *The Piano Teacher.*

Your strong command of French must allow you to direct your French actors by ear as well as you do in your native language?

Not quite. In French, I can immediately tell if the emotion is off, but I have a harder time detecting a pronunciation mistake or a regional accent that doesn't quite fit. In reality, the only French I know well is the one spoken in Paris.

In German, the title of the novel and film is Die Klavierspielerin. *But the most common word in your language for a pianist is* Pianistin. *What is the difference in meaning?*

Compared to *Pianistin*, *Klavierspielerin* feels more limited. It implies someone who knows how to play the piano but will never be a great concert performer, so the original title, taken from the novel, already signals the limitations of Erika's talent. However, we had to accept losing that precise nuance in the French and English translations.

One line of Erika's really stood out to us: "I have no feelings, Walter. And even if I did, they would never triumph over my intelligence."

It's harsh, yes, but only because it's not believable. Erika says that because it's how she wants things to be, but the film shows she can't live up to it, otherwise we wouldn't end up with what is essentially a human tragedy.

That connects with a recurring theme in your work: the gradual disappearance of emotion in the face of a harsh, cerebral, materialistic world.

I don't think so. In fact, emotions are stronger today than ever, as the film illustrates. "Cultivated" countries have tried to rid life of its chaos, but it's an illusion. The problems persist. We're still on the edge of the abyss, but we have learned to hide it better than before. That doesn't mean we've become more cerebral. Quite the opposite, in fact.

Your film opens with a direct overhead shot, a stylistic choice you previously used in Fräulein *and* Benny's Video. *It feels surprising here. It's an unusual angle for filming someone at the piano.*

It functions differently than in previous films. The idea was to create a subjective shot of Isabelle's hands, but in a stylised way, because a truly subjective camera would have resulted in a shaky image. The vertical overhead shot, which also includes the pianist's legs, creates a kind of abstracted gaze, but even in that stylised form, for me it's still a subjective point of view, like the shots of the letter that the priest writes in Bresson's *Diary of a Country Priest.*

The film's title appears more than seven minutes into the film. Why such a long pre-title sequence?

It's a technique I borrowed from some of my television films. For *The Piano Teacher*, the idea was to introduce the mother-daughter relationship before the real drama begins, after the opening credits.

Rewatching this pre-title sequence, we were struck by the way you show Alphateam, *the TV series Erika's mother is watching. You frame the screen completely and don't just show a brief excerpt; we see several shots from the series, as if we were settling in to watch it. It's quite unnerving.*

That was deliberate; I wanted to make it very clear what kind of life Erika's mother leads. She hardly ever goes out, and her only real activity is watching television. It's the same thing in the scene when Erika comes home with Walter and her mother is still glued to the TV. She even has to turn down the volume just to hear what her daughter is saying. For once, she has a distraction of a different kind.

Why that particular series?

It's the kind of nonsense you see on television all the time, a programme that mixes drama and comedy. As usual, I was given about ten different options to choose from and picked that one because I found it amusing.

You reused this technique in Caché *and* The White Ribbon, *but in* The Piano Teacher, *you seem especially fond of frontal shots where the actor faces the camera directly.*

It's a way of heightening the emotional tension of the scene. If you shoot dialogue between two characters using two cameras, you have to offset the angle a bit to do a traditional shot-reverse shot. But with non-professional actors, frontal shots don't work; they tend to look straight into the lens. I tried that with the little girl in *The Seventh Continent*, just before her mother slaps her, but it didn't work. She had nothing to look at and just gave us a blank stare. With professional actors, I place a small mark on the edge of the camera for them to focus on. That way, it's not quite a look into the lens, but it's close; almost like they're looking the viewer straight in the eye. In *The White Ribbon*, where I worked with lots of children, I avoided that setup, but I still tried to get physically as close to them as possible. It's not comfortable for the actors, being right up against the camera, but in editing, it creates a genuine connection with their scene partner.

The film also features beautiful lighting work.

That's thanks to cinematographer Christian Berger. On my sets, I almost always check the framing before a take and make adjustments if necessary. Sometimes, I move the camera less than half an inch. That can be frustrating for a crew, but mine is used to my working methods. However, I rarely interfere with lighting unless I notice a problem. I have, over the years, developed a good sense of lighting. In an interior scene, for example, I can tell if the contrast between natural light from a window and artificial light from a chandelier is too strong and will make for an artificial look on screen. In a room like the one we're sitting in now, it would be difficult to make the lighting feel natural. These are issues that cinematographers might miss because they're constantly juggling so many things. In such cases, I step in, and most of the time, I'm right. But I don't get involved in the technical settings; I wouldn't know how. I know exactly where the camera should be and could handle that myself, but lighting is a real science, and I'm grateful to have such talented collaborators.

But you know in advance what kind of lighting you want. How do you communicate that to your cinematographer?

When I sketch out the set design, I already position the lamps in specific places because I know where I'll need light. For example, if I know a character will sit in a certain spot, I make sure to include a light source there in my set plan. You can't wait until after shooting the wide shot to realise you need a lampshade by the couch for a close-up. Similarly, if a scene is supposed to be lit by daylight, I tell my cinematographer whether I want it to look like a sunny day or an overcast one. After that, it's up to him to achieve the desired effect.

You filmed The Piano Teacher *in many real locations.*

The only scenes filmed in studios were Erika's apartment, the peep-show booth, and the restroom where Erika and Walter have their first intense scene. The real locations were too cramped to film in.

There are two moments when you linger on empty spaces. The first is in the restroom scene, when you hold on a white tiled wall for a while before Walter arrives.

Yes, but the emptiness is filled with sound, with all the ambient noises you hear.

And you do it again at the end. After Erika stabs herself, you show the conservatoire's empty exterior where the only movement is from cars and the ambient sounds of Vienna at night.

I wanted to signal that it's the final shot of the film by stretching it out. As for the bathroom scene, Erika goes there to urinate, so it was normal for it to take some time. All these real-time moments were written into the script from the start.

You also shot a complex long take. The camera starts on the ice rink where Walter is finishing his hockey game, follows him as he leaves the rink, passes Erika waiting for him, then stays with the two of them as they go into the equipment room, where the key part of the scene unfolds.

That was the hardest shot to pull off in the entire film, especially for Isabelle, who had to discreetly swallow something so she could vomit later.

Did you do many takes?

Yes. We rehearsed for a long time. Benoît, who had to train how to play hockey as well as the piano, had to make sure he didn't slip when stepping off the ice. It took several takes before we got it right. Then my assistant told me she had seen the makeup artist appear in the frame just as Benoît was removing his hockey gear. There were three people helping Benoît move fast enough to get to her, and one of them—Thi Loan Nguyen, my favourite makeup artist—accidentally stepped into the frame. Isabelle and I were very upset and we started over, but never managed to get it as good. We had spent the whole day there, and as daylight was fading, my cinematographer warned us we only had time for one more take. I was furious, realising we might have wasted the entire day. And then, on that final take, we got what we needed. It had been a rough day for everyone. On top of that, Benoît was in a bad mood because he felt ridiculous in his hockey gear.

The gradual evolution of Huppert's costumes and hairstyle is striking. We move from a rigid spinster to someone trying to open up, even if her clothing choices aren't always successful.

I paid close attention to that evolution, but it owes a lot to Isabelle. Every wardrobe choice was made in agreement between the costume designer, Isabelle and me The same goes for the hairstyle. Credit also goes to the makeup artist. But if it all works so well, it's thanks to Isabelle. She captured the character's breakdown with extraordinary precision. She knows exactly what she's doing. And she can do anything.

Are you one of those directors who believe they know their characters the moment they have found their costumes?

No, because having written the character, I already know them inside out. That doesn't stop me from being very demanding with costume designers, and rarely satisfied with their suggestions. The only time I was truly pleased was with Moidele Bickel, on *The White Ribbon*. When I began to critique something, she had already realised it wasn't ideal. She's a woman of great culture, and we got along very well, but before that, I was always disappointed. That's why I've never had a regular costume designer. And honestly, when I watch other people's films, I'm often disappointed by the costumes. A costume should convey a character's psychology, yet most costume designers are mainly concerned with making sure the clothes look good on the actors, and not much else. I was lucky to meet Catherine Leterrier, who I worked with on *Amour*, and who I can continue working with into the future.

Ten

Like *The Piano Teacher*, *Time of the Wolf* was a long-gestating project. You made the film in 2003, but you wrote it ten years earlier. Do you remember where the idea came from?

In the 1990s, the subject was in the air. There was a lot of talk about disaster films, but my script was probably too expensive to attract a producer, so I shelved it and moved on. After *The Piano Teacher*, I was supposed to make *Caché*, which I had just written and which Alain Sarde had agreed to produce. We had started working on it when, at Cannes in 2001, Christine Gozlan told me they hadn't found the money and were pulling the plug. I was furious, so I offered *Caché* to Margaret Menegoz, who was interested. In the meantime, the 9/11 attacks happened, and I thought it was now or never to make *Time of the Wolf*. I explained this to Margaret, who wasn't convinced that the film would be as profitable as *Caché*. She was absolutely right, of course. Nonetheless, she agreed to produce it, though she couldn't have known it wouldn't turn out to be my best film... To give you the full picture, around that same time I had another project that didn't go anywhere, a ten-part sci-fi series for TV called *Kelwin's Book*. I've always been drawn to science fiction, and it's a real shame that series never came to life. I actually reread the script recently, and it isn't at all bad.

You've never done a TV series.

Isabelle Huppert in *Time of the Wolf.*

It seems an uphill struggle these days because here, in Austria, television isn't good. In America, on the other hand, TV—especially HBO—is often better than cinema.

What interests you about science fiction?

The chance to explore real-world problems through extreme, imagined situations. That's what I tried to do with *Time of the Wolf*, to reflect the state we're in today. We're teetering on the edge of a cliff, one we don't realise is even there.

Time of the Wolf (2003)

In the aftermath of a catastrophe, everyone survives as best they can. Anne, her husband, and their two children, Eva and Ben, head to their country house, only to find it occupied by a family that refuses to share the space. One of the intruders, initially threatening, loses control and shoots Anne's husband. Anne flees with her children, finding no help from their neighbours, though a compassionate person gives them some food. They spend nights in barns and sheds. One evening, Ben disappears. His mother and sister light a fire to help him find his way back. Ben reappears at dawn, accompanied by a solitary and sullen teenager, who gradually softens through his connection with Eva. They arrive at a train station inhabited by numerous survivors from all walks of life. The atmosphere is unwelcoming. The struggle to survive leads to increasingly aggressive and deceitful behaviour among the group. A rudimentary system of rules and organisation has been established, though it is seldom followed. Bartering is practised and overseen by a man named Koslowski, whom some regard as a prophet. The arrival of a water vendor, whose supply is insufficient for everyone, adds to the chaos. Eva, disturbed, suppresses the reality of her father's death and writes him a letter describing their situation. Soon afterwards, the group moves near a railway track, hoping to stop the next train, which represents their last hope. Anne recognises her husband's murderer and accuses him, but she has no proof and is forced to abandon her accusations. Events accelerate. A young girl secretly commits suicide. Ben, troubled by a story about a human sacrifice told by a strange man who swallows razor blades, prepares to immolate himself on a fire he builds on the tracks. A kind man dissuades him, preventing him from becoming a sacrificial victim, and assures him that everything will soon get better. Through the window of a moving train, the landscape streams past.

You open the film with a brutal act: a man murders the owner of a country house—another father, just like him—he has been squatting in.

Historically, such brutality always emerges in times of crisis.

Which explains your interest in such situations.

The opening of the film allows me to show how we revert to our animal instincts when forced to fight for survival. As soon as our usual reference points disappear, it takes very little for us to tip over the edge. That's what the young man in the animated film *Waltz with Bashir* describes. He went to war at 17 and quickly realised that if he didn't shoot first, he would be the one getting shot. This explains the squatter's behaviour at the start of the film. It's how we arrive at the time of the wolf, which is a reference to *The Edda*, the collection of epic poems about Norse mythology compiled in *Codex Regius*, the Icelandic manuscript, which includes a prophecy describing the time leading up to *Ragnarök*, the end of the world: "Time of the wind, time of the wolf, no one spares anyone anymore."

What's bold about your script is that it revolves around a single theme.

How to survive in a way that remains human. But the film does present several different situations, like the love story between the two young characters, which is unlikely to succeed but remains open-ended. Or the attitude of Anne's son, who shows great humanity but in a somewhat perverse way, by contemplating self-sacrifice as the only possible solution.

The sacrifice of the innocent to end violence echoes René Girard's thesis in Violence and the Sacred.

Yes, I thought about that.

But you ultimately chose a different ending —

—which wasn't in the original script. Initially, I had imagined the entire community of two hundred people setting off together. I actually shot that ending, but it didn't work, and I wasn't sure what else to do. I spoke to Alexander Horwath, who told me the film needed a sense of movement. That's when I remembered the Jean-Marie Straub and Danièle Huillet film *Klassenverhältnisse* [*Class Relations*], which is based on Kafka's novel *Amerika*. In the final scene they're on a moving train. That gave me the idea: what if all the characters in *Time of the Wolf* had gotten on a train, but we never saw them, and never even saw the train. We see only a landscape passing by, with no trace of human life. That, I thought, would be the perfect visual echo of what the man tells the little boy to stop him from setting himself on fire. I'm not entirely happy with the film as a whole; there are things that don't really work, but that ending is very beautiful.

Going back to the child's gesture, what purpose could his sacrifice have served? Is it fair to see a religious element in it?

I can't really say. It's really a matter of interpretation. I think each viewer will see this act differently, depending on their own conception of life and the supernatural. But it's also completely valid to see the idea of sacrifice as pointless or even absurd. That's why I decided to add the passing landscape through the train windows. That's where the film's final note of optimism lies. You wouldn't get that from the earlier version of the ending, with people walking away from the station, which suggested that things would just carry on as before. But the train window opens onto something else. Maybe not something metaphysical, but at least something

The final shot of *Time of the Wolf*.

less ordinary than watching a group of people heading off in some undefined direction. There is also hope in the moment when the character played by Thierry Van Werveke—a fascist hostile to foreigners, angry at everything—nonetheless makes an effort to comfort the little boy. In that way, my fable sticks closer to real life than mainstream films, where characters are generally one-dimensional.

When you write your scripts, do you always think about leaving room for multiple interpretations?

Always. That's my goal: to leave space for the viewer, so they can make the film their own, in their own way, with their own culture and way of thinking.

How do you respond to the reactions of viewers from cultures different from your own?

Their reactions are always interesting, but they're limited because, to be honest, my films only really reach audiences in wealthier countries. People in the Third World face different problems than the ones depicted in my films. Moreover, I think you really need to understand the cultural background of a work if you want to grasp its full meaning.

When you envision an open ending, like in Time of the Wolf, *do you list all the possible interpretations?*

No. The different readings start to multiply organically as I write the script. I don't try to name or catalogue them; it's a more intuitive process. With *Caché*, for example, I know there are several lines of interpretation. You can certainly try to read something into the final moment when Georges' son and Majid's son meet on the school steps, but if you stay realistic, there's only one explanation. I don't see it as my job to help viewers figure it out if they didn't catch it. For that final scene in *Caché*, I actually wrote dialogue for the two boys, then told them not to share it with anyone, and I threw the script away.

And you forgot what was in it?

No, I remember, but I'm not going to tell you what they said. Similarly, in *The White Ribbon*, it's never stated that a single person committed all the wrongdoings. There are multiple possible culprits. But for me, open endings are the least important aspect of my films. Wanting to pin down a single interpretation limits the film's scope; it reduces it to a psychological dimension when there are so many other ways to approach it. The point of *The White Ribbon* isn't to figure out who did what.

What are your main criticisms of Time of the Wolf?

As I mentioned, I made casting mistakes, which meant several scenes didn't work as they should have. I can give you an example that doesn't implicate a professional actor: the scene with the man who swallows razor blades. I had noticed him on the Croisette in Cannes, where he was performing this act. He was extraordinary, but he couldn't act. We cut down his dialogue, but even so, the scene never came together. It was a crucial scene because it's from hearing him talk about people who set themselves on fire that the young boy gets the idea to do the same, but since the scene doesn't work, the viewer doesn't make that connection. There were other scenes just as problematic that I had to cut, scenes centred around a character played by an actor who gave an unconvincing performance, others with an actor who didn't know his lines. But that's my fault. A bad casting decision is always the director's fault, not the actor's. In any case, I cut a lot, and that diminished the complexity of the script. There were also scenes that didn't work for other reasons, like the rape of the young girl who later commits suicide. It should have been traumatic, but the impact isn't really felt because the lighting isn't right. The film has too many flaws to work as I had hoped. On top of that, it's long and difficult to watch because of its dark, murky aesthetic. It was very frustrating. When I started editing, I felt like we were heading for disaster.

Did you realise this during editing?

I could already see during the shoot that some actors weren't working, but by then it was too late to replace them.

Why are there so many well-known actors in Time of the Wolf?

I didn't choose them because they were famous. I just thought they were the best actors for those parts — although not all were my first choices. I reached out to some actors who weren't available. That said, with few exceptions, most of them aren't major stars; they're mostly only well-known in France. Even Patrice Chéreau doesn't count as famous. He's primarily known for his directing. I wanted a real intellectual for that role, and I think he played it very well, bringing a lot of his own personality to it.

Why didn't you cast more Austrian actors, given that the film is a French-Austrian co-production?

I didn't want to end up, as I did on *The Piano Teacher*, with long scenes featuring actors speaking two different languages. It just gets too complicated. I decided all the main roles would go to French speakers, and I would keep the smaller parts and extras for the German speakers.

Time of the Wolf *is your first film shot in widescreen.*

And the only one to date. *The White Ribbon* could have been shot in widescreen too, but the format that made the most sense was 1.33. Since that wasn't possible, I stuck to the standard 1.85 format. My films usually take place in apartments or other enclosed spaces. *Time of the Wolf* is the only one that unfolds primarily outdoors, in vast landscapes, in the fog, and that required a wider frame.

The fog sequences, which are beautifully photographed, have been compared to Antonioni's Red Desert.

Antonioni was lucky to shoot in the Po Valley, where there is real fog. We had to create it ourselves using machines and then adding more digitally, because for shots that wide, there was never quite enough real fog in the frame. It reminds me of Tarkovsky in the making-of documentary for his *Nostalgia*. He's sitting in a chair, someone calls him to the set, he gets up, looks out over the vast landscape, says, "I said fog!" and then sits back down. I also thought of

Patrice Chéreau and Olivier Gourmet in *Time of the Wolf*.

Truffaut's *Jules and Jim*, which so impressed Burt Lancaster that his production company contacted Truffaut to ask how they had achieved such beautiful fog. The answer: "We waited."

Truffaut had a theory about films set during the Occupation. He said that to make them believable, you couldn't show blue skies. Did you have a similar thought process for your post-apocalyptic story?

That's what I did with *The Seventh Continent*, where the sky is never visible, except in photographs of cloudy skies hanging on apartment walls. In contrast, at the beginning of *Time of the Wolf*, when Anne and her children leave their country house after the father's murder, it's in broad daylight, just like in some of Bergman's films. Despite shooting rather heavy, dramatic scenes, Bergman often depicted very sunny locations, and once explained that as a child, his worst nightmares occurred in broad daylight.

Where did you shoot the exterior scenes?

In Austria, in Burgenland, near the Hungarian border, and for the final shot in the Waldviertel region. We had to film in locations that were very far apart. Austria is a small, densely populated country, and except in the high mountains, it's difficult to find landscapes that feel untouched. The landscape seen from the train at the end is actually a military training ground, which is why there are no houses.

Maurice Bénichou, Isabelle Huppert, Lucas Biscombe
and Anaïs Demoustiert in *Time of the Wolf*.

The night scenes are also striking. Barely lit, they show only what is absolutely necessary.

That took a lot of work. First, during filming, I was constantly arguing with the cinematographer, who was always afraid that we wouldn't see enough. Then, because he still lit it too much, I darkened it even more in post-production. I wanted a very dark film, just like real life when there's no electricity.

Like The Head of the Moor, *which also dealt with a catastrophe, politics has no part to play in* Time of the Wolf.

That's because once you bring politics into it, it's too easy to point fingers. The film becomes a polemic, which isn't what I wanted. I'm not interested in making political films tied to current events. You could argue that *Benny's Video* touches on Nazism, but only in an indirect way. I'm not drawn to message-driven political films, unless they emerge from a specific historical moment in a country. Costa-Gavras' *Z*, for example, really impressed me because it was courageous to make that film while things were still unfolding in Greece under the Greek military junta. And, of course, it's also a very well-made and powerful film. But while it might be necessary to make a political film in the midst of a revolutionary situation, that's hardly the case in Austria, where nothing ever changes. It's easy to point out the obvious mistakes made by politicians when the reality is always more complex.

There are no political figures at all in the film.

The only reference is what Maurice Bénichou's character recounts hearing on the radio, like the evacuation of certain areas. But that's how things unfold in such situations. There is no direct contact with politics; you're just dealing with orders relayed by the media, and there's no way to question them. In such moments, you're at the mercy of events, and politics becomes useless. The only vaguely political figure in *Time of the Wolf* is the one played by Olivier Gourmet, who declares himself the leader and organises the group's survival, while using the situation to his own advantage.

One of the strengths of the film is that nothing is ever spelt out. Everything is conveyed through what the characters do.

Except for *The Piano Teacher*, which is an adaptation, my films only depict behaviour; they don't include the kind of psychological explanations you find in newspapers. That's what I was saying about the article that inspired *The Seventh Continent*. The journalist filled it with justifications for the father's act, explaining that he was heavily in debt and was seeing a psychologist because he couldn't satisfy his wife sexually, that kind of thing. But millions of people face similar problems and don't end up killing their family. It's impossible to capture the full complexity of behaviour in an article, or even in a book or a film. When filmmakers try to, it's usually to reassure audiences and try to make them feel as if everything is explicable. But the truth is, it isn't.

Doesn't this way of conveying meaning through characters' behaviour require audiences to be more observant than usual?

No, because the audience doesn't need to observe; it just has to look at the fragments of reality I'm showing them. It's like real life, where we never have the full picture, only bits and pieces. Our view of the world is always fragmented. In everyday life, you can never really tell when someone is lying to you. If we were able to detect lies, no one would bother lying anymore, but since that's not the case, everyone lies, and we just have to live with that. One person says one thing, someone else says the opposite. We never quite know where the truth lies.

Did you plan for Time of the Wolf *to make audiences feel things that are usually reported on the news?*

Haneke directing Anaïs Demoustiert in *Time of the Wolf.*

No, that kind of explanation comes afterward. When I'm writing, I don't sit there thinking, "I'm going to tell this story or make this point." I start with an idea and build on it. In this case, the idea was: what happens when suddenly there's no more water or electricity? Two simple things, but once they're gone, everything about how we live changes. That premise interested me, so I explored it and imagined what would follow. But I never set out to make a statement. It's only once a film's finished that I can start talking about what it's about, and even then, I don't like doing that. It's too reductive. There's this whole obsession with pitching, which drives me crazy. You're supposed to sum up your whole project in two sentences. It's ridiculous. You can't reduce a two-hour film or a 300-page novel to a couple of lines. What's the point? To get a quick blurb in the press and stir up interest? I've always refused to play that game. I've even refused to write two-page notes of intent for producers, and some projects didn't get made because of that. So be it. The only time I gave in was for *The White Ribbon*, and even then I asked Jean-Claude Carrière to write the summary because I just couldn't do it.

When Time of the Wolf *was released, many critics cited* Andrei Rublev *as an inspiration.*

I honestly never thought of it. I love Tarkovsky's work, but he's such a towering filmmaker that it's almost impossible to go near his world without ending up imitating him. It's a shame in a way, but his genius kind of closed the door on a whole style of poetic filmmaking. You just can't attempt it anymore without being crushed by the comparison. That said, if someone asked me for my top ten favourite films today, I would start with *Mirror*. To me, it's a one-of-a-kind masterpiece; nothing in cinema history has ever topped it, not even Tarkovsky's other films. It's a miracle of a film. People have offered all kinds of interpretations, but none of them explain it fully, which, to me, is what defines a great work of art.

Another film that can't be fully grasped, because everything is hidden within it, is Caché!

Nice transition.

Can you tell us about the origins of Caché? *We read that it was inspired by a documentary you saw on Arte.*

No. I was already working on the script when I saw that documentary about the events of October 17, 1961, which gave me the political backdrop I needed. I wanted to tell the story of a man who, as a boy, had betrayed another child out of jealousy, and now, years later, he is forced to confront what he did and feels even more guilty than he did at the time. As a kid, he was just selfish, the way kids are, but now, as an adult, he has the opportunity to react differently.

So if you had seen a similar documentary set in another country that day, you might have given this theme of suppressed collective guilt a different national context?

That's exactly what the Americans attempted when they considered remaking the film. They could have used a black child whose parents were killed by extremists. Every country has skeletons in the closet, terrible things in its past that no one really wants to talk about.

Caché (2005)

Paris. Georges Laurent, the host of a literary television show, receives a videotape. It shows the street and the entrance to his home, where he lives with his wife,

Anne, and their son, Pierrot. Enclosed with it is a disturbing, blood-themed drawing. More tapes follow. The
police offer no help. One of the tapes shows the family farm where Georges spent his childhood. Georges
questions his mother about a figure he has seen in his
dreams: Majid, the son of Algerian farm workers once
employed by his parents. His suspicion is confirmed
when another tape arrives, filmed from a car, showing
the route to Majid's apartment in Romainville. Georges goes there, but Majid insists he is not the one sending the tapes. Georges hides this meeting from his wife,
but Anne receives a new tape showing Georges' visit
to Majid. To justify himself, Georges tells Anne about
how Majid lost his parents in the pro-FLN demonstra-
tion on October 17, 1961. Georges' parents had then
considered raising Majid as their own, much to Georges' dismay and jealousy. One evening, Pierrot does not
return home. Georges calls the police and has Majid
and his son arrested. The next morning, Pierrot reappears. He had simply spent the night at a friend's house.
Majid then asks Georges to come see him. Calmly, the
Algerian reaffirms his innocence, then suddenly slits his
own throat. The police confirm it as a suicide. Majid's
son later confronts Georges at his workplace, trying in
vain to convince him that he is not responsible for the
tapes. At home, Georges takes a sleeping pill and recalls
the moment when Majid, as a child, was forcibly taken
from the family estate as a result of Georges, at six years
old, falsely accusing Majid of killing a rooster, simply to
frighten him.

Outside school, Pierrot is approached by Majid's
son. The two boys talk for a while, then Majid's walks
away and Pierrot rejoins his friends.

When you started working on Caché, *were you already planning to
shoot it in France?*

From the start, I knew it would be a French film, a co-production
between several countries. I wanted to take advantage of the talent
and the international reputation of French actors. The film was a
big hit in the UK, where Daniel Auteuil and Juliette Binoche are
very popular. *The White Ribbon*, on the other hand, didn't do as

well, probably because the cast was made up of actors unknown to British audiences.

Did you have Auteuil in mind when writing the film?

Yes, I wrote the role of Georges specifically for him. I think Daniel is the best French actor of his generation. He reminds me a bit of Jean-Louis Trintignant; he always seems to be hiding something. There's something about his personality, and especially his face, that retains a sense of mystery. One day, Daniel told me he owed his entire career to the accident that broke his nose. That was a funny and modest observation from him, and quite true also. Those slightly irregular features of his make it look like there's something going on beneath the surface. Of course, that's not a hard rule; you can find plenty of actors with broken noses who are terrible, but Daniel has something unique in the way he carries himself. Even if he can be a bit of a clown at times, he's quite shy and private. I like him a lot. And he can play anyone. He actually started out doing comedy.

We appreciate your loyalty to actors like Maurice Bénichou, who had smaller roles in Code Unknown *and* Time of the Wolf, *then a more substantial one in* Caché. *The same goes for Nathalie Richard and Daniel Duval, and others who were virtually unknown at the time of* Code Unknown, *like Aïssa Maïga and Florence Loiret-Caille.*

I do the same thing in my German-language films. I treat actors the same way I treat my crew. If we work well together the first time, there's no reason not to continue, because it means we can start the next project on a stronger footing. We already know each other, so we work faster and better. Bringing in someone new is always a risk. Even if you have similar tastes and can communicate well, the chemistry might still be off. That's why, from now on, for any significant role, I only cast actors who agree to audition. If they refuse, I don't hire them. That happened once with a well-known German actor who was supposed to play the father of the girl who wants to marry the schoolteacher in *The White Ribbon*. When he wouldn't do an audition, I explained that I wasn't doubting his talent; I just needed to see whether we could work together, because if we couldn't, he might turn out to be wrong for the role. That a real risk. I'm not immune to making casting mistakes.

Daniel Auteuil and Juliette Binoche in *Caché*.

It happened with some of the actors in *Time of the Wolf* and the original lead I cast in *Benny's Video*.

Did you ask Auteuil to audition?

No. And nor with Jean-Louis Trintignant for *Amour*. I would have been very surprised if we didn't get along. I've never had any issues with great actors. Even with Isabelle Huppert, who has a reputation for being difficult, we only clashed once. It was on *Time of the Wolf*, during the scene at the train station. She was supposed to introduce herself and her kids to the people there, stating who she was. Out of nowhere, she said, "In a situation like this, I'd never say that." I told her, "But it's not you speaking. It's the character." She got upset: "You don't give me any freedom!" She was angry for five minutes, then she did the scene, and it was all quickly forgotten. When an actor is good, directing is easy.

That must be the case with Susie, your wife, who makes appearances in most of your films.

She's my Hitchcock. The only films where I couldn't fit her in were *Code Unknown*, *Time of the Wolf* and *The White Ribbon*.

She appears as early as The Seventh Continent.

From behind, in a delicatessen, behind the heroine who is buying food to share with her family before their collective suicide. Then in six more films up until *Amour,* where she is among those congratulating Alexandre Tharaud after his concert.

In Benny's Video, *she is sitting on the terrace of an Egyptian restaurant, in both* Funny Games *films she is a passenger on the neighbours' boat, and in* The Piano Teacher *she can be spotted among the audience at the private concert. In* Caché, *she appears in the background, in a pastry shop, behind Juliette Binoche and Daniel Duval—*

—alongside Marika Green, the wife of Christian Berger, who was the lead in Bresson's *Pickpocket.* In a deleted scene from *Benny's Video*—the one with the eclipse—Susie had a line, something like, "It's not dark enough!" I had to reshoot it fifteen times because she just couldn't get it right. She laughs about it now, but at the time she was upset. The same thing happened on *The Piano Teacher,* when in front of the whole crew I shouted at her. She always tells that story, and adds that, during a break, the woman next to her said, "It must be hard being married to a filmmaker."

Have you ever wanted to appear in your own films?

I did once, in *Sperrmüll.* There's a scene where an old man comes down from his apartment to get into a taxi, but a young man rushes in and steals the taxi right under his nose. The extra who was supposed to play the young man turned out to be terrible so I fired him, and since we had already wasted enough time, I decided to play the part myself. That's the only time I've appeared in one of my films. And since that film was a total disaster, I decided, out of superstition, never to appear in my films again.

What about in other people's films?

I played a small role in Michael Kreihsl's *Charms Zwischenfälle* in 1996. In one scene, a man, played by Kreihsl himself, stands in front of me with a slab of butter in his mouth. I open the refrigerator for him to put it inside, and we see that there are already about twenty identical slabs inside, all with bite marks. Then he asks me for money and I throw him out. I had a lot of fun doing that scene, but I terrified the whole crew. The director had me sit on a bed with no mattress, barefoot. There was no light on my legs, so you couldn't tell that I was barefoot, so I asked them to light my feet. The cinematographer hated me for it.

Why did the director ask you to play that role?

He was a friend.

And since then, you haven't acted in any other films?

No, but I would be willing to play a monk because I think their hoods are very stylish. Or a psychiatrist. Those are the only two roles I could see myself playing.

Back to Caché. *Once again, you highlight the gap between reality and perception, but by using digital technology, you blur the lines even further, starting with the opening sequence, where you trick us by filming in full frame what turns out to be a videotape watched by the protagonist.*

From the very beginning, I wanted the audience to realise how easily they can be deceived by images.

Did the idea to shoot the entire film in high-definition digital come to you while writing the script?

Yes, because *Caché* is the opposite of *Benny's Video*, where there is a clear difference between the cinematic image and the video footage. Here, I wanted the audience to fall into the multiple traps I set for them, and to do that, the story scenes and the video recordings had to have the exact same look.

Before writing the script, did you research advancements in digital technology?

Yes, I discussed it with my cinematographer, Christian Berger.

Was this the first digital film that he had shot?

Yes, and for all of us, it was a nightmare. At the time, digital cameras weren't as advanced as they are today, and we had to watch what we were shooting on a tiny screen. We encountered every conceivable technical problem. For example, the camera's fan made an unbearable noise, so we had to cover it with a blanket, but then it would overheat, so we had to stop filming regularly to let it cool down. For the scene where Georges first visits Majid—which we see twice: once in the present narrative and once as surveillance footage from a slightly different angle—we used three cameras.

I was watching three screens and noticed that the third one was blurry. I was told it was just due to the cable and that the image wasn't actually blurry, it just looked that way on the monitor. I didn't believe it, and I was right. It was blurry. Despite being digital specialists, none of the numerous technicians on set could fully control the equipment. It was still all pretty experimental at that point.

By using video, you found a new formal approach to familiar themes. You show that even an intellectual, like Georges, can behave in a primitive way when he realises his job might be on the line.

His job is his whole life, and he's ready to fight for it. But the real problem starts earlier, when his behaviour causes him to fall into the trap. He's so sure it's Majid who sent the tapes that he goes straight to threatening him, instead of apologising or admitting he has completely forgotten what happened back then, and saying that he's now ready to help. If he had done that, the whole situation might have been defused.

On the contrary, when he offers to help by giving him money, it's another way to further humiliate him.

Georges can't bear being accused because he is repressing his own guilt. He can't even admit it to his wife, and he lies to her about visiting Majid.

Caché *is about lying as a fundamental survival mechanism.*

Just as it often is in real life. Everyone has things in their past they would rather not talk about, and most people try to forget them as fast as they can.

Your main character behaves the same way in his professional life. During the editing of his literary show, he asks that certain segments be cut.

You could call that standard professional practice.

But it's no coincidence that you show it in the film.

Of course not.

Just like having Mazarine Pingeot—the illegitimate, "hidden" daughter of François Mitterrand—on the show. Were you aware of her story when writing the script?

No, it was Margaret Menegoz who suggested Mazarine Pingeot to me, explaining who she was. I immediately decided to include her.

Some critics have compared your protagonist to Oscar Wilde's Dorian Gray, the polished public image hiding a much darker self.

That's going a bit far. After all, he hasn't committed any crimes. As a child, he didn't grasp the consequences of what he did, and when it all comes back to him as an adult, he feels trapped and reacts in an unpleasant, but very human, way. Unable to accept his own guilt, he shifts the blame onto others, which is an understandable response. Then, when Majid commits suicide, his guilt resurfaces. Suddenly Majid becomes a true victim and Georges' character is caught in a near-tragic trap. That's not anything he could have foreseen because people we hurt in life don't usually go on to kill themselves. It's like someone who drives too fast all the time. The day they hit a child and kill them, everything changes, but the accident was the result of a behaviour that, until then, hadn't caused any real damage. That's the complexity of life. Behaving badly doesn't automatically make you inhuman.

In that sense, Caché *seems very clear-eyed about the inescapability of human guilt. This is powerfully underscored by the final shot— a wide frame amidst the bustling crowd outside a school with the meeting between Georges' and Majid's sons—which we have already mentioned. It isn't an easy shot to read, and some viewers didn't even notice the specific characters within the frame.*

Especially those watching on a television screen. It's a wide shot, and the characters are tiny figures. Even in the cinema, some people didn't notice them. But I never considered framing it any other way.

Perhaps because, at the bottom of the image, we see the roof of a car parked on a side street next to the school. The framing seems somewhat unpolished, more like something you would expect from a security camera than from one of your usual setups.

That ambiguity actually works both ways. If something we assumed was real turns out to be a video recording, then the opposite could also be true.

The last shot of *Caché*.

That distinctive framing might suggest that it was filmed by the person responsible for the tapes, or maybe it represents some kind of timeless, all-seeing eye looking down on humanity.

No comment.

Has anyone ever given you what you'd call the "correct" interpretation of that ending?

No, because there is no one correct interpretation. That's the point. I designed the ending to invite different readings, so by definition there can't be just one. People can see whatever they want in it. That's how life is. We analyse things, thinking they will lead us somewhere, but in the end, we never really know.

But you must have your own take on it.

Not exactly, but I do know what's in that little exchange I wrote for the two children outside the school.

We get the feeling that you're never going to tell us.

Correct, because doing that would ruin it. And besides, it's not really what the film's about. That moment is just a way to draw the viewer's attention. Audiences today are so used to American films and television that they don't always get it. Susie received countless calls from her friends praising the film, only to admit that they didn't understand the ending.

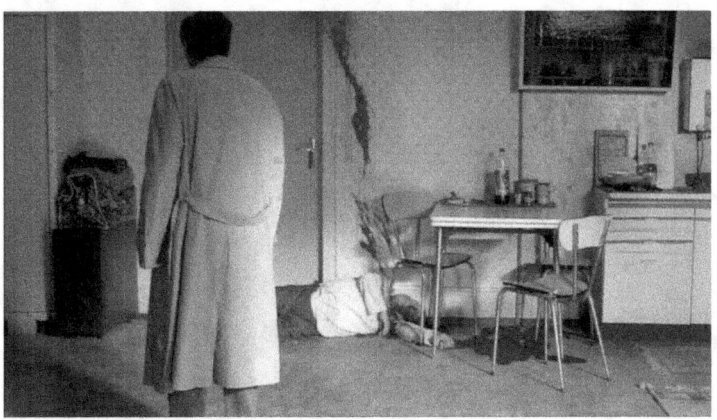

Daniel Auteuil and Maurice Bénichou in *Caché*.

Going back to the "film within the film," the footage of Georges first visit to Majid's apartment isn't as smooth as the frontal shot we see earlier.

Right, because the lines of the composition are no longer perfectly aligned. The third camera was focused on Auteuil alone, for his reverse angles. It was tricky to set up; both actors were moving, and we had to position each camera so that it wouldn't show up in the frame of the other two. Naturally, we shot it all in a studio. The set, along with its carefully staged disorder, was designed specifically to hide the placement of the cameras.

Was the house where Georges lives built in a studio?

Yes, which meant we could design it exactly as we needed it. Even so, we based it on the real interior of the house we used for the exterior shots. I actually stumbled upon that house by chance, walking past it on the way to see another one. What caught my eye immediately was the way it stood out on the street; it looked totally different from everything around it. In terms of the script, filming there meant using a part to represent the whole. It needed to feel like a place where someone could feel completely safe. Its whiteness gave it a luxurious 1930s Art Deco feel, and on a practical level, the real house had an artist's studio, which made it really easy to get soft, even lighting across the entire set. As soon as I saw the outside of the house, I knew I could use it to create a very specific kind of lighting atmosphere.

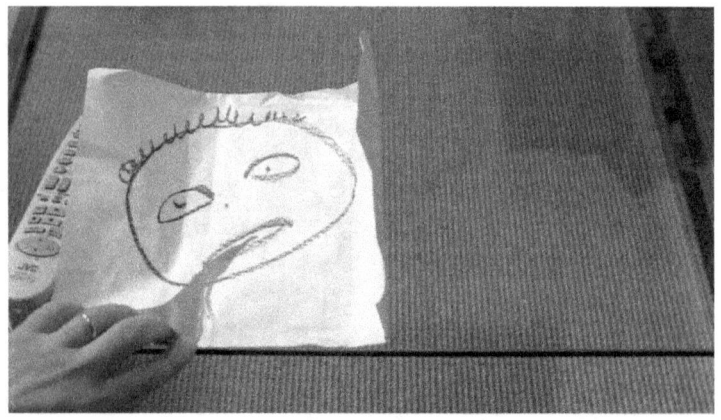

Caché.

The paradox is that this neutral, diffused lighting creates a sense of unease.

A typical film noir lighting setup would have been too obvious. You have to work against the audience's expectations. And sometimes the best way to show something is to hide it.

How important is sport to you? It keeps showing up in your films: ping-pong in 71 Fragments, *golf and sailing in* Funny Games, *ice hockey in* The Piano Teacher, *swimming in* Caché, *horseback riding in* The White Ribbon.

Sport, for me, always represents pressure—the pressure to act, to engage with the world. Personally, I've never been that into the idealised view of sport. I love skiing, but I do it for fun, not to win anything. Elfriede Jelinek actually wrote a play about sport called *Ein Sportstück*. She has a complicated relationship with it too, and like me, she shows that you don't get anywhere in that world unless you give in to the intense pressure it puts on you. It's a great metaphor for how people live under capitalism. In *The Piano Teacher*, Jelinek made Walter a sportsman to emphasise his primal nature.

The only scene where sport leads to genuine accomplishment in any one of your films is the swimming competition won by Pierrot in Caché.

That scene also provides a rare happy moment for his parents, who momentarily forget their troubles. But even in the training sequence, it's clear that the child isn't immune to the kind of pressure I'm talking about.

Pierrot raises another unanswered question when he starts suspecting his mother is having an affair with Pierre.

Yes, and on that note, I asked Juliette to act with Daniel Duval, who plays Pierre, as if he were really her lover, and to act with Lester Makedonsky, who plays her son Pierrot, as if he weren't. That way, the audience never gets a definitive answer.

Pierre and Pierrot?

Maybe that's not a coincidence…

Among the motifs you use repeatedly in your films is the phrase "I love you." While traditionally, this expression is accompanied by swelling violins, in your films it doesn't trigger grand emotions.

But it does carry emotion—just not in the usual way. In my films, those words only come up in moments of crisis. They're used to help, to comfort, to calm someone rather than simply expressing sentimental feelings. And since my films are about personal behaviour, it makes sense that "I love you" shows up now and then. Actually, the phrase I probably use most in my films is *Entschuldige* ["I'm sorry" or "Excuse me"]. I bet no other director uses it so often. The same goes for Ich weiß nicht ["I don't know"].

In Caché, *you use cinematic language to try to show what is happening inside the protagonist's mind. For example, when Georges receives the drawing of the bloody mouth, he suddenly recalls, in a flashcut, Majid as a child.*

I wanted to show how memory works, how it's triggered by associations. Every memory starts with a sensation, and in this case, it's the drawing that sets things off. But the image Georges sees is totally removed from context. It's only later in the film that the context slowly reconstructs itself, and both Georges and the viewer start to understand what they're really seeing.

Who did the anonymous drawings that are sent to Georges?

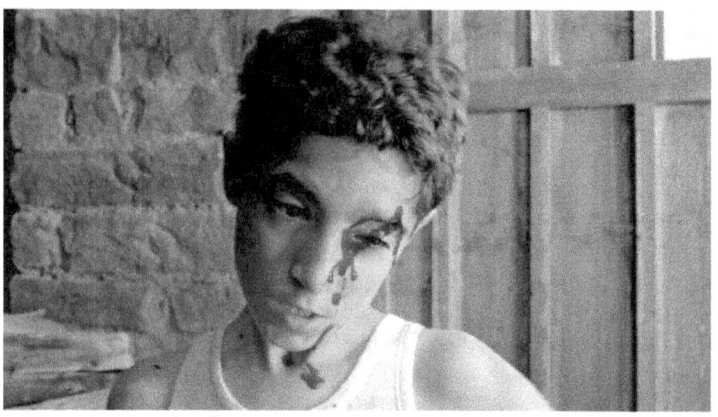

Malik Nait Djoudi in *Caché*.

I designed them myself. I sketched each one, and someone from the set decoration team finalised them, always in a childlike style.

Later, you show us the dream with the two children and the rooster, as seen by Georges. You've said before that you don't like dreams in cinema because they often lack credibility, but you're certainly interested in cutting together these kinds of dreamlike images.

It's a good way of telling a story efficiently. It also creates tension. The audience works to make sense of it all and wonders what they're looking at; it reminds them of something they saw earlier. It's a classic technique. What makes it unusual here is that the sequence begins as a flashback, the memory of something that actually happened: Majid really did cut off the rooster's head. But gradually, the editing and camera angles shift that realistic flashback into something more like a nightmare.

It's the only dream in the film. Had you planned others?

Yes, later on in the story I planned another dream sequence, based on a nightmare I had years ago. At the time, I had just broken up with someone and was on vacation in Greece with a new girl-friend. I felt terribly guilty about the breakup. In the dream, my ex came swimming back to me, out of a puddle on a slab of concrete. I panicked and tried to push her head down with my foot, but all I managed to do was squash her head, which immediately reassembled and kept bleeding. The more I tried, the more guilty I felt.

I wanted to adapt that nightmare to show Georges' relationship with Majid. We shot it all but I had to scrap the scene because of technical issues.

When you started writing the screenplay, had you seen David Lynch's Lost Highway? *That film also features a couple being harassed by anonymous video recordings of their house.*

I had seen the film, but it didn't cross my mind once while writing *Caché*. That said, it's entirely possible that the influence went to work on my subconscious. It doesn't matter. If it helped me develop my story, so much the better.

If, when you're writing a scene, it suddenly reminds you of another film, do you force yourself to go in a different direction?

Yes. I'm suspicious of references, which are often a form of theft.

But in Georges' library, you prominently display the DVD box set of Maurice Pialat's films, easily identifiable with his face on the spine. Is that some kind of tribute?

I used my personal DVD collection for that scene. It makes sense that, given his cultural background, Georges would have that box set, but it's also a tribute to the director I consider the most interesting of all the French filmmakers, after Bresson.

What about Alain Resnais?

I love his early films—*Hiroshima Mon Amour*, *Last Year at Marienbad*, *Muriel*—which had a big impact on me, and I really liked *Same Old Song* too. But Resnais' work is more intellectual, whereas Pialat's films are grounded in reality. He moves me deeply, and stands apart from French cinema, which always struck me as a bit artificial. Though it's hard to compare them directly, Pialat is like Cassavetes. There's a lived-in, spontaneous quality to the performances and the energy of the scenes that is just extraordinary. Actors who are unremarkable in other films become sublime in his. Dominique Besnehard in *À nos amours*, for example. I haven't found anything equivalent to his genius in any other French filmmaker.

You know that his working method was the opposite of yours? No storyboards.

Yes, which is why I tell my students that I can show them how I make films, but that doesn't mean it's how they should make films. You can get great results by filming in a completely different way to how I do things. It all depends on what you're trying to achieve. One thing is certain: you can't improvise meticulously composed shots.

The compositions in Caché *are particularly meticulous. Would you agree that the long takes in the film reinforce the sense of entrapment, as if the characters can't escape the frame?*

Yes.

It's especially evident in the scene where Georges comes home in the evening. His wife and their friends are already there, and he locks himself in the kitchen and breaks down in tears.

That was a very difficult scene for Daniel to perform, further complicated by a major camera issue. We were supposed to move from the living room to the kitchen using a dolly, but there was a tiny step at the kitchen threshold that made the camera jolt. If you watch the DVD extras, you'll see the whole thing, including me shouting at the camera crew. I was furious because everyone had the storyboard well in advance, and it was only at the moment of shooting they told me the shot couldn't be done. I felt there was no excuse. If they had properly prepped what I had planned on paper, everything would have worked. It took them a long time to come up with a solution, which was to make a quick movement when Auteuil enters the kitchen and shuts the door. The whole shot was technically very complex; there was a lot of dialogue, multiple character movements, and Daniel breaking down in tears in the kitchen. We ended up doing thirteen or fourteen takes. It was exhausting for everyone, even more so for Daniel, who had to go through all that emotion again and again just because of a camera glitch.

By linking a personal lie with a broader national denial, Caché *once again feels like the work of a humanist.*

I have no objection to that statement. It's better than being called a moralist, which some people try to pin on me, and which annoys me. But honestly, I don't really care. It doesn't stop me from making the films I want to make. You can't please everyone.

Haneke directing *Caché*.

Whether you please everyone or not, you're one of the few film-makers today offering a truly personal perspective on contemporary society.

Don't forget about Bruno Dumont. The thing is that the production landscape has changed dramatically over the past forty years, and even if more filmmakers today wanted to engage with social issues, they would run into problems of funding. If I weren't already established, I'm sure I wouldn't be able to finance the films that matter to me, whereas when I started out, it was still possible.

Eleven

Don Giovanni at La Défense — Gérard Mortier's support — Directing opera singers — Christoph Kanter's trumpet-shaped set — Mickey masks and a rape on stage — The Commendatore returns in an office chair — Why I have never shot commercials — The pleasure of teaching directing — We are short on good screenwriters

In 2006, in Paris, on the occasion of the 250th anniversary of Mozart's birth, you staged your first opera, Don Giovanni, *first at the Opéra Garnier, then at the Bastille. Who came up with the idea?*

Gérard Mortier, who was then the director of the Paris Opera. He had already invited me to stage an opera, *Katja Kabanova*, when he was in charge of the Salzburg Festival. I was flattered by his offer, but since I didn't speak a word of Czech, I had to say no. I could have handled an Italian opera because, between the few words of Italian I know and a good German translation, I knew I could manage, but directing a Czech opera without understanding a single word of the language seemed impossible. Still, my contact with Mortier had been established, and once he was settled in Paris, he asked me again if I was interested in directing an opera. I was keen on *Così fan tutte*, but Patrice Chéreau had just staged it in Aix-en-Provence, and the production was set to be performed in Paris. Instead, Mortier suggested *Don Giovanni*. My first thought was the usual line you hear, that it's an opera you're bound to screw up because it's so complex, but after thinking it over and reading through the libretto again, I felt I had found a good way in, so I took the plunge.

When did you get the idea to set Don Giovanni *in a modern context?*

Peter Mattei, in suit and tie, as Don Giovanni.

From the outset, I knew I wasn't going to do a traditional staging, one of those classic versions we've seen a hundred times. Even when directing for the theatre, I always considered the three time periods that every production is tied to: the period in which the action takes place, the period in which the author lived, and our own time. For *Don Giovanni*, I was particularly interested in the importance of social hierarchy, which underpins the relationships between the characters. I asked myself what its equivalent would be today, and I landed on the power of money, which is even more dominant in our time. That led me to make Don Giovanni a corporate executive, but only after verifying that this reinterpretation would work for all the characters. The other challenge was the set design. In a traditional staging of *Don Giovanni*, there are lots of different sets. In our case, we needed to imagine a single setting where the entire story could unfold.

Why did you insist on a single set?

Because I like the classical structure that relies on the unity of place, even though maintaining that unity isn't always easy. I remember that the great theatre director Rudolf Noelte often opted for a single set, and it worked beautifully. In my own case, I realised it could be done when I came up with the idea of setting the whole thing inside a corporate office. At the same time, I was a bit nervous because this was my first opera production, and it was happening at Garnier, where every production attracts a large audience of connoisseurs.

It isn't the first modernised version of this opera.

No, there have been lots of others. I watched recordings of them to make sure I had something new to offer.

Among the productions you saw, were there any that, like yours, explored Don Giovanni *from a socio-economic perspective?*

There was one, Peter Sellars' version, that I found moderately successful. He staged all three Mozart operas with Da Ponte librettos: a brilliant *Marriage of Figaro*, a very good *Così fan tutte*, and a less successful *Don Giovanni*, mainly because of the final act. He cast two striking black twins as Don Giovanni and Leporello—a fantastic concept, obviously not one I could copy—and set the production in the Bronx, with drug dealers. The constant costume changes and disguises were fantastic, up until the last act, which, in my opinion, didn't work. Most *Don Giovanni* productions I have seen are musically coherent but much less convincing in terms of staging.

What's it like directing an opera at Garnier? Were you free to carry out your ideas?

Before signing the contract, I presented my vision to Gérard Mortier, who gave it his full approval. He backed me all the way through and helped however he could. For example, I wanted to have a say in the casting, which had already been finalised when I arrived. I reviewed all the performers and found them all spot-on, except for two I didn't know: the singers playing Masetto and Zerlina. They turned out to be disastrous in the first rehearsals; not vocally, but as actors. I warned Mortier, who insisted I keep them. I rehearsed with them far more than with the others, but after ten days, it still wasn't working, and I convinced Mortier to replace them. It wasn't easy. The singer playing Masetto was an American who had to be sent home with full compensation. His understudy, David Bižić, took over and was excellent. For Zerlina, we got lucky. Mortier knew a young Polish singer, Aleksandra Zamojska, who had already performed in Salzburg and was available. She arrived just ten days before the premiere and was perfect. A real miracle, because ten days is far too short a period of time for me, given how demanding I am with singers. Since they aren't professional actors, I show them every gesture they need to make. They bring their own ideas, of course, but most of the time they appreciate having clear, detailed direction. I didn't use storyboards but did sketch diagrams of their movements in relation to the music. I try to anticipate everything. If you're working with talented performers, it always comes together.

How long did you spend rehearsing?

Six weeks, though you have to subtract the final ten days, by which point everything had to be working smoothly, and during which additional rehearsals with the orchestra start. That's why, for my next production, *Così fan tutte*, in Madrid, Gérard Mortier granted me the eight weeks of rehearsal I asked for. That's highly unusual because it's very expensive. Performers are usually contracted for two or three weeks, covering about ten performances. In the weeks leading up to that, they're expected to be available, but with my approach, they start work long before the performances begin and have to be paid accordingly.

Have you ever worked this way for your films?

I don't rehearse films. Cinema is the opposite of theatre. In theatre, you have to rehearse because, once the show is ready, it has to run on its own, night after night, without the director. In cinema, you work on a sequence of moments that are recorded once and for all. I don't rehearse before shooting, though other directors do and achieve excellent results. There are no rules; that's just my way of doing things, but I find that if you rehearse too much, there is a danger of getting too comfortable, and you lose the tension that makes things come alive. In theatre, tension resurfaces when the audience is present. That's not the case in film. The only time I rehearse is with non-professional actors and children, to give them a sense of security before facing the chaos of a film set. With professionals, I prefer to make use of their spontaneity, their initial instincts. In fact, I usually end up choosing either the first take, or the twentieth or twenty-fifth, when they circle back to the freshness of the first one. Another issue with rehearsals is that they exhaust actors. That said, Ingmar Bergman worked with stage actors in his films and rehearsed them for weeks in the theatre before shooting everything in just three weeks. And he made extraordinary films.

A digital model of the single set designed by Christoph Kanter.

Did you also have a hand in the musical direction of the opera?

I had to discuss things in advance with the conductor because my staging included many pauses. The most obvious example is before the famous "champagne Aria," when Don Giovanni mistreats Leporello. When he opens the window and we hear street noise, we wonder if he's about to jump—which isn't in the libretto. It's a recitative, so there's a bit more flexibility there, but only if the conductor agrees, because those pauses have to be carefully coordinated. Back in the day, everything used to be played and sung straight through without interruption.

Did you choose the conductor, Sylvain Cambreling?

No, he was selected by the Paris Opera. I went through the entire score with him to indicate what I wanted to do, particularly where I was deviating from tradition, always asking for his opinions. One modification he struggled to accept was my decision to reduce the peasants' chorus to a quartet. Another was during the party scene. There are usually three small orchestras onstage, musically sparring with each other, but it was impossible to include multiple orchestras in my set. Instead, I used three recorded pieces, played through a radio, which had to either transition seamlessly with the live orchestra or overlap with it. Initially, Sylvain was against this idea, but he eventually came around, as there was no real alternative. For the 2012 revival, the new conductor, Philippe Jordan, wanted to remove all the pauses. I told him that if they were reviving my 2006 staging, they had to keep it as it was. He tried to negotiate a compromise, but I refused. They're welcome to stage a new production, but if they want to use mine, they have to respect it fully.

Your staging included some bold choices. The first is that single set, designed by your regular film production designer, Christoph Kanter, which is stunning. Was he your first choice?

Yes, and he also designed the sets for my *Così fan tutte* in Madrid in 2013.

Was Gérard Mortier on board with this?

Yes. I explained to him that, in the world of opera I was an outsider, and that to feel comfortable, I needed to surround myself with collaborators I was used to working with. That's how I was able to bring on Christoph, as well as Annette Beaufays, the costume designer for *The Piano Teacher*, who is also the head costume designer for all the major theatres in Vienna and is always travelling the world for her work. That reassured me. Since we chose to set the opera in the corporate world, we decided on a design inspired by the architectural style of La Défense, Paris' business district. The only major issue we faced was with the head of set construction, an otherwise very likable Italian, who was about to leave the Paris Opera to continue his career back in Italy. He insisted on building the set there, claiming it was too large for the Garnier workshop. When the pieces arrived at Garnier, most of them didn't fit together properly, which caused real headaches because the carpenters were still working on the set while we were rehearsing on stage. It also drove up production costs. The only time I actually had the full lighting setup for the entire production was on opening night. The lighting director, who had worked with Patrice Chéreau and many others, was so frustrated that at one point he just walked out. Nothing was working, and he couldn't do his job properly. This set issue was the biggest challenge of the production. It delayed us and caused a lot of stress. I was worried that we wouldn't be able to get everything done in time.

Another bold choice was your use of darkness, something you're known for in your films.

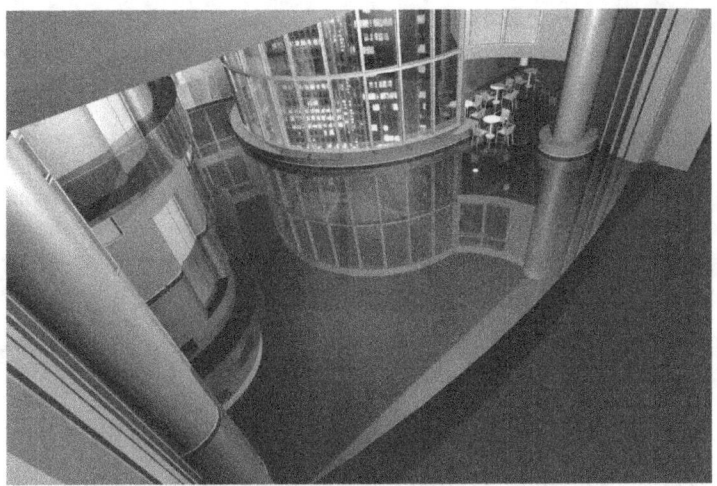

The set seen from above.

Mortier asked me several times if I could brighten things up a bit, but I had to say no. The set lent itself to that kind of lighting. As always, there were spots in the auditorium where the view wasn't great, but I made an effort to ensure audiences could see well enough. Also, the set was shaped like a trumpet, which helped project the voices better in a space where the acoustics aren't exactly ideal.

Some people felt that your staging was better suited to the Bastille, where the production was revived the following year.

I actually think the contrast between the set and the space at Garnier was more striking than at Bastille, where our set blended in more easily.

Another audacious choice was replacing the traditional Venetian masks with Mickey Mouse masks. How did you come up with that idea?

I was looking for masks that would suit a cleaning crew in La Défense, something they might find amusing for a party and that would be easily found in stores. Mickey is the ultimate symbol of fun, but the sheer number of masks creates an unsettling effect.

These playful yet distinctly American masks, worn by cleaners, led some to describe your interpretation of Mozart's opera as Marxist.

The world of *Don Giovanni* fits perfectly within an ultra-capitalist setting. Mickey Mouse, as an emblem of America, reinforces that idea. A lawyer warned that we might run into copyright issues using those masks, so Mortier formally requested permission from the Disney corporation, which they denied, but I was stubborn, and Mortier backed me, saying we would take our chances. If we were sued, it just meant they had no sense of humour.

Your most daring choice is undoubtedly the emphasis you place on sexuality. There is even a rape on stage.

That's in the opera.

Yes, but you show the young woman completely nude, from the front, and you emphasise the violence. The scene is rarely staged that way.

I think that nowadays, in certain circles of power, men have developed a sexuality that is fast and brutal. Don Giovanni, placed in the world of finance, could only behave that way. As for the nudity, the young woman is naked for only a second. Don Giovanni rips off her clothing and his colleagues immediately cover her with whatever is to hand.

But such a scene is usually taboo in opera.

Perhaps, but I'm sure it's been done like that elsewhere. Recently, at the Wiener Festwochen festival, there was a classical music performance where everyone was nude, including the pianist. In theatre, that sort of thing doesn't shock people anymore.

It's also common in contemporary dance, but at Garnier?

Mortier wasn't concerned. No one opposed it. My only challenge was finding a performer who was willing to appear nude, even briefly. All non-singing roles required a specific casting process. My film casting agent, Kris de Bellair, spent weeks finding extras. Garnier's in-house casting agents weren't very happy when Kris went into the suburbs to find North African and African extras, people who had often never set foot in an opera house before but who were delighted to participate.

Another bold sexual choice is the kiss on the lips between Don Giovanni and Leporello. That isn't in the libretto.

True. It's in the scene known in German as the "champagne Aria." Why that name? There's no mention of champagne in the libretto, but at some point, someone decided that Don Giovanni should hold a glass of champagne. It's a moment when Don Giovanni is in a frenzy of despair, so I had to make him do something excessive. He considers suicide, then overcomes that impulse and lashes out at the people around him. Just as he stabbed the Commendatore with a knife, he throws himself on Leporello and kisses him on the mouth. It's an act of humiliation following a moment of weakness and despair in front of his servant.

This violent and sensual character is paradoxically placed in a set dominated by shades of blue and grey.

Black, actually—which reflects those very cold, impersonal corporate environments. The contrast is deliberate, of course. This is also evident in the scene where Don Giovanni takes Donna Elvira's coat while singing, wraps himself in it, then lies down on the floor. I think that's the strongest moment in the whole production. It was beautifully performed and enhanced by the conductor's decision to bring in an additional mandolin player just for that piece. The way he played it was stunning. It's all the more touching because it contrasts with the icy setting.

Singing while lying down is also unusual.

It's difficult to sing in that position because it disrupts natural breathing. Shawn Mathey, who played Don Ottavio and was supposed to sing part of an aria lying down, chose to stay standing because he was worried he might miss a note, but Peter Mattei as Don Giovanni and Christine Schäfer as Donna Anna were so technically skilled that they could adapt to anything.

In the final act, you also came up with something new for the return of the Commendatore.

When I was deciding whether to stage the opera, I knew it would all hinge on whether I could come up with a strong concept for the Commendatore's return, a scene that can easily tip into the absurd. If you want to keep things believable, you have to avoid ghostly clichés, which is why Peter Sellars' version didn't work, because he gave the apparition a religious dimension. If the world you're depicting is one where God no longer exists, you can't suddenly make Him reappear at the end, which is why I chose to depict the Commendatore as a corpse sitting in his office chair. His voice comes from a tape recording, and his daughter moves his hand for him. In the end, it's Donna Elvira—the other woman he has betrayed—who delivers the fatal blow to Don Giovanni, before the employees throw him, still alive, out the window. I felt it worked very well that way. And in the scene where the Commendatore invites Leporello to follow him, there was no need to deal with the awkwardness of a talking statue. We just had to open the door to the boss' office.

Another striking moment in the finale is this revolt of the minorities, represented by North Africans, Africans and women.

At that point, we go beyond realism, because there are far more people in that scene than there were at the party earlier. It's the image of an entire social class rising up and taking revenge.

It brings to mind Code Unknown, *where you also addressed immigration and social integration issues.*

As you know, that's the reality of the massive office complexes of Paris, where the cleaning staff is almost exclusively Arab and black. I wanted my staging to reflect the social reality of today.

In your staging, as in many others, including Joseph Losey's film version, the same moment in the second act is cut. Why?

It's the scene in which Zerlina tricks Leporello into letting his guard down, which often gets cut because it really doesn't work. Initially, I wanted to keep it, but the singer who ultimately played Zerlina arrived so late in rehearsals that I didn't have time to sort it out.

In 2013, your plan is to stage Così fan tutte *in Madrid. Will you be modernising it as well?*

I think so, but I don't yet know exactly how to anchor it in the contemporary world. When I first suggested staging it to Garnier, it wasn't because I had a brilliant concept for adaptation; it was simply because I loved the music so much that I wanted to live with it for a while. That wasn't the case with *Don Giovanni*, which

Christine Schäfer (Donna Anna) and Shawn Mathey (Don Ottavio)

I wasn't as familiar with. But by listening to it every day, I discovered lots of details that I had never noticed before. Of the three operas that Lorenzo Da Ponte wrote for Mozart, *The Marriage of Figaro* is my favourite, but I wouldn't dare stage it because I don't know how to address the issue of *droit du seigneur* [a medieval custom in which a feudal lord had the right to sleep with a subordinate's bride on her wedding night] in a modern context. Peter Sellars managed it by setting the opera in a luxurious penthouse overlooking Central Park, with an American ambassador living among his female employees, and that was very funny, but I don't want to repeat what's already been done. The only one of the three Da Ponte operas that can be easily transposed to the present day is *Così fan tutte*. It's as timeless as a Marivaux play.

Do you like The Magic Flute?

I love all Mozart, but I would be incapable of staging that opera. You need a great deal of imagination and the ability to come up with original, fantastical images. And that's just not me.

Are there other operas tempting you?

Since *Don Giovanni*, I've been offered a dozen different operas by various composers, and I have said no to them all because I don't want to be pigeonholed as an opera director. Most opera directors have studied music and know the scores inside out. There is an enormous amount of preparation involved, working through the score bar by bar, which takes a lot of time, and it's not particularly well-paid. I would rather make a film... I'm no longer a young man, and in the years I have left, I want to focus only on what I know how to do.

For someone whose original ambition was to become a concert pianist or composer, directing opera seems like a good way to express that passion.

Yes, but there aren't many operas that interest me enough to stage them. I could see myself directing *Fidelio*, Beethoven's only opera, but again, it's difficult to find a credible contemporary setting. I've never seen a good staging of it. I've also been offered Wagner, but his music doesn't nourish me enough to live with it for months.

You must have enjoyed working on Don Giovanni *because though you said you are done directing theatre, here you are having agreed to stage a second opera.*

That's as much because of Mozart as of Mortier, who reached out and has always supported me. I feel I should be loyal to those who have been loyal to me.

Did your experience with Don Giovanni *influence the direction of your subsequent films?*

No, they are two completely different things. It's the same with the theatre work I did for twenty years, although it was through the theatre that I learned how to work with actors. On stage, actors have more freedom; if they don't want to do what I ask, they simply won't do it. You have to persuade them, seduce them into doing what you want. In cinema, the director is the ultimate authority because everyone knows there's no time to waste on discussions. Film actors, as a result, are much more cooperative. That's why I always tell my students to do theatre. Go anywhere, stage a small play, work with actors, even if you end up getting booed! That's where you'll really learn something about acting. Filmmaking really doesn't teach that. Film students tend to blame the actor when a scene doesn't work. I always tell them: the problem isn't the actor, it's *you*, in how you're directing them. Either you picked the wrong actor or you failed to guide the performer towards what you wanted.

Is directing opera singers even more demanding than working with film actors?

No. It's always demanding if you want a certain level of quality. Maybe it was harder for me because it was unfamiliar territory. When I moved into cinema, I was already used to television. Opera was something entirely new, which is why I was quite nervous when I started out. I didn't know how to communicate with singers, how far I could go before alienating them. But I quickly realised that they're very open-minded and curious, and *want* to be guided. It's actually easier than working with theatre actors. In film, since I write my own scripts, actors can't really criticise me. In any case, when people praise the performances in my films, it's mostly thanks to my experience in theatre. To answer your question: I actually think opera and cinema have more in common than theatre and cinema. As I've said before, I'm someone who plans meticulously; I know exactly what I want for every shot in a film. That way, the crew knows precisely what to do. Opera is similar in that we have to follow the music. It's the guiding thread that can't be altered.

Have you ever considered directing commercials?

Never. I've had several offers, but always turned them down. I could say it's because of professional ethics, but it's more that I'm incapable of working on something that doesn't interest me. Remember my disastrous attempt at directing a Labiche farce? Even if the advert were for a cause I support, like human rights, it would still be the opposite of what I do in cinema, which is to foster doubt rather than hammer home truths. Besides, I don't feel comfortable with short films. I see this with my students; it's harder to make a good short film than a good feature.

You often mention your students in our discussions. How long have you been teaching film, and where?

I started teaching in 2002 at the Vienna Film Academy, which is part of the faculty of fine arts and music. I teach for the pleasure of it. It also keeps me connected to younger generations and helps me stay in touch with what interests them.

What does your teaching involve?

I teach directing and screenwriting, through seminars and one-on-one work with each student. I run two seminars: one focused on film analysis, the other on working with actors, shot composition and storyboarding. I also mentor each student through the short films they have to make, from scripting to final editing. In their final year, students develop a feature-length project of at least forty minutes, which can serve as a calling card. Several have managed to get their first feature films produced this way.

How many students take your classes?

There's no set limit, but generally, about twenty per cohort. For directing, the group is smaller; usually two or three students, except in 2011 when we had an exceptionally strong year and selected six. Only one was Austrian; the others came from Serbia, Poland, Ukraine and America. The Academy is open to students from all countries, but fluency in German is required.

What do you start with in your directing course?

It depends. I try to respond to students' expectations, and begin by asking them, "What do you want to learn in this course? What are your weaknesses?" The answer is often the same: working with actors. It's true that student films are generally technically

Haneke teaching at the Vienna Film Academy.

competent but rather weak when it comes to directing actors, so we organise rehearsal sessions and they act out scenes with each other. We also bring in students from the Reinhardt Seminar, the drama school, and even professional actors. That's how one of my students was able to make a film with Ulrich Mühe and Susanne Lothar. We let them direct. We watch, we correct. I always say: the only way to learn directing actors is to *do* it. I draw their attention to the importance of having a good ear, something that develops over time.

Is there a theoretical component to your courses?

No, it's a hands-on, practical programme. Even when it comes to film analysis, I make them write detailed critiques of the films we watch, then we discuss them. I eventually handed this part of the course over to my assistant because the first-year students' level was so low that it frustrated me too much. As I mentioned, the first films I show are Tarkovsky's *Mirror*, Bresson's *Au hasard Balthazar* and Cassavetes' *A Woman Under the Influence*. Then come propaganda films: Riefenstahl's *Triumph of the Will*, Petersen's *Air Force One*, Costa-Gavras' *Z* and a film by Eisenstein. We screen one film every two weeks, about twenty per year. That gives us the chance to show students quite a few great films they generally haven't seen and which tend to unsettle them, except for one or two students who have already seen everything, but who won't necessarily be the most talented directors.

Can you tell when some of your students just don't have the talent?

You can immediately spot students who are talented, but that doesn't mean they will go on to have a career. If they're too self-absorbed, they won't be able to adapt to others, and as a director, you have to know how to adapt. I'm not talking about conforming to what others expect from you, but knowing very clearly what you can and cannot do. To answer your question, I'm very impatient and sometimes tend to think that certain students will never make it. But that's not true; they just need time. We've seen students who only found their footing after years of struggle. Then, all of a sudden, they break through and everything starts to fall into place. Besides being impatient, I'm also very direct. If I don't like something, I say so immediately. That way, my students know I never lie to them. Because of this some are afraid of me; others like me a lot. Either way, when I'm working with students, I always remain true to who I am.

How many hours do you teach per week?

My classes are scheduled on the first two days of the week, from 10a.m. to 6p.m. When I make a film, I try to shoot in the summer, during the break, though that wasn't possible for *The White Ribbon* and *Amour*, so I had to take unpaid leave.

How long does the directing course last?

Three or five years. After five, students earn the title of *magister.* But honestly, five years is too long. We have students who are still here after ten years because they took time off to work and then came back to finish their studies. Most enrol in the five-year programme. During our first meeting, I always tell them that if they don't go out and do things beyond the classroom, nothing we do at the Academy will ever stick. I encourage them to get as much hands-on experience as possible, even if it means making coffee on a set. They learn much more from working with professionals than they ever could from their professors. I share my own experiences with them, but they also have to go out and learn for themselves.

At the end of their studies, does the Academy guarantee employment for its students?

No, but we do what we can to help. For example, two of my students are currently making their first feature films with Wega-

Haneke teaching at the Vienna Film Academy.

Film. Of course, I can't force anyone to hire my students; I can only introduce them, say that they have an interesting script, and ask the producer to read it. It's up to the producer to decide if they want to make the film. The biggest problem today—and not just in Austria—isn't a shortage of directors but a lack of good writers. Most directors are skilled at their craft, but the films are terrible because the scripts are so weak. I always remind my directing students: "One day you will depend entirely on writers!" I think directors are vastly overrated. If a script is bad, there is nothing a director can do. When people say, "A film by...," they should actually be referring to the screenwriter.

Twelve

The origins of *The White Ribbon* — The photographs of August Sander — Reconstruction or re-creation — The colours of black and white — In praise of digital imagery — Emotion versus interpretation — I don't want to educate the audience — Working with children — Lies in the service of truth — Ingmar Bergman and *Village of the Damned* — A lesson in sound mixing — The Palme d'Or and behind the scenes at Cannes

How did The White Ribbon *come about?*

Many years before I made the film, I had a contract for a two-hour television film with the Austrian channel ORF. The network's script editor, aware of the scope of the project, assured me that we could extend the runtime if necessary, but when I submitted my script—which by then was a three-part miniseries—he had retired, and his replacement insisted on sticking to the two-hour limit in the contract. I refused, and the project was shelved. Then, while filming *The Piano Teacher*, some ORF executives called me and said they and Westdeutscher Rundfunk wanted to talk with me. I assumed they wanted to revive my project, so I met them during my lunch break. It turned out they wanted me to make a three-part telefilm—about Metternich! They were really keen because they had already invested a lot of money in it, but I just wasn't interested. Several years went by before a new director at the ORF contacted me. This time, she wanted to produce my trilogy, but as a two-parter. I explained that we could either keep the three-part format as originally planned or condense it into a single feature, but splitting it into two simply wouldn't work. She never understood my reasoning, and once again, the project was abandoned until I mentioned it to Margaret Menegoz, who loved the script and immediately wanted to produce it, on the condition that I cut an hour. I promised to try and managed to remove 25 minutes;

any further cuts seemed impossible without altering the structure. Margaret insisted that the film couldn't exceed two and a half hours because that's the maximum length to ensure the greatest number of daily screenings in cinemas. I can't remember if it was her idea or mine to bring in Jean-Claude Carrière, but he agreed right away to help with the cuts and came to Vienna. In two afternoons, we came up with a solution. Since we couldn't trim the plot itself, Carrière had the brilliant idea of removing all the scenes showing the children playing together. I thought they were good and provided an important glimpse into the kinds of games children played at the time, but in terms of the sense of mystery I wanted to maintain, it was a smart choice to cut those scenes, which made the children's relationships too easy to decipher.

The White Ribbon (2009)

An elderly schoolteacher recalls. Between 1913 and 1914, in a small village in northern Germany, a series of unexplained incidents unfold. It begins with the village doctor's horse mysteriously falling after tripping over an invisible wire strung between two trees. Soon after, a farmer's wife falls to her death from her attic, where a floorboard had rotted. Other, seemingly minor events gradually spread unease throughout the village. The pastor punishes two of his five children, Martin and Klara, for coming home late, and Martin in particular for his growing tendency to masturbate. As a consequence, both must wear a white ribbon, a symbol of their path back to purity. During the harvest festival, Max, the eldest son of a tenant farmer working for the baron, vandalises his employer's cabbage field, blaming him for his mother's death. Shortly thereafter, Sigmund, the baron's child, is found in the woods, bound and beaten. Eva, a nanny working at the baron's estate and recently put in charge of his new-born twins, is immediately dismissed. She seeks refuge with the schoolteacher, who has shown her kindness and sees this as an opportunity to grow closer to her. He asks for her hand in marriage, but her father insists they wait twelve months before marrying. From this point, the incidents escalate. The doctor, now recovered, returns to the village and resumes his affair with the midwife who once cared for his children, only to later humiliate and dismiss her.

Soon after, he begins sexually abusing his teenage daughter, Anna. Meanwhile, the steward's wife gives birth to a baby who quickly falls ill. This is followed by the burning of a barn and the farmer's suicide by hanging. The baron's wife confesses that she has a lover in Italy and intends to leave to join him. Karli, the midwife's mentally disabled son, is found tied to a tree, his eyes nearly gouged out. The schoolteacher, disturbed and determined to understand what is happening, conducts his own investigation. He concludes that the village children are behind the incidents. He presents his theory to the pastor, who is outraged and expels him from the village. The midwife, too, leaves town, intending to report her son's testimony to the police. Rumours begin to swirl... On June 28, 1914, Austria declares war on Serbia following the assassination of Archduke Franz Ferdinand in Sarajevo. Germany follows suit, declaring war on Russia and France. As the villagers gather in the church, a profound silence settles over them.

Did the first draft of the script already contain the notion that even a good idea, when turned into a rigid system, becomes an ideology, and that ideologies can be dangerous?

Yes, I would say that was the whole point of the script, though I only really realised that once I started writing. I don't work like some writers who pick a contemporary issue—the economic crisis, for example—then build a story around it. For me, something has to hit emotionally and become the driving force behind my thinking. With *The White Ribbon*, I initially imagined a choir of blond-haired characters in northern Germany, in a black-and-white setting, children singing Bach chorales and punishing people in their lives who don't practise what they preach. That was my starting point, perhaps unconsciously shaped by my political thinking, although my goal was never to make a political film, but simply to tell a story.

How did the idea for the film come to you?

I have no idea. That's the hardest question to answer because I never really know. It just fell from the sky. It's like a composer creating a melody; where does it come from? Impossible to say. Sometimes an image pops into my mind, as was the case with *The*

White Ribbon, but that's rare. More often, I get the idea for a story first, then develop it.

The White Ribbon isn't your first historical film, although here you're exploring a period and a culture you had never tackled before. What research did you do?

Before I even settled on northern Germany, I was mainly focused on the subject of education and read a lot of books on the subject, as well as on rural life. I found it all fascinating, and it certainly enriched my approach to the script. When it comes to a historical story, there are lots of details you can't make up, for example the scene where the farmer's son destroys the cabbage field to avenge his mother's death. That came straight out of one of the books I read, as did a proverb I had the steward recite in the film: "The wheat is harvested, we want to be paid. Woe to the miser. We'll have his head!"

Where did you come across the idea of the white ribbon, which symbolises a return to purity after a transgression, in a book?

Yes, I found it in a 19th-century author's writings on child education, although I read so many books, I can't remember which one.

Could it have been by Alice Miller?

No, I don't think so. I'm familiar with her work and have probably read everything she wrote. She never gives concrete, practical examples. The books that were most useful were the ones that described real-life cases. I was struck by the idea that all too often, in education, good intentions lead to trouble.

Do you study photographs from the era when determining The White Ribbon's *visual style?*

I was already very familiar with August Sander's photographs, which represent an ideal for me. They have an extraordinary sharpness and clarity, something you didn't really get in cinema before digital technology. In postproduction, we went back over every face, even in wide shots, to enhance the sharpness. It was extremely meticulous work. In the early scene where Anna, the doctor's daughter, tries to comfort her brother Rudolf on the staircase after their father's riding accident, there was a tear on Anna's face that wasn't visible enough, so we digitally enhanced it.

Was the decision to shoot in black and white influenced by the fact that early 20th-century photos were in black and white?

Partly, yes. Since we only know that era through black-and-white images, using that palette gave our reconstruction a sense of authenticity right from the start. But there was a second reason: distance. Black and white creates a kind of remove that rules out any naturalistic approach, and that kind of remove was essential for this project, because it's simply not possible to recreate the period exactly as it was. The black and white constantly reminds the viewer that they're not seeing a fake version of reality but a deliberate recreation.

But The White Ribbon *wasn't shot directly in black and white.*

Correct. Given the light sources we wanted to use — candles, oil lamps, torches — none of the black-and-white film stocks we tested gave us the results we were looking for. When filming a candle, for example, only the flame was visible; everything else was pitch black. This is because the film industry has largely abandoned black-and-white film stock, and companies like Kodak have stopped improving its sensitivity. Meanwhile, new colour film stocks are released every six months. We ran endless tests to find the one that suited us best.

Did you also test digital cameras?

No, Christian Berger and I had too many bad memories from shooting *Caché*. We didn't want to relive that nightmare.

How do you go from shooting in colour to having black-and-white theatrical prints?

We shot on colour film, then transferred it to digital and converted it to black and white. The black-and-white digital version was what we used for editing. During filming, I had a truck with two monitoring screens, one in colour to check certain details, the other desaturated to get a sense of how it would look in black and white. It made a huge difference. Before shooting, Christian Berger and I experimented by watching several films set in the same era as *The White Ribbon*, but with the colours removed. One of them was *Unforgiven* by Clint Eastwood. The results were as disastrous as I had expected. Any hidden light source added to boost the glow from a lamp was glaringly obvious, whereas, in colour, such tricks went unnoticed. Colour distracts the eye; black and white highlights everything that is fake. We had to take this into account.

From a financial perspective, did choosing black and white pose a problem?

Of course. All the producers were against it, especially the television networks. Margaret Menegoz was the first to convince French television to broadcast the film in black and white. The Germans were much more hesitant because their contract required a colour version. I knew that if the film was well received at Cannes, German television wouldn't dare broadcast it in colour without making fools of themselves. That said, if they hadn't backed down, I wouldn't have worked on a colour version. They would have had to figure it out with my cinematographer. The best part was that when the film aired on German television in October 2011, it set audience records, with 4.5 million viewers watching it in black and white. The same happened in Austria, where 800,000 viewers tuned in, which surprised everyone.

The digital version screened at Cannes was astonishingly sharp, but in 2009, most theatres weren't equipped for digital projection and you had to produce 35mm prints. How did you handle the transfer?

We spent a lot of time adjusting the contrast and fine-tuning the blacks and whites to match the look we had achieved digitally, but the depth of field just isn't as good on analogue film, and you lose a lot of the image's texture, which, in digital, almost gave it a 3-D feel.

Did you also draw inspiration from Sander's photographs for the costumes and faces?

Not just Sander's. All photographs from that time show faces that are very different from today's. Whenever possible, I chose actors and extras with features resembling those of the early 20th century, although there weren't many professional actors with those features, so we had to rely on hairstyling and accessories. In photographs from 1913 and 1914, for example, you never see a girl with her hair falling over her face. They all pulled their hair back, with or without a barrette. And they all dressed the same way, which created an extraordinary similarity among them. In the film, the midwife and the doctor's daughter appear to resemble each other, though if you look closely their features are actually quite different.

Did you have actors in mind once you finished the script?

At that point, the only roles that had been cast were that of the midwife, played by Susanne Lothar, and the pastor, played by Ulrich Mühe. I like writing for actors I admire, but it can some-times backfire, which is what happened when Ulrich died from an aggressive form of cancer. To replace him, I thought about the big names of German theatre and cinema, but none of them fit. Either they seemed too neurotic or they just didn't have that natural authority, that kind of presence that makes a room go quiet when they enter. Then one day, I met Burghart Klaussner, who immediately fit the image I had of the character. Even though he created a very different pastor than the one Ulrich Mühe would have played—he would have been softer, younger, more nervous—I was very happy with my choice.

For the role of the Baron, you chose Ulrich Tukur, a highly regarded actor and musician in Germany.

That was a difficult role to cast because I needed someone like Josef Bierbichler, but with a more aristocratic air. It had to be very masculine man, someone who would feel more at ease with his horses than his wife. That kind of actor doesn't really exist here. Ulrich Tukur struck me as the best fit, even if he was a little on the young side for the role.

How did you find the children?

That was my biggest concern. I was afraid of showing up on the first day of shooting without the seven children I needed for the main roles. An adult actor can always be replaced by another of roughly equal talent, but that isn't the case with children. Finding young people who can act on film isn't easy. We gave ourselves six months. My casting agent, Markus Schleinzer—who has worked on several of my films and has since directed his first feature, called *Michael*—filmed about seven thousand children with his team of assistants and students. I narrowed that down to about thirty, who I worked with directly. We also enlisted casting directors from television. It was through them that we found Leonard Proxauf, who plays Martin, the pastor's son. He had already starred in Toke Constantin Hebbeln's film *Nimmermeer*. He's strikingly hand-some, with a fantastic face, and appears on the film's poster, but more than anything, he was very moving in auditions, especially

Leonard Proxauf in *The White Ribbon*.

in the scene where he is accused of masturbating. The same agency also introduced us to the children who play the steward's two sons. Everyone else was handpicked by us. For smaller roles, we mixed children who had some filming experience with others who were cast on location by my team.

And for the adult extras?

That was the job of Schleinzer's second assistant, a Romanian who had done the same job on *Time of the Wolf*. For that film, she went home to find the actors who played the Romanian family. They were so happy with the experience that they spread the word, so when she went back with her video camera for *The White Ribbon*, every door was open to her. It helped that the small fees we paid the extras amounted to significant sums compared to Romanian wages. Two whole busloads of extras were cast that way. They all looked like real peasants—their faces weathered by the sun, unlike German farmers, who, because they work the land with modern tractors equipped with air-conditioned cabins, tend to look more like city folk.

Did you recruit any extras in Germany?

Of the two hundred people we needed for the big celebration scene, about half were locals. My assistants travelled through the region, and whenever they spotted someone with an old-world face, they invited them to audition. I had a wall covered in photos, and from that, we were able to build up the groups we needed.

What was your approach to writing the dialogue?

Writing in the local dialect of the time was out of the question because we would have had to subtitle the film for German audiences, and it would have been too difficult for the actors, who came from all over Germany and already had to drop their regional accents. Only Josef Bierbichler kept his Bavarian accent to play the steward, which made sense, as stewards in those days often travelled far from home to take up work. I had to dub Branko Samarovski, who was also in *The Rebellion*, because his Austrian accent was so strong.

We read somewhere that you were inspired by the literary style of Theodor Fontane, the Prussian author of Effi Briest, *particularly when it came to the dialogue.*

Not so much for the dialogue as for the voiceover, which employs a more elevated language.

Did the idea of having a narrator come to you right away?

Yes, for the same reason as using black and white. It creates a certain distance from the events being shown.

It also helps emphasise that what the schoolteacher is recounting isn't, as he says himself, "true down to the last detail." That ties into a central idea in your films—that any so-called truth is always relative.

Exactly. I always try to keep audiences on their toes. With this film in particular, it was crucial to maintain perspective on the possible guilt of the children. As adults, not all of them would go on to become Nazi torturers in the camps. The characters, for the most part, are quite distinct and not simply portrayed in a negative light.

Where did you shoot?

In Northern Germany, where Protestantism is very present. I could have set this story in Austria, in Burgenland, where there are Protestant communities, but that wouldn't have been as representative. And Northern Germany was also an obvious choice because, from the outset, I had imagined a flat landscape where you can see for miles.

Who did the location scouting, you or your team?

My production designer, Christoph Kanter, who drove nearly forty thousand miles in his car over several weeks, stopping in every village to take thousands of photographs. He's very organised, meticulously recording in his computer maps and photos of all the places he visited, keeping track of every road he took. It soon became clear that filming in the western part of the country was impossible because everything had been renovated. Initially, we considered Poland or even former Czechoslovakia, but that was too complicated. We then looked in former East Germany, but during the years of communism too many buildings had been rebuilt and altered. We did find the village of Netzow, in the Prignitz region, about 120 miles northwest of Berlin, which has a wide main street and, right in the middle, a church towering over everything. Like everywhere in the former GDR, the streets were paved over and full of potholes. Fortunately, the government had promised to repair them the following year, which is why they let us remove the asphalt and cover the streets with sand to give them the look they had at the start of the 20th century. We also took down electrical poles and television antennas, and disguised over a third of the village with set facades, which we attached to the front of the houses.

What materials were used for these sets?

The facades in front of the existing houses were made of painted wood, but the doctor's house, with its garden, was entirely built in stone so that it could be fully lived in. Right next to it, where the midwife lives, was an old dilapidated house undergoing renovation, which we had to refurbish. The biggest challenge was the castle. We had extensive documentation listing all the castles in Germany, but they had either been fully renovated and turned into hotels or were in total disrepair. The one we picked was near the Baltic Sea, about 120 miles from Netzow, a distance which complicated things. The interior was in terrible shape, but the exteriors were more or less usable, apart from the garden, which was a mess. Since it was too expensive to rebuild the surrounding buildings, we used digital effects to erase the corrugated metal roofs, frame by frame, in the shots where they appear. Inside the castle, everything had to be redone, including the staircase. The only thing we kept was the wood panelling in the main salon.

Netzow, the main setting of *The White Ribbon.*

Wouldn't it have been easier to recreate this interior in a studio?

No, because the size and layout the actual space perfectly suited our needs. That said, we did build the interior of the pastor's house in a studio in Leipzig. For the exteriors, besides the doctor's house, we also constructed the steward's house with its grand staircase in a barn that Kanter transformed. The amount of work he put into this film was incredible. He even compiled a book with photos of all the sets before, during and after his team worked on them to show the producers where their money had gone. Even the vegetables you see in the fields were planted by us months in advance so they would be ready by the time we were filming.

Your wife, Susie, is credited among the technicians who contributed to the set design.

She decorated two of the rooms in the castle, the one where the baroness plays the piano and the one where she has her big argument with her husband. It was a delicate job because both rooms were completely empty. Susie also took care of little details, like how meals were served back then.

How did you create the impression of changing seasons?

We filmed in summer, except for a few shots of the village with the church under snow, which were filmed in winter. It didn't snow that year, so we had to use machines to create artificial snow. A few flakes did fall one night, but they only lasted half a day at most and we had to add fake snow because it had already started melting. All the other snow shots were done digitally. Because of the trees, we also filmed the scene where the young farmer discovers his father hanged in winter.

How long did the shoot last?

Three months, but the set designers started two months earlier and kept working while we were filming the village scenes. The schedule was extremely tight.

You insisted that the film's subtitle, Eine deutsche Kindergeschichte, *remain untranslated for non-German-speaking countries.*

Yes. I was concerned that its translation—"A German Children's Story," not "A Story for German Children"—might give foreign audiences the impression that the film was about a specifically German issue, which it isn't. The subtitle inevitably makes Germans reflect on their own history, but I wanted non-German-speaking viewers to feel that this fable could just as easily have taken place in their country. Moreover, I wanted the subtitle to be written in *Sütterlinschrift*, the script my grandmother used, which was standard in Germany and Austria until the early 1930s. This type of script has now completely fallen out of use. I can still read it, but I can't write it.

Why did you set the action in 1913-14?

As a German speaker, I wanted to explore the childhood of the generation that, twenty years later, brought the Nazis to power. But at the same time, I didn't want to make it too narrowly focused. I wanted to show that elevating an ideal to an absolute and turning an idea into an ideology is always dangerous. Of course, what is happening today with Islamist extremists is different in many ways, but the core of the problem remains the same.

The children's vengeful behaviour seems to stem from the rigid Protestant education they receive.

It's important to understand that this kind of education wasn't unique to Protestantism. In the Middle Ages—a period that has always fascinated me—educational practices were horrendous. More generally, throughout the world, before the 19th century, children's education was really quite brutal. Babies were literally

Burghart Klaussner, Ursina Lardi, Fion Mutert
and Ulrich Tukur in *The White Ribbon*.

swaddled so they wouldn't move, and as soon as they were old enough, children were put to work. *The White Ribbon* deals with the problem of education beyond Protestantism. When I tell a story, I try to remain as open as possible and connect with audiences on an emotional level. If that sparks reflection, so much the better, but I'm not trying to teach anyone a lesson.

The film seems to speak to our doubts about education. If, in the past, education was too rigid, things have swung too far the other way, since the 1970s.

If there were a perfect formula, everyone would be using it... Education is one of humanity's greatest challenges. How do you take a naturally self-centred creature and transform it into a social being? That has always been a struggle. It's easy to say that the pastor's authoritarianism in *The White Ribbon* is inhuman, but many parents from my generation, who rejected all forms of authority after 1968, didn't do their children any favours. On the contrary, many of those kids grew up feeling lost and unable to find their place in society.

What stands out are the contradictions in the characters. The doctor is excellent at his job, but in his private life—

—he's despicable, yes. It's a matter of perspective. For his patients, what matters is that he's a good doctor, but you wouldn't want to be in the shoes of his wife or daughter. The truth is, we never really know a person's true nature, except perhaps in the case of artists, whose true selves emerge through their work. Even then, every artist, just like every individual, has a public face, a private face, and a third, unconscious face that even they are unable to fully grasp.

Your characters are all rather complex. The midwife, for example, played by Susanne Lothar, isn't just a victim of her cynical lover. She shows remarkable insight when she tells him, "You must be very unhappy to be capable of such cruelty."

That one line explains the doctor's entire character. As for the pastor, contrary to what some have said, he's not a bad man. You have to believe him when he says that striking his children gives him no pleasure. If he does it, it's because he is convinced it's necessary, which is why he gets so upset when the schoolteacher accuses the children of the crimes. He can't let that idea take hold because it would destroy everything he has been trying to build in his family and community. But deep down, ever since he found his bird crucified on his desk, he knows the truth. You never see the pastor explicitly accuse his daughter, but you do get the sense that he knows it must be her. He can't say anything because he has to keep up appearances. But he's a broken man.

The communion scene is constructed on what is unsaid.

It shows his inner struggle. He wonders whether he can forgive her, because if he gives her communion, it means he absolves her.

How did you approach the scene where Rudolf, the doctor's son, learns about death from his older sister, Anna?

That's the kind of question every child asks sooner or later. In the past, when three generations lived under the same roof, the answer often came by chance, with the death of a grandparent. I don't remember exactly how I learned about it myself, but for everyone, discovering that we're mortal is a great shock. That realisation usually comes around age four or five. A certain intellectual capacity is needed to grasp the notion that something that *was there* no longer is.

The scene becomes especially moving when the child realises he has been lied to, that his mother didn't leave on a long journey, as he had been told. How did you direct Miljan Chatelain, who is incredibly touching in the role?

It wasn't that difficult for him because, under the direction of Markus Schleinzer, he had already rehearsed the scene many times with Roxane Duran. Plus he's just very talented. I noticed him during the final rounds of casting. With a child who isn't talented, no amount of explanation or effort will make it work, but Miljan instinctively understood what we were asking of him.

Did you use multiple cameras to shoot the scene?

No, just one. We started on him and he played the whole scene continuously, then we filmed the young girl. We did multiple takes, with breaks in between, because after twenty minutes in that kitchen, with the camera in his face, he wanted to move around, so we stopped and let him wander in the garden, then started up again. You need patience when working with young children because they can't focus for long periods. Having to repeat lines bores them, and sometimes throws them off. But everything went well, thanks in part to Schleinzer, who was always there to reassure him.

Did you know Schleinzer had such a talent for working with children?

I knew he was talented, but maybe not to that extent. He had already done some casting for me with non-professional actors and it had always worked well. He has a great way of communicating with people.

Aside from the need to take breaks, do you direct children in the same way as adult actors?

With children, the simplest approach is to show them directly what they need to do. If we have to do something again, I explain it with simple words, like asking them to be "a bit sadder," for example. I always say that when an actor has to play a lion on screen, the professional *acts* like a lion, but the child *is* the lion. That's why it's crucial to do extensive research to find children who naturally fit the roles. Through experience, I've realised that children are much harder to direct under the age of eight, probably because that age marks a developmental milestone.

Thanksgiving celebration for the summer 1913 harvest
in The *White Ribbon.*

*On the theme of children and death, there's that strange scene
with Martin, the pastor's son, who balances on the edge of a bridge
parapet before explaining to the schoolteacher who rushes over to
him: "I gave God a chance to kill me. He didn't. That must mean
He is pleased with me."*

I could never have come up with that one myself. I found it in one of
the books on education that I read, but slightly reworked the facts.
It was originally about a child who wanted to test whether he was
bad in God's eyes, as his father had claimed while punishing him.

*This appeal to God's judgment echoes the note left on the mutilated
body of Karli, the midwife's son: "For I, the Lord your God, am a
jealous God, punishing the sins of the fathers upon the children to
the third and fourth generation."*

I invented that. I started with that well-known biblical quote as a
way of explaining why this disabled child had been tortured. It's
an act of punishment inflicted on a child, but directed at the adults.

The film was originally called The Right Hand of God.

That wasn't my first idea; it was one of the options I thought about
when I was worried *The White Ribbon* might sound like a film
about a tailor. I dropped it when someone said, "Yes! The Right
Hand of God. That's because of the pastor, right?" Plus, as a title,
it felt a bit heavy-handed and overdramatic.

When it came to the misdeeds in the film, did you set a specific number of them while writing?

No. This isn't *Se7en*—although to build tension, I did need a variety of incidents or accidents. And I needed each one to be surprising, so the audience would be compelled to think about who might be the culprit. Who dislikes the doctor enough to make him fall from his horse? People in the village know he mistreats his daughter; she could have talked about it with her friends, but we can't be absolutely certain. I had to imagine situations that would allow for speculation. Some incidents might also simply be accidents. It's by mixing it all together that I could get closer to reality, where not everything has an immediate explanation.

At times, though, you do clearly designate a culprit, like Klara, the pastor's daughter, who kills her father's caged bird—while at other moments you merely stoke our suspicions by repeatedly showing the children gathered together. In the scene where the teacher catches them trying to peek inside the midwife's house, you unsettle us even more by partially obstructing our view when his back and the half-closed gate hide part of the group. This way of denying us a full view of the action very much fits your storytelling style, in which you reveal events in fragmented, incomplete pieces.

That's how I work: by hiding things to make the audience curious. I do the same with sound, letting you hear things you don't see, which means you have to imagine what's happening. These are things I think about as early as the scriptwriting stage.

And yet some viewers were quite insistent that the children were guilty of everything.

That's their reading of it, and yet there are events in the film that can't be explained with such certainty. The farmer's fall could have been an accident, the barn fire as well. Or it could have been an act of revenge by the steward's children, who we see watching the flames from their window. Conversely, the pastor's three children seem surprised by the fire. There's a contradictory presentation of facts, leading to multiple interpretations. I get bored when everything is over-explained, which happens all too often in films.

In any case, whenever we see the children together, the audience feels a certain unease.

Christian Friedel and Leonie Beneschin in *The White Ribbon.*

That was the goal. After each new misdeed, the children are there, always as a group. What's unsettling is how serious they look. They never laugh, and seem weirdly grown-up.

Most representative of this unsettling maturity is Leonard Proxauf, who plays Martin, the pastor's eldest son. His face—handsome and stern—expresses a kind of repressed anger.

It's an incredible face. Even in real life, he isn't an easy boy. He hated filming the scene where he's tied to the bed and after each take demanded he be untied. All day long he kept that hard look, never smiling. He's really quite extraordinary in the film.

Who decided to use his face for the poster?

I did, because he's so expressive. With the tear running down his cheek, he captures exactly the feelings that all the children in this situation are experiencing: fear, anxiety, but also a sense of accusation. There's something about him, like a child who's been hit before and won't let anyone near him again.

Many filmgoers have drawn comparisons with Village of the Damned, *the 1960 film by Wolf Rilla, in which children unite to commit some fairly unpleasant acts.*

I wasn't familiar with *Village of the Damned* when I made *The White Ribbon*, but people talked about it so much after the film's release that I ended up watching it, and I thought it was quite good.

The script is solid, the tension never lets up, and the black-and-white cinematography is superb — much better, frankly, than what we achieved before sharpening our footage in post-production.

With the final shot of your film, it feels as if you're placing the story in the broad sweep of history, with all the characters gathered in the church on the eve of World War I. The choir sings the Protestant hymn composed by Luther, Ein feste Burg ist unser Gott.

Yes, but in any religious community in Northern Germany at that time, everyone would have gathered to sing that hymn. It's a militant act on their part, as the lyrics attest:

> Ein feste Burg ist unser Gott,
> ein gute Wehr und Waffen;
> er hilft uns frei aus aller Not,
> die uns jetzt hat betroffen.
> Der alt böse Feind,
> mit Ernst er's jetzt meint,
> groß Macht und viel List
> sein grausam Rüstung ist,
> auf Erd ist nicht seins gleichen.

> A mighty fortress is our God,
> A mighty shield and weapon;
> He helps us free from every need
> That hath us now o'ertaken.
> The old evil foe
> Now means deadly woe;
> Deep guile and great might
> Are his dread arms in fight;
> On earth is not his equal.

I felt it was ideal for the conclusion of the film.

And the decision to bring together all the protagonists?

That was a deliberate theatrical choice, like the chorus at the end of an opera.

There's a sense of collective guilt in that final shot, especially with the slow fade to black.

The final shot of *The White Ribbon*.

The ending echoes the opening of the film, which also fades in slowly, pulling us into the past. The final fade brings us back to the present.

It might evoke a nightmare coming to an end, prompting us to imagine how this generation will behave two decades later.

That's one way to interpret it, but I limit myself to showing a slice of life between 1913 and 1914. For me, everything ends with the narrator's final sentence: "I never saw anyone from the village again." He says nothing about what happened afterward. And neither do I. It's up to the viewer to reflect on such things.

Thanks to the distancing effect created by the voiceover of the schoolteacher, whose tone suggests a certain age, the film comes across as a warning against the possible resurgence of a future ideology, potentially as destructive as Nazism or Stalinism.

Exactly. The narrator is old enough to have lived through Nazism and probably other forms of extremism, like the Baader-Meinhof group. As I mentioned, I met Ulrike Meinhof in 1970 when I was working as a script editor for television. Raised in a very religious environment, she was very much a product of her Protestant upbringing and displayed great moral rigour. Having grown up in that Protestant culture myself, I had always associated it with a certain austerity, but it was through Meinhof that I made the connection between this moral rigour and the danger of acting fanatically in the name of a cause. In a way, that encounter may even have been the origin of *The White Ribbon*'s screenplay.

Your direction of The White Ribbon *alternates between functional tracking shots, classic shot-reverse shot and longer takes, which gives the film a quasi-musical rhythm.*

Yes, but this rhythm was established in the scriptwriting phase. When I later break down the film shot by shot, I simply follow what I have written. For me, every situation described naturally calls for its own distinct visual approach. For example, a scene involving children—like the one we discussed, in which Rudolf learns of his mother's death—could only be shot in shot/reverse shot. I would never have achieved such truthful performances in a single long take. The same applies to all scenes involving non-professional actors. As for tracking shots, I only used them to follow people moving across the village square or along paths. It's quite a straightforward approach.

Has your passion for music helped shape the rhythm of your story-telling?

Rhythm is something you either have in you or you don't. It's hard to teach. This is something I see very clearly with my students. Some have an innate sense of how to structure a script. Unlike directing actors, which you can learn by doing, rhythm takes a particular kind of talent. It's like singing: you either know how to do it or you don't. It's hard to explain, but as soon as I've written a scene, I already know how to film it. Adjustments are sometimes needed depending on the location, but in the studio, I have the sets built according to my shot breakdown. In *The White Ribbon*, when Martin fetches the cane with which the pastor will punish him, I wanted that to be one long shot, slowly building tension. Christoph Kanter and I designed the set around the camera movement.

Were there any scenes where you used multiple cameras?

Just one: the scene near the end with the schoolteacher and the pastor's two children. A three-person shot/reverse setup is tricky to edit because each actor moves slightly differently, making the cuts harder to match. Most of the time, I prefer to use a single camera. With two, you have to pull back to avoid catching the

Rainer Bock in *The White Ribbon*.

other in the frame, and that often means sacrificing some of the scene's intensity.

The front-facing close-up, which lets us really get into a character's inner world, is a signature of your filmmaking, one pushed to perfection in The White Ribbon.

Bergman had systematised this technique long before I was using it.

Bergman feels like a significant influence on The White Ribbon. *Beyond the use of close-ups, the film evokes certain compositions from his 1963 film* Winter Light. *In the scene where the pastor hesitates to give communion to his daughter, for example, the medium close-up of Burghart Klaussner, centred in the frame, with a slightly blurred large cross to his right, resembles Bergman's imagery. Would you count* Winter Light *among the Bergman films that influenced you?*

Yes, it deeply impressed me when I first saw it, just like *The Virgin Spring*, *The Silence* and *Through a Glass Darkly*, but I wasn't consciously referring to it in *The White Ribbon*. The sense of austerity you noticed comes really from the use of black and white. *Caché* is just as rigorously framed as *The White Ribbon*, but it's less noticeable because it's in colour. It's no coincidence that Christian Berger was nominated for an Oscar for *The White Ribbon*'s cinematography. In black and white, image composition becomes

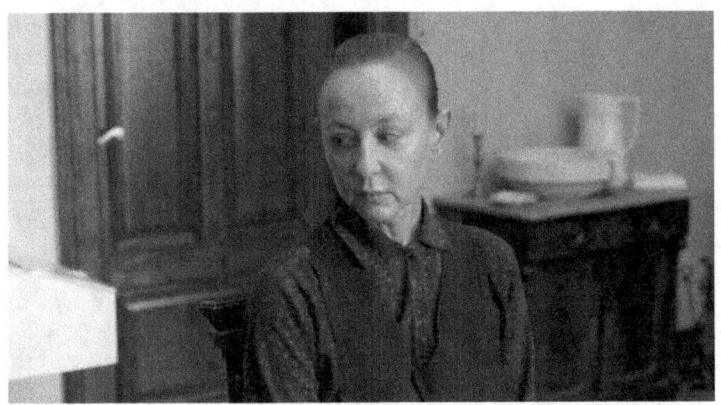

Susanne Lothar in *The White Ribbon.*

much clearer and, therefore, more striking. Bergman's greatest films are his black-and-white ones. If no one ever talks about the cinematography of *Scenes from a Marriage*—which I greatly admire for being his least pretentious and most brilliantly acted film—it's because it's in colour, making everything appear more ordinary.

The lighting in The White Ribbon *is impressive, particularly the way it plays with darkness, like the sequence where Rudolf descends the stairs and discovers his father, the doctor, molesting his sister. How did you collaborate with Christian Berger on that?*

For all my films, I follow the same method. When constructing the set, I decide where the real light sources will be placed. When designing a bedroom, for example, I choose where the bedside lamp will be, then the other light sources, before even starting work with the actors, as this affects how they move and where they stand. In fact, even in the storyboards, I mark the lamp positions using a specific colour, then work with the cinematographer and his team to refine all the details needed to achieve the sensations I want to convey on screen. For the scene you mentioned, Rudolf had to descend the stairs in darkness so that when he opened the door to his father's office, he would be suddenly struck by the light coming from inside, just as he is by what he's looking at. We put a small light source at the top of the first floor and another in the bedroom in order to minimally illuminate his movements before he finds his father and sister. In any scene that relies on darkness, you need a small ray of light to create contrast. If you simply dim the lights on set, everything turns grey, and the effect is lost. It's a difficult effect to achieve. In the scene where the schoolteacher, sitting at the harmonium, is visited by Eva after being dismissed, the light from his oil lamp wasn't strong enough to illuminate him when he got up to join the young woman, and we spent half a day testing solutions before finally figuring it out: follow the schoolteacher's movement with a Chinese lantern fitted with a light. This trick created unrealistic shadows on the wall which we had to correct digitally. In the scene where the baroness plays the piano accompanied by the flutist, we enhanced the light from the two candles with a spotlight placed above the actors, and then, in post-production, removed the patch of light it cast on the carpet.

You give as much importance to sound as to image. This is especially striking in The White Ribbon, *particularly in the outdoor countryside scenes, where we hear a multitude of sounds: wind rustling through the leaves, birdsong, chickens clucking, flies buzzing... How do you approach the sound mix?*

We always start with the live sound recorded during filming. If the dialogue is good, we keep it, but everything else is redone in post-production. In exterior scenes, microphones never capture the sound of wind very well. We look for existing sounds to replace it, or, if the sound engineer has enough time, he records isolated sounds corresponding to the various sources visible on screen, including the wind. Everything is recorded on separate tracks so we can adjust the intensity and volume of each sound during mixing. We amplify a bird's song here and lower the sound of a fly there. It's all a question of nuance. I remember asking for a character's swallowing to be clearly audible, but not too pronounced, because that tiny sound contributed discreetly to the emotional tension. It's about finding the right level for every sound, which takes time. We spent two months on the mix of *The White Ribbon*, whereas on my first films, because we didn't have the money, the process was finished in a week or so. You also need a technician with a good ear, as well as the patience and willingness to follow me down this path. Jean-Pierre Laforce is brilliant because he has the discipline and never stops until the job is done right. We're always experimenting, trying out sounds that have no real-world equivalent. We might take the sound of an eagle in flight and double its speed to see if it produces the effect I'm looking for. In *71 Fragments*, in the scene where the father gets up at night to check on his sick child,

The White Ribbon.

I thought that, in absolute silence, it would be interesting to hear the sound of a branch tapping against the window. We went down to the garden, cut a branch, and tested different ways to produce that sound. For me, foley technicians are true artists. They arrive with a suitcase full of seemingly worthless objects and create amazing sounds from them. Of course, all of this requires preparation. Jean-Pierre and Guillaume Sciama, my sound engineer since *Time of the Wolf*, have always delivered for me.

So unlike filming, improvisation can play a relatively significant role in sound mixing?

Yes and no. We only add things and improve what already exists, though sometimes that can go quite far. If I don't like a line of dialogue — even a single syllable within a word — we search for an equivalent from another take. We can even change the meaning of a line by selecting a take where a key word is delivered with different inflection.

Do you create a storyboard for the sound?

No, but after editing the images, I go through the film with the editor, the sound engineer and the mixers to identify areas where the soundtrack can be improved. Guillaume and Jean-Pierre then have a few weeks to gather all the sounds we'll need. They present me with different recorded tracks and we decide what works through trial and error. Of course, not everything can be anticipated, but I generally know what kind of atmosphere I want for each scene. We also have to consider dubbed versions, where the sound design has to be adjusted to match different dialogue tracks. If a glass is placed on a table during a certain line, we have to ensure the sound is on a separate track, and sometimes we remove sounds entirely. This was the case in the nightmare scene in *Amour*, where, when Trintignant opens the door and steps into the hallway, I removed almost all the ambient noise. Since that's unusual, it unsettles the viewer and forces them to pay closer attention. It's a lot of work, but I find it much more enjoyable than filming, which is always stressful.

Do you have a personal sound library that you make use of from one film to another?

No, but I have occasionally reused an exceptional sound, including the snoring of the mother in *The Seventh Continent* after she takes pills to kill herself. It was a real recording of a dying person that Karl Schlifelner discreetly captured in a hospital. A sound like that can't be recreated.

Sound mixing also allows you to edit sounds as you would images, to create dissonance, for example in the scene where the school-teacher plays the harmonium to comfort Eva, you transition to—

—the grunt of a pig in a farmer's pen. I liked doing that. I thought it matched the rhythm and prevented the scene from becoming overly sentimental. It was also a good way of introducing the farmer's refusal to forgive his son for destroying the baron's cabbage field.

The beautifully raspy voice of the narrator, performed in German by Ernst Jacobi, contributes to the film's musicality. Did you give him any particular direction?

That's his natural voice. I chose him for two reasons: first, because there aren't many elderly actors still working in German-speaking countries; and second, because his voice was a credible contrast to Christian Friedel's unusually high-pitched voice as the young schoolteacher. A radio director I know suggested Jacobi. At first, I hesitated because he had been offended when I offered him a small role in *Funny Games*, as the neighbour who helps Mühe launch a boat. He had sent me an angry letter, chastising me for offering him such an insignificant role, so I feared another rejection,

Haneke directing *The White Ribbon*.

but he accepted. He found the script very moving, and said it reminded him of his youth. We worked together in Munich for three days. I knew the exact duration of each piece of narration and timed him with a stopwatch. If it was too long or too short, we re-recorded it until it fit perfectly. It wasn't easy, and I often had to calm him down when he got frustrated when he made a mistake, but the result was worth it. He even recorded the text for the American release. The Americans didn't dub the film, but they wanted the voiceover to be in English, with a German accent. That seemed believable to me; the narrator could have emigrated to America. Jacobi put in a lot of effort, since he wasn't as comfortable in English. We hired a coach, and it took him nearly a week. All for nothing, in the end, since the Americans scrapped the whole thing.

We liked Jean-Louis Trintignant's voiceover in the French version.

It was Margaret Menegoz's idea to approach him because he has a beautiful voice and also because she knew I had always wanted to work with him. He was directed by Hervé Icovic, who handled the dubbed version and had previously supervised the French versions of my films. For *The White Ribbon*, Icovic sent me tapes with three voice options for each role. I was the one who chose Daniel Mesguich, Dominique Blanc, Jean-François Stévenin, Didier Flamand and the others. I was worried about the children, but got lucky because the ones playing the doctor's children, as well as little Gustav, the pastor's youngest son, were bilingual and dubbed themselves.

When the characters play music, it's Schubert, Schumann and Bach.

As should be expected in one of my films. On his harmonium, the schoolteacher plays a piano piece by Schumann until he's interrupted by Eva, who has been dismissed by the baroness. To cheer her up, he then plays Bach's *Sicilienne*. At the piano and on the transverse flute, the baroness and the tutor play a passage from a variation on a lied from *Die schöne Müllerin* [*The Beautiful Miller's Daughter*]. It was a variation I didn't know very well, as I'm not a great fan of the flute. I originally wanted a violin, but Michael Kranz, the actor chosen to play the tutor, didn't know how to play one, and that would have been obvious right away. He didn't know how to play the flute either, but it was easier to fake. Even so, it still took him several weeks of rehearsals to get the gestures right. As for the other music, there are also the dances during the village celebration, all of which are period dances from the region, the handwritten scores of which we found in the area. We only allowed ourselves one liberty: to re-orchestrate them for several instruments, even though they had originally been written for solo violin.

We haven't yet talked about your ultimate prize, the Palme d'Or. Can you tell us about your Cannes experience?

It was very enjoyable, although I was very nervous, as I always am when selected for Cannes. For me, the most dramatic experience was *Funny Games*, not so much because it was my first time in competition but because of the uproar that followed the screening. Some audience members screamed in fury, others shouted "Bravo!" I knew there and then that I wouldn't be winning any awards, but I still had a good time, and when everyone applauded after the screening of *The Piano Teacher*, I wondered where I had gone wrong. During the screening of *The White Ribbon*, I sensed that the reaction would be positive and I was right, but I also knew that after several minutes of applause, I would start to feel uncomfortable. I never know how to react in those kinds of situations, even though, of course, it makes me very happy. After the official screening on Thursday, I stayed nearby, at the Hotel du Cap Eden Roc in Cap d'Antibes, hoping we might win an award. On Sunday, the day of the awards ceremony, Margaret Menegoz called to tell

Haneke winning the Palme D'Or for *The White Ribbon.*

me that we had won something, but we didn't know what. For *The Piano Teacher*, I had been asked to bring back Isabelle Huppert and Benoît Magimel. It turned out to be for their acting awards, but since I was also summoned, we wondered if we had won the Palme. I later found out that there had been intense debate among the jury members. Some were very opposed to my film, but those who defended it argued that if I wasn't given the Palme, I should at least receive the Grand Prix, and my actors should win the acting prizes. Four years later, in 2005, I received the Best Director award for *Caché*, and for *The White Ribbon* I wondered if I would receive one of those prizes again. During the ceremony, as each award was announced, the tension mounted, and I only started to relax once the Grand Prix went to Jacques Audiard's *A Prophet*, which was the favourite of the French press. Winning the Palme d'Or was incredible. But honestly, just being invited to Cannes, and especially receiving a prize, is already an immense joy.

The White Ribbon was honoured multiple times, winning a Golden Globe and a European Film Award in Berlin, always edging out Audiard at the last moment.

Audiard is very likable and has a terrific sense of humour. At the Oscars, where we were both nominated for Best Foreign Film, we were seated at the end of the row, one behind the other. At the beginning of the ceremony, he joked that once again he had put on his tuxedo just to celebrate me, and when we found out that the Oscar was going to Juan José Campanella's *The Secret in Their Eyes*, he turned around and said to me, "Loser, loser!" That was funny, and actually really quite charming.

Thirteen

A second Palme d'Or — *Amour,* inspired by my aunt's death — Choosing a closed setting over fake naturalism — Cutting off the music — I recreated my parents' apartment — How to film a terrifying nightmare — Reuniting with Darius Khondji — The mystery of Jean-Louis Trintignant and the courage of Emmanuelle Riva — Pigeon takes flight — Unblocking inspiration

At the 2012 Cannes Film Festival, fate had it that Amour *was competing against, among others, Jacques Audiard. How were you experiences of your second Palme d'Or?*

It was obviously very gratifying, but until the very last moment, I had no idea what prize I would receive. As you know, after *The Piano Teacher* won the Grand Prix and the acting awards, the festival changed its rules regarding multiple prizes, and when Margaret Menegoz informed me that the film was among the winners, she added that Nanni Moretti, the jury president, requested that I bring my two lead actors, Jean-Louis Trintignant and Emmanuelle Riva. He explained his reasoning when he presented us with the Palme and again during the jury's press conference.

Upon receiving your Palme, you stated that Amour *is "in some way an illustration of the promise" that you and Susie made to each other, should one of you ever find yourselves in the same situation as Riva's character. Is that what pushed you to make the film?*

I don't think so. I had two motivations: my desire to work with Jean-Louis Trintignant and my interest in the subject. I was deeply affected by the suicide of my aunt, who had raised me. That's really what got me thinking seriously about the topic. The main theme of the script isn't death or old age, it's the question of how to cope with the suffering of a loved one. A year before she died, my aunt, then 92, attempted suicide by taking sleeping pills. I arrived in time

Haneke, with Emmanuelle Riva and Jean- Louis Trintignant,
winning the Palme D'Or for *Amour*.

to save her. When she woke up in her hospital bed and saw me, she
reproached me and asked, "Why did you do this to me?" Before
that first attempt, she had asked me to help her die, but I told her
I couldn't because I was her heir, which meant I might have gone
to prison. But mostly I didn't help her commit suicide because I
wouldn't have had the strength to. She found her own way, and I
intervened in time, but for her second attempt, she waited until I
was away at a festival, and that time, she succeeded.

Was she seriously ill?

She suffered from excruciating rheumatism. She lived alone in her apartment and was determined not to end up in a nursing home. She was fully lucid, but every morning, it became harder and harder for her to get up, and she feared her condition would worsen. She said she was tired, that there was no hope that things would improve, and she didn't want to go on living that way—which is what Emmanuelle Riva's character experiences in *Amour* and what Trintignant's character struggles to accept. It's an incredibly difficult situation to endure.

Amour (2012)

A team of emergency responders forces its way into an apartment. In a bedroom lies the corpse of an elderly woman, surrounded by flowers placed around her head on the pillow. In a concert hall, Georges and Anne, a couple in their eighties, await the beginning of the performance. After the show, they visit the pianist, Alexandre, in his dressing room before heading home, still enchanted. But upon their return, they find an unpleasant surprise: the lock to their apartment has been tampered with. The next morning, during breakfast, Anne suffers a stroke. Their daughter, Eva, who lives abroad, visits her parents. Her father tells her that after undergoing tests, her mother underwent surgery that that went badly, and that she is now paralysed on her right side. Eva is overwhelmed by the situation. Georges takes care of his wife every day. During a surprise visit, Alexandre, the young piano prodigy and Anne's former student, is shaken to see her in this state. Anne struggles more and more with her condition and attempts suicide. Some time later, Anne suffers another stroke, this time leaving her bedridden and nearly speechless. Eva is notified, but she can only offer advice that proves futile. Her father tells her that her concern is of no use to him. He will continue to care for his wife himself. The need for a nurse becomes unavoidable. Anne refuses to accept the increasing loss of her independence. One day, Georges tells her a childhood story, then suddenly smothers her with a pillow. He buys several bouquets of flowers and cuts off the heads, then he seals

the windows. Returning to the bedroom, he hears a noise
in the kitchen. It's Anne, finishing the dishes. She invites
him to go out with her. He takes his coat and follows her.
Eva returns to her parents' now empty apartment.

*Why did you choose to open the film with the death of Riva's char-
acter?*

It's a way of creating tension, a technique I used in *71 Fragments*,
where the audience is told at the outset that a series of murders
has taken place. I remember Veit Heiduschka, the producer of that
film, shouting at the end of the first screening: "This is crazy! You
can't reveal the ending right at the start!" But it isn't as if I invented
anything new. It's a common device.

In Amour, *you opted for a closed setting. Almost the entire film
takes place in the couple's apartment.*

Because artistically, it's more interesting. I wanted to steer clear
of the kind of false naturalism that comes from showing hospital
rooms and medical treatments. That belongs strictly to television
drama. What interested me was depicting the internal conflicts that
arise from watching someone you love suffer.

The apartment feels like a kind of love nest.

That's how most elderly people live, just like Jacques Brel describes
so heartbreakingly in his song *Les Vieux*. I would even say that
they are forced to stay together because no one else really understands them. That's what I show in the film through the character
of the daughter, played by Isabelle Huppert, who shows up full
of good intentions that don't help in the slightest. I'm not judging
her. She feels responsible for her parents, but she's at a loss and she
falls back on clichés that don't help anyone.

*Alexandre, the young pianist, isn't very comfortable with illness
either.*

He never expected to find his former teacher in a wheelchair, and
is clearly overwhelmed. He is just as unsettled when she asks him
to play the piece she had once taught him, especially since, at that
moment, his professional pride takes over because he hasn't played
that piece in a long time and he fumbles through it. His behaviour

reflects the discomfort that younger generations feel around old people. They don't know how to interact with the elderly because they're not used to it. In the past, different generations lived together, so young people were familiar with old age and its challenges. These days the elderly are more numerous, but they live out of sight.

In the postcard he sends after his visit, Alexandre at least has the courage to write: "It was a beautiful and sad moment." He refuses to ignore reality, unlike Huppert's character, to whom her father explains that they don't have time to cater to her worries and good intentions. Your direction seems to echo this idea, that there is no time for sentimentality!

And yet the elderly couple still share genuine affection. That's the gentleness of old age.

We even hear Anne say, "Life is beautiful, for so long!" It's a line that might come as a surprise in a Haneke film. It seems to signal a shift in your filmmaking since The White Ribbon, *as if you are introducing not necessarily moments of happiness but at least moments when your characters are able to enjoy life.*

From the start, I was never opposed to depicting moments of joy. I just always felt that mainstream cinema had so overused them in such an exaggerated way that it was difficult to film happiness without slipping into kitsch. The ability to portray something uplifting without falling into that trap comes with artistic maturity, which might explain why I now allow myself a bit more gentleness.

And, in so doing, more complexity.

It's not that I didn't want complexity in my early films, but my Austrian trilogy was more about presenting certain models. That didn't stop a German critic from writing a long article—one I found really quite moving—arguing that, contrary to popular belief, those three films were actually very tender because they took the protagonists' suffering seriously. But it's true that those films weren't naturalistic. *Amour* isn't either, but its characters feel more human than archetypal. That seems to be an evolution in my cinema since *Code Unknown*. In that film, as well as in *Caché*, there were already moments of tenderness, weren't there?

Zun Fern die Stele Campen

28. Bild
Bad. Vorraum. Anbau.   Innen/Dämmerung

Bad. *Licht im Bad abblände. Rest kaltes Dämmerlicht*
Georg, in Pyjamahose, mit nacktem Oberkörper, putzt sich die Zähne. Es
KLINGELT. Georg spuckt aus, wischt sich den Mund ab und geht in den

Vorraum
zur Tür.

        GEORG: Ja? Wer ist da?

Keine Antwort. Georg ist sehr irritiert. Aus dem Off ruft

        ANNA: Georg?! Was ist? Wer ist da?

Georg öffnet die Wohnungstür. Aber draußen hat sich das im Halbdunkel liegende
Treppenhaus verändert, Lift und Liftkabine existieren nicht mehr, bloß das Zugseil
pendelt noch im leeren Schacht. Wände und Treppen haben weder Verkleidung
noch Farbe, teilweise sind die Wände aufgestemmt, alles vermittelt den Eindruck
einer Baustelle. Georg ist fassungslos, versteht nicht, was passiert ist. Zögernd
verläßt er die Wohnung, macht ein paar Schritte in den Raum.
Im Off, entfernter, die beunruhigte Stimme von   *Schärfe m===i auf Georg*

        ANNA: Georg? Was ist denn?!

Georg wendet sich nach rechts, geht zögernden Schritts den Gang entlang, der sich
nach ein paar Metern erneut nach rechts in einen weiteren langen, spärlich
erleuchteten Gang öffnet. Auch das hat Georg noch nie gesehen. Es ist sehr STILL
geworden. In der Tiefe des Raumes ist der Gang mit dunklem Wasser
überschwemmt.
Georg macht ein paar Schritte in die Tiefe dieses Raums. LEISES GERÄUSCH
SEINER SCHRITTE IM WASSER.
Georg bleibt stehen. Sieht nach unten auf seine Füße. Sie stehen bis über die
Knöchel im Wasser. Darunter schimmert das schwarz-weiße Muster des
Bodenbelags durch. Das Wasser ist schmutzig, von Schlieren durchzogen.
Georg schaut fassungslos von seinen Füßen in die Tiefe das Raums. STILLE.
Da schiebt sich lautlos von hinten eine Hand vor seinen Mund und hält ihn wie im
Schraubstock. Panik.
Georgs GUTTURALES STÖHNEN wirft uns in die folgende Szene.

A script page from *Amour…*

Yes, but they seem more numerous and more fully embraced in
Amour.

Perhaps.

With the caveat that the love between this couple leaves no room
for a third party, as shown by the exchanges with the daughter and
the visits from the concierge.

Exactly. When faced with the concierge, Georges feels vulnerable
because any visit disrupts the delicate balance he has built. His
apartment is a kind of fortress. The moment a foreign body enters,
there's a risk of destabilisation.

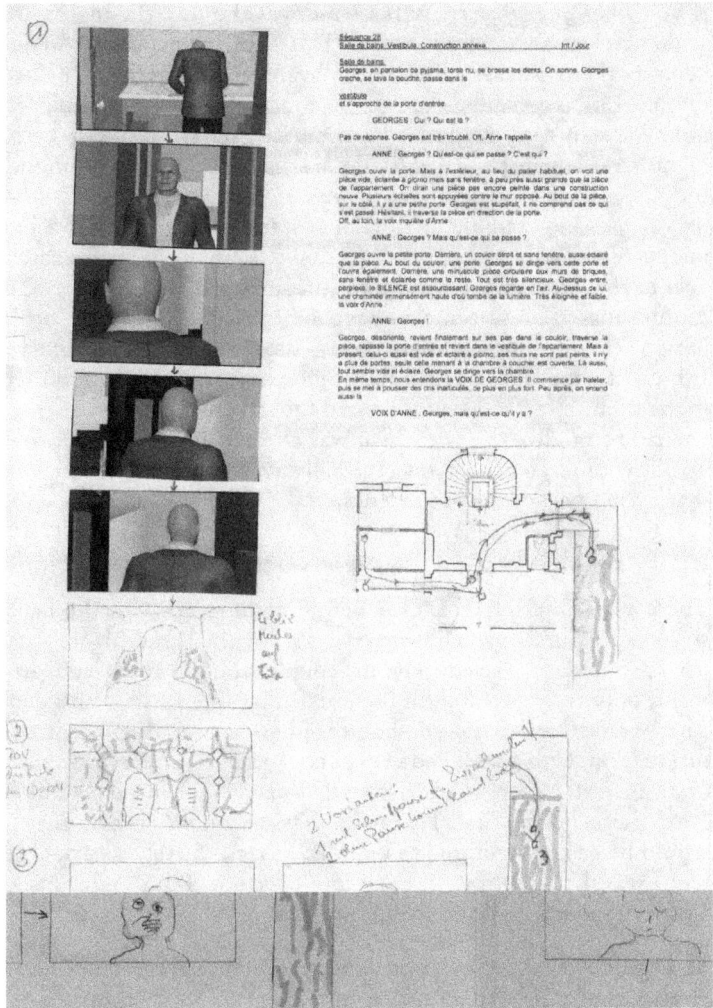

…and its translated, storyboarded version created on a computer.

That's what sets off the nightmare sequence, which isn't initially presented as such to the viewer. When Georges thinks someone has rung the bell, he goes to open the door and realises the elevator is gone, then walks down the corridor, and everything begins to feel increasingly strange until the corridor fills with water and a hand suddenly grabs him from behind, covering his mouth. The hand signifies suffocation.

If you like. But what really mattered was the way the nightmare sequence was introduced. Just as in *Caché*, when young Majid beheads the rooster—the sequence begins like a flashback before revealing itself as a nightmare—here, too, we start with an ordinary moment before it turns into something surreal. The challenge with nightmares in cinema is that if they are made too overtly symbolic, they lose their psychological power. In Hitchcock's *Spellbound* or *Vertigo*, for example, the dream sequences are artistically and intellectually impressive, but they don't feel like real nightmares. You have to remember that, to the dreamer, a dream is reality. To capture that in on screen, you have to begin with something ordinary, then slip into the nightmare. That's not easy. For *Amour*, I thought about it for a long time before settling on what you see in the film. In fact, once we finalised the structure of the sequence, we had to modify the set, which was already under construction. To allow the water to get into the hallway, we had to install a tank that wasn't part of the original design.

Originally, there wasn't going to be any water in the nightmare?

There were multiple versions. Before coming up with the hand suffocating him, I had considered a burning bed, and before that, it was something else entirely: the couple would leave their apartment, only to return and find that its entire interior had changed. That would have required shooting the scene at the end of the production, with a weekend in between to allow the crew to redecorate the set. When we finally settled on the version in the film, I was initially sceptical. I worried that it wouldn't work, that it would be too complicated to pull off. In fact, the day we shot the scene was the only time we went into overtime. But looking back, I'm very satisfied with the result.

Was this nightmare a way of creating a kind of mirror of the film's ending, which also has a dreamlike quality?

Yes, I needed the nightmare to prepare audiences for the ending. There are several scenes that work on this principle and echo each other, like when Georges listens to Alexandre's CD, and in the reverse shot we see Anne playing the piano, even though we just saw her bedridden. The audience is momentarily puzzled before understanding, when Georges turns off the CD.

Did Emmanuelle Riva have to learn the piano for that shot?

She had to learn all the movements to play like a real musician. On set, she was really playing the piano, but what we hear on the soundtrack is the performance by Alexandre Tharaud.

What is she playing? A piece from Alexandre's album?

Yes. That album features Schubert's *Impromptus.* In the concert scene at the beginning of the film, Alexandre plays the first *Impromptu.* It's that same piece the couple listens to together when they play the CD. But in the scene where Georges dreams—or remembers— Anne at the piano, she's playing the third *Impromptu.*

Why did you choose Tharaud to play her former student?

Because out of all the pianists I auditioned, he turned out to be the best actor.

During his visit, when Alexandre sits down at the piano to play Beethoven's Bagatelle *at Anne's request, you cut the scene before the piece is finished.*

As I do throughout the film.

Which anticipates the upcoming scene where Anne asks Georges to stop the CD playing Schubert's first Impromptu.

That's for a different reason. She can't bear to listen because it reminds her too painfully of what she has lost, which her husband completely understands. Going back to your earlier point, I wanted every piece of music in the film to be interrupted. In this film, the music is always cut short.

Is that why Georges himself stops playing too, when he is at the piano?

Yes, but what's going on in that scene is a bit different again. From her bed, Anne hears him playing a Bach chorale: "Ich ruf zu dir, Herr Jesu Christ, ich bitt, erhör mein Klagen!" ["I call to you, Lord Jesus Christ, I beg you, hear my cries!"] When he stops, she asks why. He doesn't answer, but we see him react, just slightly, to what she had said. Maybe he has given up praying.

The characters are music lovers because you're one yourself and know that world well.

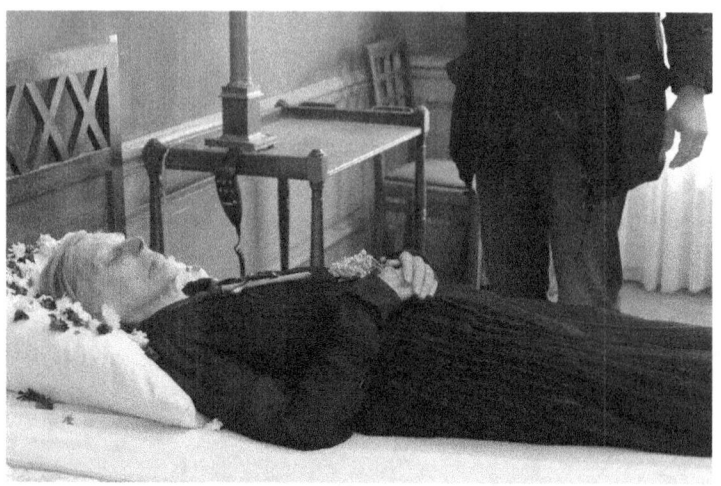

Emmanuelle Riva in *Amour.*

Yes, and it also allows me to use music within the scene itself, as in *The Piano Teacher*.

As you had done in Lemminge, *with the two children who are musicians. Did it ever even cross your mind to give them a different profession?*

It wasn't out of question, but this felt more effective, more beautiful. When you're an artist, you have a certain kind of spiritual freedom that you don't necessarily have working a desk job, and when everything falls apart, maybe the loss hits harder than it would for a businessman who has spent his life under constant stress. Of course, artists also experience pressure, but generally in a more fulfilling way.

What's surprising is that, for people who have spent their entire lives in music, we see them listening to it very little.

Musicians very often don't listen to music, just as filmmakers don't necessarily watch other people's films. My father-in-law was a musician and didn't own many records. He would listen to radio broadcasts when a great conductor like Karajan or Mitropoulos was on, but always in a very professional way, score in hand, never simply for pleasure, as I often do. It's rare for a musician to play music at home just as background noise; most can't stand it. When we have guests, Susie likes to put on music, but I always ask her not to when musicians are visiting, because it makes them uncomfortable.

Just as you never show violence directly in your films, the progression of the illness here is handled through suggestion. The sudden appearance of the IV drip suggests that Anne's condition has worsened.

I preferred to show the illness evolving through changes in the setting, rather than through the characters' behaviour or dialogue. Since the whole film takes place in one apartment, I couldn't rely on different characters and locations like I did in *The White Ribbon*. While writing the script, I had to find a new way in every scene to signal the passage of time, whether it was the same day, the next, two weeks later, or a month. I also used what's visible outside the windows, through the sheer curtains, to help with that. The whole story unfolds over about a year.

One of the strengths of the screenplay is in the subtle way you show the progression of the illness through these telling details.

The challenge was to show the illness advancing through situations and objects while still keeping it medically realistic. Early on we see Anne in a wheelchair that her husband has to push. Later, she's using a motorised one, which she gradually learns to control and which gives her a bit of independence. As part of my research, I got to know all the kinds of equipment older people rely on to get by, like that nightstand, bigger than the one she knocks over, where she can keep her medication.

This realistic approach to objects is essential for making the progression of the illness believable. But you also manage to give each one dramatic significance.

That was exactly the challenge. When adult diapers become part of her daily life, the key for me isn't to show the object itself, but rather Anne's face and the look of humiliation that comes with it.

Before writing the script, did you make a list of all the day-to-day things that someone who's had a stroke typically goes through?

Yes, but more importantly, I had to figure out the character's mindset so that each situation would feel meaningful. You can't just show daily routines that everyone is familiar with or can easily picture: washing, eating, bodily needs... Physical problems always trigger emotional reactions, and that's what I wanted to capture on film.

As the illness relentlessly progresses, you include two montage sequences, one showing the empty apartment, the other focusing on paintings.

Each of those sequences comes at a moment when, even in the writing phase, I felt I needed what in music is called a *fermata* — a pause — to give the film some air after a difficult scene. The series of shots of the empty apartment comes right after Anne is hospitalised. They show how everything can vanish in an instant, and there is an added sense of unease because it all takes place at night. In daylight, the effect wouldn't have been the same. The sequence of paintings follows the scene where Georges slaps Anne while forcing her to drink, even though she wants to die and spits the water back out. That, for me, is the most violent scene in the film, and it raises the central question: how does one cope with the suffering of a loved one? To express that, without leaving the confines of the apartment, I came up with the idea of showing paintings, large, empty landscapes or ones with two isolated figures. I knew exactly the kind of paintings I wanted, but finding them was no easy task. My production designer, Jean-Vincent Puzos, initially showed me photos of Scandinavian paintings that were perfect, but they belonged to various museums, and we couldn't borrow them for filming. Since we wanted actual canvases, not photographic reproductions, Puzos went looking for new ones. He brought back a large selection, but I rejected them all because, for obvious reasons, he had chosen inexpensive works, and it showed. In the end, we used some that were a bit pricier and looked better, but I still wish we could have used the Scandinavian ones.

Are those the paintings that decorate the apartment?

Yes, but over the course of the film, they mostly go unnoticed. If you look very closely you might recognise one or another during a panning shot, but I didn't want them to stand out until that specific montage where they all appear. The only painting that's clearly visible is the one in the bedroom, above the bed. It's also the first one that appears in that montage sequence. Initially, I had planned to show the paintings according to the time of day they depict,

Isabelle Huppert in *Amour.*

from morning to night, but that felt too symbolic, so I removed all the twilight scenes. In the end, I went for something else: a sense of space gradually opening up, with landscapes that become more and more expansive.

Was that meant as a counterpoint to the characters' inability to escape their condition? Like in The Seventh Continent, *where the sky could only appears in photographs?*

I don't want to offer an interpretation. What matters is that this series of paintings comes right after the scene with the slap, just as the montage of night shots of the empty apartment begins following her stroke. For both of these sequences, we have to move beyond simple psychological explanation and into something more existential.

You mentioned your production designer Jean-Vincent Puzos. Why didn't you work again with Christoph Kanter?

He was already tied up on a large German production. But in any case, we needed someone who knew Paris well. Puzos is Spanish, but he grew up in Paris and speaks perfect French, and he often works with American productions shooting in France. It was my cinematographer, Darius Khondji—who had already worked with him—who recommended him. I met with other production designers before hiring him, but he was the only one who came to our first meeting with a notebook full of notes and images connected to what he had read in the script. I could tell right away he was a professional. On top of that, he's very friendly and funny, and a hard worker. Working with me might have been a bit complicated for him, since he wasn't used to a director who gets involved in everything, and I don't think he always enjoyed that. He also didn't know that I always complain when I first see a set. People who know me understand it's not personal; you just need to make the changes I ask for, like repainting walls that are too dark. Still, my relationship with Puzos remained very friendly. He brought a lot to the film, including helping me develop the idea of the water and the hand that suffocates Georges in the nightmare scene. If I make another film in France, I would definitely want to work with him again.

His set design is phenomenally realistic in Amour.

He even had a real oak bookshelf made. Usually in film, you use cheap wood and paint it so it looks like oak onscreen. That kind of realism thrilled me. I personally arranged the books on the shelves by subject and in alphabetical order. Even though there's no shot where you can read the titles on the spines, I'm convinced that this sort of detail registers on screen. Similarly, Puzos found period windows to install in the set, and he laid down a real antique parquet floor. Since I had specified that I didn't want the floor to creak when the dolly rolled over it, he added several layers of soundproofing material.

Everything on that set seems to really work.

Even the elevator. The set was built four or five metres above the studio floor so the elevator could actually go up and down. You see it arriving in the opening sequence, when the policeman enters the apartment. We had to commit fully to realism so that nothing would feel like a studio set. Puzos works with a brilliant painter at aging the furniture, and Susie worked on the set dressing. She knows what I like and was the one who arranged the paintings, the ornaments, every little decorative detail.

There are lots of photographs in the living room. What do they show?

I found two of them online, pictures of Rubinstein and Horowitz pulling funny faces, in the spirit of that famous portrait of Einstein sticking out his tongue. There's also a photo of Cortot, another

Alexandre Tharaud and Jean-Louis Trintignant in *Amour.*

pianist, several autographs from composers, and some family photos. For those, as well as the ones in the album that Anne flips through, we used personal photos that the actors brought in. Emmanuelle had many, whereas Jean-Louis mostly had film stills, including some with his real-life wife, so we replaced her face with Emmanuelle's. We also used a photo of Isabelle Huppert at fourteen, and a few of Emmanuelle as a teenager.

How did you decide on the layout of the apartment?

The general layout is actually based on my parents' apartment, including the small room next to the kitchen. I chose that setup before writing the script because it was easier for me to imagine scenes in a space I already knew well. Whenever I had a new idea, I immediately knew how to incorporate it into the setting. That familiarity with the space was a real source of inspiration when I was writing.

Could you give us some concrete examples?

It was by recreating the long hallways of my parents' apartment that I got the idea for those extended shots of Georges slowly making his way back and forth whenever Anne asks him to fetch something. The prominence of the small side room also comes from something real, which is that after my mother died, my stepfather locked up their bedroom and moved into that little room.

Did your production designer point out potential structural or stylistic differences between Parisian apartments and the kind you knew in Austria?

Not really. The layout of the spaces is pretty much the same. The furniture is different, of course, but its arrangement within the rooms is very similar. Essentially, our set corresponds to a kind of apartment you find both in Paris — in Haussmann-era buildings — and central Vienna.

But surely you didn't recreate your parents' apartment in such detail only out of convenience.

Maybe it made the whole thing more emotional for me.

Perhaps this is reinforced by you giving some of your own memories to Georges, like the story about summer camp.

The summer camp memory he tells Anne before killing her is something I actually lived through, just like the story about the cinema that he recounts in the kitchen. But that's what we always do when we write: we draw on events that happened to us personally, things we have thought about at one time or another. Anything else and you risk falling into cliché. I never feel the need to point out which parts of my films come from my private life. The story told in *Amour* isn't that of my parents, even if my mother also tried to commit suicide several times.

Suicide is a recurring theme in your films, but here it's framed through the lens of euthanasia.

I wasn't especially looking to deal with that issue, but, of course, the film does raise the question of whether people have the right to end their lives. The character of Georges is more ambiguous. I'm not saying he's right or wrong; it isn't my place to judge, but his wife says it very clearly: she wants to die, and she can't do it herself. His promises — that he will take care of her, that she will get better — don't help at all, as is often the case in situations like this. That's what interested me: how do you handle something like this, even with the best intentions in the world? Did he already know, when he walked into the bedroom, that he was going to kill her? Maybe, maybe not. It's up to the viewer to ask the question and decide.

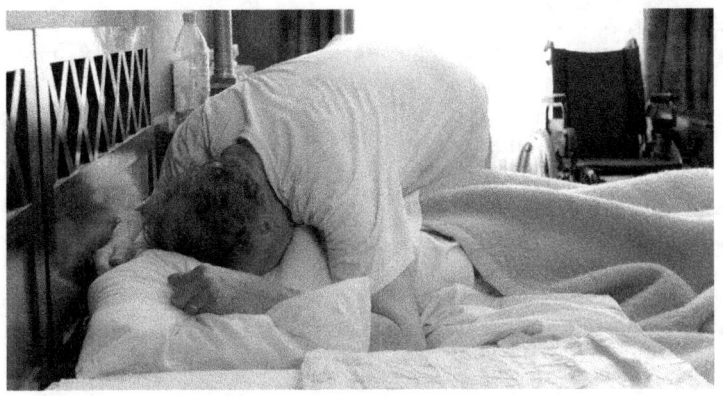

Emmanuelle Riva and Jean-Louis Trintignant in *Amour.*

Which explains why you filmed that scene in a single, continuous shot. When the husband picks up the pillow, it becomes a genuine act of love. He is finally giving her what she asked for.

There you go again, interpreting…

But you invite that interpretation by showing such a deeply moving gesture. When Georges suffocates Anne with the pillow, he buries his own head in it, as much to increase the effectiveness of the act as to offer her one final embrace.

That's one way of seeing it, but the reality was more mundane. Jean-Louis had broken his hand a few days earlier, and we had to take that into account. In the other scenes, it was enough to conceal his swollen hand, but for the suffocation scene, he had to exert a certain amount of physical strength. We had to find a way to make the scene credible without him having to use his injured hand too much. Several solutions were explored. At first, we made a firm pillow with a hole in it so Emmanuelle could breathe, but it turned out to be too hard, and if we had used it, it would have bruised her face. Fortunately, I was once again filming the scenes in chronological order, and that gave us time to rehearse, with my assistant and I taking turns playing Georges and Anne. On the day of the shoot, we finally found the right position: once the pillow was placed on Emmanuelle's head, Jean-Louis would lean on his left elbow, giving her enough time to turn her face to the side to breathe. Then he could press down on the pillow with his whole body, softening the pressure with his right hand resting on the bed, while giving the illusion of pressing even harder with his head. That's how the effect became more striking than if he had simply pushed with both hands. Jean-Louis was extraordinary. On top of the physical demands of the scene, he also had to deliver the film's longest monologue right before. We did three takes of that single-shot scene. I chose the third, which was perfect. By the time we finished that take, there was a very real emotional charge in the atmosphere.

How did you work with Darius Khondji, your cinematographer, on the lighting?

I wanted realistic lighting, so he opted for a setup with lights that could be adjusted electronically and quickly. He worked very closely with Jean-Vincent Puzos. One of the reasons we built the set elevated above the studio floor was also to accommodate the green screen outside the windows, so we could have depth of field lit by lights mounted at the top of the set. There was a courtyard visible through the kitchen window that we constructed on set at the bottom of a ten-metre-deep pit.

Did you run camera tests?

We spent a long time discussing formats. Should we shoot on traditional analogue film or digitally? I was on the fence, but Darius favoured digital because he had access to a brand-new camera, the Alexa RAW, which was supposed to offer higher resolution than anything available previously. We tested the camera for a full day, and while I wasn't really convinced because the focus was off, Darius was enthusiastic. After what I had gone through in post-production on *Caché* and *The White Ribbon*, I was very wary of shooting on digital. I didn't want to be experimenting on this film; it had to work smoothly, without delays. Darius kept insisting that with this camera everything would move quickly, that we would get a final image immediately on set and would just have to tweak it slightly in grading, so I finally gave in. But Roman Polanski, who was doing the same tests at the same time for *Carnage*, was smarter and gave up on the Alexa in favour of shooting on film. Throughout the shoot, we faced enormous problems. Every time I looked at the dailies, I thought they looked awful: out of focus, with off-colour tones. It was a disaster. Still, we managed to put together a decent first cut by sharpening the whole thing. Then we had to go through very precise colour grading. I usually do this

Haneke on the set of *Amour.*

with the cinematographer, but Darius and I had argued so much about image sharpness that going through and discussing every shot together would have taken weeks. I never thought the image was sharp enough, and at one point even went to an ophthalmologist to check my eyesight. It turns out my vision was perfect. In the end, I let Darius do his own pass on the grading, then I did mine the way I wanted, here in Vienna, and he came in a for a few days to take a look. I had done the grading for the American remake of *Funny Games* without him because he wasn't available. That way of working isn't unusual. Most of the time, cinematographers go straight from one shoot to another and only have a few days to review the final image.

How important is colour grading to you?

Traditionally, grading focuses on colour itself, but it also plays an important role in shaping dark scenes. Jürgen Jürges, the cinematographer of *Time of the Wolf*, lit the scenes too brightly out of fear that nothing would be visible, so it was me who, during grading, removed much of that light. Nowadays, with digital, you can do almost everything. You can remove blemishes, erase a painting, replace it with another, and, of course, adjust the lighting. That wasn't the case before. That said, digital has its downsides, especially when, on set, you film something and say to yourself, "We'll fix that in post…" You can end up wasting a lot of time thinking that way. Still, it should be acknowledged that in terms of sharpness, digital technology allows improvements that were impossible in the old days. If I had filmed you in the past, and in the rushes noticed that you were slightly out of focus, I would have had to draw a small circle around you to increase the contrast and sharpen the image. If you had moved, I would have had to correct that slight blur frame by frame. Today, it's enough to mark a single point on your faces, and the machine—like a military drone locked on to a moving target—will follow that point, sharpening the image even when you're moving. We used that technique extensively for *The White Ribbon*. For *Amour*, to get the image as sharp as we needed it, we had to increase the contrast in every shot where the characters were too far from the camera. That required using a noise reduction filter because when you increase contrast, you also increase visual noise, especially in dark scenes. In the end I was satisfied with the result, but I decided never to use a video camera again.

In Amour, *your entire direction revolves around the two actors. Did you know they had already worked together?*

Yes, just once, in a short segment of an Italian film I didn't know [Gianni Puccini's *Io uccido, tu uccidi* (1965)], which they themselves had more or less forgotten. It was Riva who told me about it one day, over lunch.

Why were so determined to work with Trintignant?

Because he's an actor I've always liked very much. I have forever been fascinated by him. Like I said about Daniel Auteuil, Trintignant gives the impression that he's hiding something. Besides his looks and talent, there is something indecipherable about him. Maybe it's that famous voice of his that everyone always praises. For me, it's always been his eyes. When he looks at you, it feels like he's really *seeing* you, and that can be quite unsettling. It's probably where some of his quiet power comes from, the kind you see in his face, whether in *Z*, where he exudes great authority while remaining calm, or in *And God Created Woman*, where behind the seemingly naïve young man there's a kind of deep, inexplicable knowledge. That's the miracle of his personality and the hallmark of a great actor: being able to bring out things that no one else can. And now, with the face of someone who has lived such a long life, he has a beauty and richness that you never tire of looking at.

The close-ups, including, at the end of the film, the stubble on his unshaven face, really emphasise how time has left its mark.

We wanted to show how, at that point, he was becoming increasingly unkempt because he doesn't have the time or strength to take care of himself. We even added a bit of stubble digitally because after a weekend of not shaving, his beard wasn't noticeable enough.

How did you choose Riva?

I had auditioned lots of French actresses for the role of the mothers in *The Piano Teacher* and *Caché*, so I set about doing it all over again for *Amour*, but with the advantage of being able to eliminate straight away those who clearly weren't right. I had noticed Riva back when *Hiroshima mon amour*, one of my favourite films, and a cult film for my generation of Austrians in the 1960s, came out. I always thought she was an extraordinary actress, but after Resnais' film, she more or less disappeared from view here in Austria. For *Amour*, I watched excerpts of films featuring other actresses of the same age, but none of them really fit, and I kept coming back to my memory of Emmanuelle. As they aged, many French actresses became precious grandes dames, but Emmanuelle remained strikingly beautiful, and she was exactly who I needed for the film. I auditioned several other actresses, who were good, but Emmanuelle stood out and I quickly cast her. I'm very happy with her performance. Everything went smoothly during the shoot, and I think, even in terms of their physical proportions, she and Trintignant make a beautiful couple.

Which scene did you ask her to perform for the audition?

The kitchen scene, when she has her first stroke. I thought it was the hardest to play because Anne doesn't understand what's happening to her. She tries to fight it, then tries to drink her tea, then the tears come. I always use the toughest scene in auditions, so I can be sure the actor can go all the way.

When you first presented the project to Trintignant and Riva, did they have any hesitations about what they would be required to do?

Jean-Louis outright asked me if we couldn't switch the roles, so that *he* would play the one who was ill! Emmanuelle, during our first meeting, told me how much she loved the script. When I asked

Jean-Louis Trintignant in *Amour*.

if there was anything she was afraid of, she mentioned the scene where she had to appear nude in the shower. I told her that the nudity was essential. She understood, and said she would try to experience the moment not as Emmanuelle Riva but as Anne. On the day of the shoot, after we had set up and rehearsed the shower scene, when I gave a signal to the costume assistant to remove her robe, Emmanuelle still tried to dodge it. "Do we really have to do this?" she asked. When I reminded her of our earlier conversation, she didn't push back.

You shot the scene so that while it's clear that Riva is naked, the nurse's body shields her from view.

That scene was genuinely hard for Emmanuelle to shoot. She complained of being cold, even though we had heated the set, and I filmed as quickly as possible to reduce her discomfort. I did two fairly long takes so I would have enough material to choose from. It wasn't the kind of scene I could direct down to every detail. I had asked the actress playing the nurse to shield Emmanuelle's body as much as possible, but not entirely, so it wouldn't feel fake. Likewise, for the toilet scene where we see her underwear pulled down, we had to find an angle that was clear enough for the audience to understand what's happening, without making it feel crude. Shooting those scenes was a very courageous professional act on Emmanuelle's part, proof of someone who loves her craft and is fully aware of her responsibilities. But I think she still took pleasure in making this film. In fact, she made a connection between the titles of Alain Resnais' film and mine, saying: "It's a

Emmanuelle Riva in *Amour.*

lovely coincidence that between my first film and my last is the word *amour.*"

Was the title Amour *difficult to come up with?*

It took a while. I couldn't really call the film *Les Vieux* [*The Old People*] because of the Jacques Brel song, so I made a list. First was *Ces deux* [*These Two*], which someone corrected to *Ces deux-là*, but I didn't really like it. Then came *Quand la musique s'arrête* [*When the Music Stops*] because, as we have discussed, music is being constantly interrupted in the film, but that felt a bit too sentimental. Then, during a lunch with Margaret Menegoz, the word *amour* was mentioned, and Trintignant thought it would be a perfect title. He felt it captured the whole film. I was immediately convinced, but would never have dared to use that title for a traditional love story. In fact, it turns out that no one had. I checked online, and under the title *Amour* found only a Belgian short film from 1922, and nothing else since, except for Luca Guadagnino's 2009 film *Amore*, with Tilda Swinton.

How did you work with Trintignant? Did you shoot many takes?

Not many, even though, given his age, Jean-Louis sometimes had memory or mobility issues. We took the actors' age into account in the production schedule, spreading the shoot out over eight weeks to allow for regular breaks.

What kind of direction did you give Trintignant for the scene where he tries to catch the pigeon with the blanket?

We shot two setups — one in the kitchen, the other when he goes out into the hallway — and used two cameras. Since the pigeon moved toward the door several times, we were able to combine different takes in the edit. It took a lot of attempts because it isn't easy to catch a pigeon, even though we scattered seeds on the floor to guide the bird's movement. For the shot where the pigeon had to fly off, I gave Jean-Louis a cane to try and shoo it away, but he was too gentle to use it effectively. Eventually he managed to catch it.

The way he caresses his wife's hand while telling her the summer camp story echoes the gesture he makes with the pigeon.

That was Jean-Louis' idea. I had only asked him to take Emmanuelle's hand. I don't think it was something he planned; it came to him spontaneously.

The first time the pigeon appears, Trintignant manages to make it fly out the window. The second, he closes all the exits and tries to catch it. Is it a symbol of death returning?

You can see it that way if you want, but you can also look at it in a more straightforward way. The first time, Georges manages to get the pigeon out, but then it comes back, and again, he gets it to fly off. It's all quite ordinary. The second time, the pigeon is stuck in the apartment because all the windows and doors are closed, except for the skylight, which is left open so air can circulate. Everything else is shut because Georges doesn't want the neighbours to smell Anne's decomposing body, so it really depends on whether you read the scene psychologically or metaphorically. Just like with the ending of the film, I leave it up to the viewer to decide.

But the ending seems very clear. When you connect it with the beginning of the film, there aren't many possible interpretations.

What's certain is that Anne is dead, but we don't know what has happened to Georges. Since we don't see him in the opening scene, anything is possible. Did he leave? Is he in the small back room? Is he dead somewhere in the apartment, or elsewhere? Did he imagine all of this? Did Anne come to get him? You're free to believe whatever you like.

To us, what seems certain is that after fulfilling his wife's final wish, Georges has nothing left but to join her—at least in his imagination—in the kitchen, where he finds her young and healthy, before leaving with her. It feels like the beginning of a new union, between love and death.

I've got nothing against that reading, but Georges isn't necessarily dead. He may have simply left, since in the opening scene we see that the front door hasn't been sealed shut. I like when very concrete details of everyday life help us get closer to the truth of a character. I made a point of showing Anne and Georges at the beginning of the film seated in the audience at a concert. They're just two people in a crowd, because their story could happen to anyone.

There is also the matter of the lock on their apartment door, which they find broken when they return from the concert. At first glance, it seems like a minor event, since nothing was stolen, but symbolically it's their happiness that has been violated. Audiences link that moment to the opening shot of the film, when the firefighters break down the front door, and, in retrospect, to Anne's stroke itself.

I can even tell you that I imagined the broken lock specifically as a trigger for the stroke. A stroke is always the result of a series of minor stresses. I remembered my aunt had a stroke after getting extremely agitated upon returning from vacation and discovering her toilet no longer worked. In itself, a damaged lock isn't a major issue, but at a certain age, it can become one. In the film, Anne doesn't sleep the following night; she's clearly preoccupied by the door, and the next morning, over breakfast, she has her stroke.

The scenes in Amour *all flow beautifully, but those of us who followed your work on the film know how complicated its genesis was. At one point, you were so stuck in the writing process that you completely abandoned the script and turned to another project. What happened?*

I was struggling with the screenplay, feeling like I just couldn't get a real grip on the subject. Then, by chance, I came across an article mentioning a Canadian film on the same theme: Léa Pool's *The Last Escape*. I immediately got the DVD and discovered how closely its story—an elderly man, increasingly ill, being cared for by his wife—resembled mine. The film shows how the illness reshapes their daily life. In the end, the family, who remain very close, organises a fishing trip for him, since he has always loved fishing. Everything is beautiful and idyllic around them when, suddenly, the old man jumps into the water. His son and wife then decide not to move, not to try and save him. In terms of its context and form, the film was quite different from mine, but on top of my writing difficulties, it really threw me off. I decided to give up completely on what became *Amour* and turn to another project, but the moment I started working on that new script, I kept thinking about the story of my elderly couple, and one day, just like that, everything just clicked, and I was able to finish the script pretty quickly.

Fourteen

A single set and a mix of eras in *Così fan tutte* — Singers expressing complex emotions — Silences and living tableaux — Pulling off a good recording — *Happy End* after scrapping *Flashmob* — The bourgeoisie of Calais — A family ensemble film — Kassovitz joins Huppert and Trintignant — Shooting on a smartphone — Finding the humanity in everyone — Unanswered questions — Tribute to editor Monika Willi — A summing-up film

The phenomenal success of Amour *meant that you ended up traveling the world with the film, including to America, where it won the Academy Award for Best Foreign Film. At the same time, you directed another opera, once again collaborating with Gérard Mortier. This was the* Così fan tutte *you had proposed to him in 2006, but which you had set aside in favour of staging* Don Giovanni *instead.*

In 2012, Mortier was set to take over as director of the New York City Opera, New York's other major opera house, after the Metropolitan, and remembered that I had once told him I wanted to direct *Così fan tutte*, so he extended an invitation. But when the budget allocated to his programming was cut by nearly half, Mortier chose to abandon the project and accept another offer from Madrid's Teatro Real, then asked if I would be interested in mounting *Così* in Madrid instead. I would have preferred New York, but I agreed.

From the outset, was the production conceived for both the Teatro Real in Madrid and La Monnaie in Brussels?

Yes, I think that was the plan. Mortier knew La Monnaie inside out, having previously run the place, where he played a significant role in turning it into a major opera house. For the Brussels revival, I had some concerns—not about the singers, who were the same

Così fan tutte.

ones we had in Madrid, but about the chorus, which is always tricky to put together locally. Luckily, I had some of the extras from Madrid re-hired, and that helped me hide a few chorus members who didn't really blend in. Some of their costumes no longer fit, so Moidele Bickel, my costume designer, made adjustments. We also had to bring in a few new extras. Around twenty made the trip from Madrid, but five or six said no, mainly because of the low pay. The Spanish extras who did come were mostly in it for the joy of being part of the show.

You worked with Bickel on The White Ribbon.

She's the only genius I've ever met in this profession. Her work was extraordinary. Sadly, she died in 2016, shortly after her partner. She was already ill and deeply affected by his death, as well as the losses of great directors she had worked with—Patrice Chéreau, Klaus Michael Grüber, Luc Bondy. She was a tireless, demanding and dedicated professional, and we got along extremely well.

The costumes in Così *span multiple eras: Fiordiligi and Dorabella are dressed in a modern style, while Don Alfonso's ensemble reflects the 18th century, as does Despina, whose costume is reminiscent of Watteau's* Gilles. *This all gives the production a timeless quality.*

That was my initial concept for the staging, which also extends to Christoph Kanter's single-set design. As I've said before regarding *Don Giovanni*, when staging a past work today, three time periods have to be considered: the era in which the story is set, the era in which the opera was composed, and the present day, when the production is created. The director's task is to find their own way of uniting these three levels in a meaningful and compelling way for the audience. It was tricky with *Don Giovanni*, but I believe I managed it. For *Così*, I started with the idea of a wealthy man hosting a costumed ball in his château to celebrate its renovation. As is typical in such events, guests interpret the dress code in their own ways. Some follow the suggestion to dress as 18th-century nobles, others arrive in modern attire.

The costumes seem to carry a certain symbolism. Fiordiligi wears a beautiful red dress, Dorabella a black outfit, and Despina, in white, is dressed as a Pierrot.

We weren't aiming for specific symbolism; the characters' outfits don't carry particular messages. Fiordiligi's red dress was chosen for aesthetic reasons. Juxtaposing her against a woman in black and another in white was purely a visual decision. It also suited their respective personalities.

Why the contrast between Fiordiligi's very feminine and sexy outfit and Dorabella's more masculine attire?

That wasn't planned. The singer, Paola Gardina, had a naturally tomboyish quality, so we decided to accentuate that by dressing her in black trousers and a jacket, contrasting with Anett Fritsch's sexy red dress and long hair.

Despina, on the other hand, directly refers to Watteau's Gilles.

Yes, but that idea really came to us only when Moidele and I saw Kerstin Avemo, who is so slim and has strikingly platinum blonde hair. We thought she could perfectly echo Watteau's painting, so we stylised her as a white Pierrot. It was a way of moving away from the usual portrayal of Despina as servant in a little tutu and apron. The Pierrot costume not only suited her but also had the advantage of being timeless and socially ambiguous. You couldn't really place it. The whole thing actually started with Despina's arias, which sound rather silly if you take them at face value, but if she's singing them to tease her partner, they suddenly get much more interesting. Similarly, I have always found it somewhat naïve when Fiordiligi and Dorabella show off their medallions, gushing over how handsome their lovers are. But if they do it to provoke Guglielmo and Ferrando, the scene gains another dimension. One

The annotated score…

provocation leads to another. What begins as a playful game turns into a trap in which they all become ensnared, victims of their own behaviour.

In your Così, *these dynamics were possible because the six main roles were played by exceptional singers.*

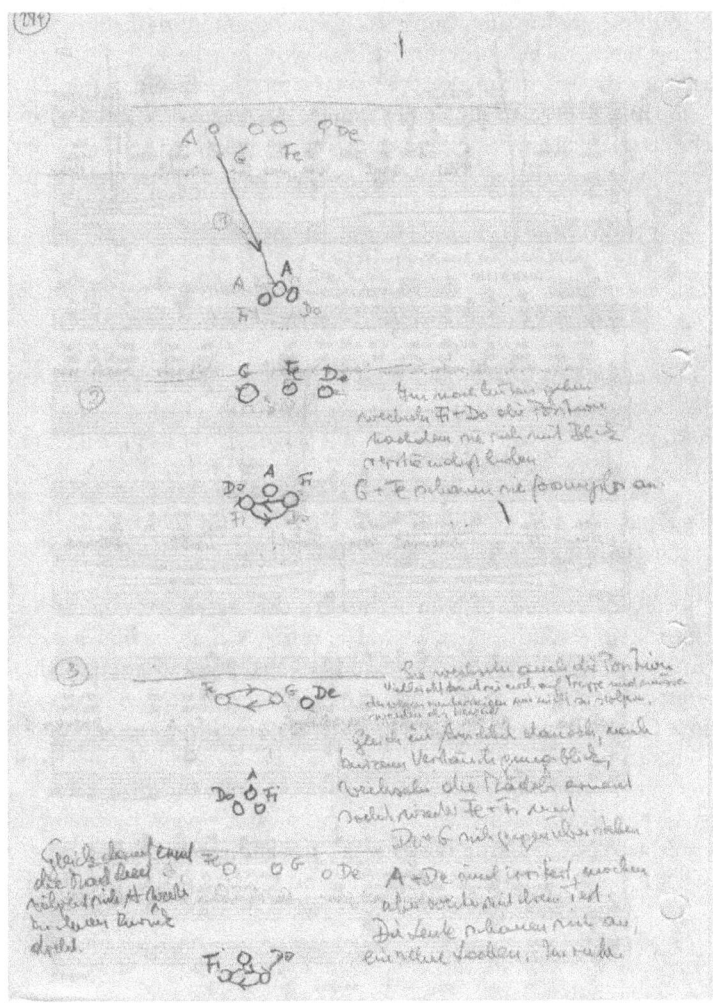

...and storyboard of *Così fan tutte.*

Yes, we were lucky to find them. Several months were devoted to auditions. Around forty singers were considered for each role by the Teatro Real's team, who assessed their voices. I selected the ones best suited to express the opera's complex emotions. For me, acting ability was a crucial requirement.

Had your performers previously acted to such an extent in an opera?

I couldn't say for sure, but it's not that common in opera. Everything tends to be approximate, and you just have to hope that the performers can make their characters believable. After *Don Giovanni*, where I struggled to achieve everything I wanted within the standard six-week rehearsal period, I demanded and was given eight weeks for *Così*. Even then, we worked seven to eight hours a day, whereas the norm is six hours, dropping to four toward the end. Gérard Mortier backed me all the way.

Do you prepare a storyboard, or at least a written breakdown for your operas, as you do for your films?

It's the same approach. At home, I listen to the music and follow the written score. In my notebook, I have the music on one page and, measure by measure, I note my staging on the opposite page, which includes precise gestures and movements for the singers.

You worked out with your performers during rehearsals all the small realistic gestures they make on stage?

Not every gesture, of course, but it's the search for nuance that interests me. With opera, it's more difficult than in film because you have to follow the music and respect its rhythm, and adapt your performance accordingly. At a given moment, you have to be in a precise place to make a specific gesture. One step too many, one second too late, and it all falls apart. You can choose to do away with all detail and just stick the performers at the back of the stage and let them sing, which is often what happens. If the singers can't act but the music is beautiful, the audience will still believe what it is seeing and hearing. But if you want to really move them, something more is needed.

Speaking of emotion, we saw Anett Fritsch, who plays Fiordiligi, crying on stage.

Yes. She and Kerstin Avemo were completely committed. They had great trust and paid great attention to detail.

At one point, you even asked her to sing while lying on the floor.

It's not as difficult as you might think. I used to believe it was, because some divas refused to do it, but it's a myth. In reality, lying down actually allows the voice to project with greater strength because the sound reflects off the floor.

One striking aspect of your staging is the contrast between the very realistic acting of the performers and the geometric compositions, where symmetry predominates.

But that's embedded in the opera itself. You can't go against the symmetrical effects in the music and libretto without weakening their impact.

The numerous movements and tableaux vivants created by the characters also highlight some beautiful lighting work, from the blue sky above the terrace to the warm yellows of the fireplace.

That was especially challenging to pull off because of reflection issues on stage caused by the large sliding glass doors of the terrace. Our German lighting designer, Urs Schönebaum, who is very well known in his field, did a magnificent job.

As with Don Giovanni, *Christoph Kanter designed a single set, despite the multiple locations indicated in* Così's *libretto.*

Kanter and I developed the general concept, and as with *Don Giovanni*, we decided to use a single set for the entire performance. Since we wanted a realistic setting, it was impossible to change sets four or five times during the opera without requiring pauses, and pauses in opera are deadly, so I had to think of a way to bring together all the different locations of the story into one unified set.

The set is somewhat reminiscent of Resnais' Last Year at Marienbad, *with the château and garden, the mirrors in the bar, the prominence of white.*

I hadn't thought of that! It's true. We have a classical-style set with modern-day characters. The background is in the style of Andrea Palladio's classical villas—columns and all—and in the foreground there's a sleek, modern fridge that actually opens and from which comes cold lighting, in contrast to the warm glow from the classical fireplace.

Even more than in your previous opera, you incorporated silences into your staging of Così.

More than in *Don Giovanni*? I don't know... But it's never for show. Silence, at the right moments, can really heighten the emotional impact of a scene. In *Così*, when Fiordiligi and Ferran

Così fan tutte.

do embrace on the floor and the others enter, the couple doesn't notice them, even though Guglielmo, Fiordiligi's fiancé, is right next to her. Their duet, which overflows with passion, ends in complete silence. No one moves during the kiss. It's a silence that speaks a thousand times louder than if the music had immediately resumed. As in other moments of the performance, silence allows the audience to fully absorb what they are witnessing.

Was conductor Sylvain Cambreling, who had already directed Don Giovanni, *on board with this?*

Yes, from the start. Initially, Thomas Hengelbrock was supposed to conduct *Così*, but he ended up unavailable. It was good to reunite with Sylvain.

You placed more emphasis on the recitatives than usual.

Così is an opera built around conversation. If you don't understand the recitatives, you're going to miss the story. They provide the meaning and drive the action forward, so instead of treating them as secondary, as is often the case, I really made them a priority. They're essential to the realism of the opera.

You also surprised us with moments where the chorus and extras suddenly freeze.

I limited that effect to two scenes: the quintet in Act I and the final quartet, the only moments where things take on a more metaphorical tone.

The Madrid stage is extremely wide, whereas the Brussels stage is much smaller. Did this pose a problem?

The Brussels stage was significantly smaller. It was particularly noticeable with the positioning of the Watteau painting, which almost disappeared into the wings. Audiences seated on the left couldn't see it, but we really had no other choice. We had to make do.

Did you have any involvement in the filming by Hannes Rossacher for the video release and television broadcast?

It was a huge disappointment. The director was known for his recordings of rock concerts, particularly for the Rolling Stones, and he had done some good work. He arrived in Madrid with twelve cameras to film three performances but he shot them all in essentially the same way, with cameras constantly in motion, which is completely unsuitable for an opera. When it came time to edit, we had very few choices, since it was almost the same footage three times over. I had trusted him and didn't want to get involved in the filming process, but when he showed me a rough cut he had put together with his editor, I was very upset. I tried working with them, but it just wasn't working. That's when I called my usual editor, Monika Willi, who, fortunately, was available. She did a remarkable job, selecting the best shots from the three performances and twelve cameras. Thanks to her, when you watch the final version, it feels like a brilliantly filmed performance, but that's entirely thanks to Monika.

Don Giovanni *wasn't recorded?*

No, because of the limited rehearsal time we had. To record something properly, you have to plan from the very beginning. Later, of course, I regretted not having a record of it, but by then it was too late. When the production was revived at the Opéra Bastille, there was never any question of recording it, but the cast had been changed without my input and I was offered an unacceptably short rehearsal period, so I refused to be involved, and the result, at least from the excerpts I saw online, didn't impress me.

After Così fan tutte, *you went back to filmmaking, but despite* The White Ribbon *and* Amour *being so acclaimed around the world, you were unable to get your next project,* Flashmob, *off the ground. What was it about? What happened?*

It was an ensemble film, like *71 Fragments of a Chronology of Chance* and *Code Unknown*, that weaved together multiple intersecting stories, culminating in a flash mob. One of these stories was inspired by a rather large woman I met who found her partners online. She told me that many black American men preferred plus-size women. I don't know why, but that's what she told me. She had experienced several unusual relationships and gave me permission to use her stories as a starting point, though I ended up reworking her character and her experiences quite significantly. Forest Whitaker agreed to play her partner, and half of the film was going to be shot in the United States, making it an American co-production. That's where things started to fall apart. I came to realise that my European producers were wary of collaborating with American studios, as they didn't want to deal with the complexities of the American system, and to protect themselves, they bumped the budget up so high that it became impossible to finance. I could have persisted, but I gave up because I had already spent two years searching for the right actress to play the main part and was uncertain if I could find anyone. You can't cast just anyone opposite Forest Whitaker. It wasn't just about finding a certain body type; I needed an actress who could match his talent. We looked in Austria and Germany, as I wanted the film to be in both German and English, but when we couldn't find an overweight actress, we expanded the search to France, with no better luck. In the end, I abandoned the project, not wanting to waste more time and with no way to push back against the producers.

How did Happy End *emerge from the impossibility of making* Flashmob?

The collection of stories in *Flashmob* formed a complex web, the elements of some of which I incorporated into the screenplay of *Happy End*. The story of Eve, for example, the teenage girl in *Happy End*, was in *Flashmob*, but in a different context. Several years ago, I read a newspaper article about a girl who had poisoned her mother and posted details online. That really stuck with me. The mother was ultimately saved thanks to some acquaintances who alerted the police. They happened to see the video on the Internet and made the connection to a woman living nearby whose health had been visibly deteriorating. What intrigued me was that this girl had been talking so openly online about what she was doing. It certainly says something about the way we live today. *Happy End* really started when I had the idea to revisit that story and combine it with my desire to work again with Jean-Louis Trintignant, who didn't have a role in *Flashmob*. The rest came together fairly quickly.

The idea was that all the characters would belong to the same family?

That was a major difference from *Flashmob*, and an added challenge, since I had to develop the story within the confines of a single family, whereas in a traditional ensemble film you have the freedom to introduce characters from different walks of life. On the other hand, the advantage was that I could bring three generations together under one roof and adhere to the classical unities of time, place and action.

Happy End (2017)

Footage filmed and narrated on a smartphone: Ève, a teenage girl, shares her hostile feelings toward her mother, whom she wants to "silence." She takes her mother's medication and tests it on her hamster. Convinced by the results, she administers a high dose to her mother, who is hospitalised in a comatose state. Thomas Laurent, her father, takes Ève in at the family's grand townhouse in Calais, where Georges, the stern patriarch, and Anne, his daughter, live. Anne runs a large public works company with her son, Pierre. Their business, already struggling, faces additional trouble when a construction site collapse results in a worker being critically injured. Anaïs, Thomas' second wife, welcomes Ève as her own child, but the teenager remains wary. After an unsuccessful attempt to access assisted suicide in Switzerland, Georges crashes his car into a tree, but only manages to injure himself. Thomas, head physician at the hospital, oversees his recovery. At night, he exchanges passionate erotic emails with Claire, his mistress. When Pierre tries to negotiate with the family of the injured worker, he is violently assaulted by the victim's son and retreats to his apartment, where his mother confronts him. He is advised to obtain a medical report documenting his injuries, which ultimately prevents the case from going to court. Ève's mother dies, and the girl permanently moves to Calais. Now in a wheelchair, Georges ventures into the streets, seeking help from migrants to end his life. Failing that, he tries again with his barber, again without success. Faced with mounting financial trouble, Anne turns to the British bank where her partner, Lawrence, works. She secures the funding, agreeing in return that Pierre be removed from the company's leadership. For Georges' 85th birthday, a gathering is held at the Laurent residence, featuring a viola da gamba concert by Claire. Ève, meanwhile, having discovered her father's erotic emails on his computer, swallows a handful of pills. Recovering in the hospital, she tells Thomas of her fear of being placed in foster care if he ever left Anaïs. She also speaks of her father's emotional detachment from everyone. Not knowing how to respond, Thomas encourages her to talk with Georges, who confesses his past: he smothered his paralysed wife to end her suffering. He asks Ève if she has any secrets. A distressed Ève confesses to having once tried to poison a girl she loathed at summer camp. Anne and Lawrence announce their engagement. At the celebratory banquet, Pierre, who sees himself as a failure, arrives with a group of migrants. Anne manages to calm him, though the gathering remains unsettled by the incident. As Lawrence and Anne invite the migrants inside, Georges asks Ève to wheel him to the pier. Standing in the waist-deep water, he hesitates. Ève films him with her smartphone from a distance. Anne and Thomas rush toward them.

Why set the story in Calais?

Because in France, the word "Calais" has come to stand for the issue of immigration and the way we turn a blind eye to the real problems of the world. I can't make a film about migrants; I don't know their lives first-hand. But I can make a film about our blindness and indifference to suffering of any kind. The characters in the film each reflect different sides of that indifference. Everyone is wrapped up in their own problems, which gives them an excuse not to think about what others might be going through. We acknowledge hardship and might donate a little money, but then move on because, ultimately, we don't care. I'm not talking about that small group of people who actually go out into the field and get involved. That kind of commitment is rare. Most of us, myself included, are indifferent. We make the occasional donation, but mostly to ease

Fantine Harduin and Jean-Louis Trintignant in *Happy End*.

our conscience. I have an ambiguous view of all the characters in the film. The family is just like us. We're all self-centred, dishonest and hypocritical. And at the same time, we're hurt, sad and lonely.

Like Pierre?

I don't know. It's not my place to judge these characters or decide who is the best, or the least bad. We're all quite contradictory in our behaviour. The best example is Ève, who seems hurt and vulnerable. The question is: did she really intend to kill her mother? And take Anne, Isabelle Huppert's character, who never seems to give an inch. During her meeting at the bank, she has to accept her son's dismissal in order to save the company. And yet, underlying the scene is the question of who ultimately comes out on top. With this contract, did she strike a better deal than Lawrence, played by Toby Jones, and the bank?

The same ambiguity can be found in the character played by Jean-Louis Trintignant. He's a tough man, shaped by the social class he represents, but when he's with his granddaughter Eve, toward the end of the film, he shows her real tenderness.

That's the film's love scene.

Of all your films, Happy End *might be the one where the idea of letting the audience form its own opinion is most pronounced.*

That principle has always guided the writing of my screenplays. Perhaps it's more successful this time. I hope so. As always, we know very little about the motivations behind people's behaviour. The film is full of examples. We don't know why Anne lives alone. Who is the father of her son? It's like real life, where we know so little about others. That's what keeps us interested. In my scripts I have always tried to capture the ambiguity and contradiction you find in life. Why did Ève poison her mother? Did she really want to kill her? Did she just want to shut her up and her death was just an accident? Why did she try to kill herself? Was it guilt? Did she not think through the consequences? Or is she just miserable in her new life? All of that remains unresolved.

And as usual, when writing the script, you followed your usual method, first carefully laying out the combination of the different elements of the plot on a board.

I didn't start writing until I had mapped out the structure with index cards, moving them along different narrative lines.

Was it always the plan to open the script with smartphone footage?

Yes. From the start, we ruled out showing the teenager filming like it's some kind of crime drama. Another key aspect of the opening sequence is how it sparks curiosity. At first, the audience doesn't fully understand what's happening; the clues come gradually, when the person using the smartphone reveals that she is filming her mother. This commentary is unsettling because it anticipates the action, as when she announces what her mother is about to do in the bathroom a moment later. We sense that she is suffocating under the strict, orderly life imposed on her. This disconnect in the opening shot is a way of unsettling the audience, prompting them to question what they are seeing.

And what they are seeing isn't neutral. On one hand, audiences are immediately plunged into the action, and on the other, they wonder what kind of film they are watching, what kind of online programme they are tuned into.

It's actually a mobile app inspired by Snapchat. The idea is to share images and words that disappear automatically after a few seconds.

Fantine Harduin and Mathieu Kassovitz in *Happy End*.

For a brief moment, anyone connected at that exact time can see them, but it's really all down to chance. Once it's gone, it's impossible to retrieve what was posted. It has become a popular app among young people, the perfect way to say or show anything without consequences, from obscene photos to death threats. It's the ideal tool for all kinds of exhibitionists and voyeurs, knowing that at any moment, anything could appear. I had never heard of the app, but did some research online when I began developing the story.

More than ever, you immerse the audience in the action without introducing the characters. It's up to them to pay attention and figure out who's who and what's happening.

That's the case in all my films, and it's how real life works. When you meet someone for the first time, you rarely know who you're dealing with. Before we really know someone, we have to rely on what they tell us, without knowing if they're lying. And it's always more complicated than that. You can spend years with someone and suddenly discover an entirely new side of their personality. That's what makes life so interesting, that we never fully know another person, even after living alongside them for years. In some cases, we're forever in the dark about someone. As I said, in *Happy End*, it isn't even clear whether Ève really meant to kill her mother when she gave her the pills. Maybe she just wanted to shut her up, as she writes in her comment on the phone.

She doesn't seem too upset about the fate of the hamster.

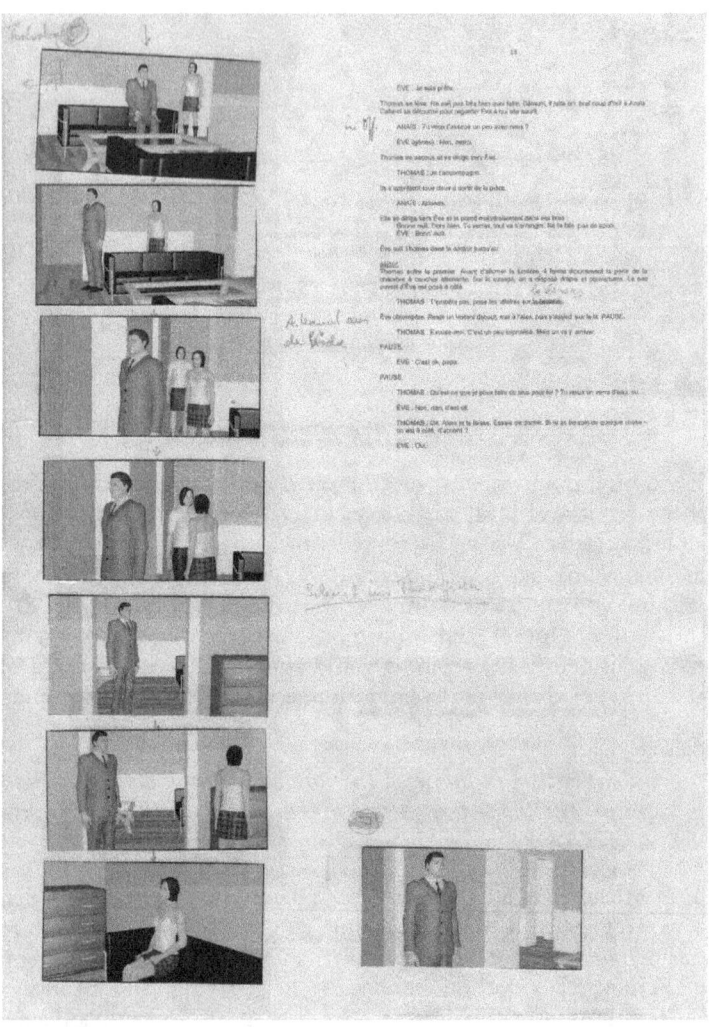

Storyboards for *Happy End.*

But is the hamster really dead? She gave it the same antidepressants her mother takes, and it stopped moving. But might it wake up again? That's what actually happened on set. For the record, to reassure sensitive readers, a veterinarian was present and administered a mild sedative designed to put the hamster to sleep for just a few moments.

Beyond the question of whether she meant to poison it or not, the way Happy End *opens is clever because it demands the audience's full attention.*

We gradually get to know the characters. We first hear Thomas, played by Mathieu Kassovitz, in a voiceover at the hospital. In his second scene, when he picks up Ève and her luggage, we see him, but he doesn't speak. We only really understand who he is two scenes later, when he helps his daughter to bed. Every scene adds a new layer of understanding, allowing the audience to form their own judgments about the characters while keeping them engaged. It's up to the audience to find answers to their questions, otherwise the film becomes didactic. When a director's opinion of the characters is so transparent, I lose interest. I just have no desire to keep on watching.

Did you play with the public image of certain well-known actors, like Trintignant, Huppert and Kassovitz?

No. I've never cast an actor based on their public persona; that doesn't interest me. The only thing that matters to me is how they act. I wrote *Happy End* with Trintignant and Huppert in mind simply because I love their work as actors.

Did you write Kassovitz's role with him in mind?

No, but I cast him early on because, among actors in his age range, he was the only French actor who stood out. I needed someone who could come across as intelligent, credible as a surgeon, and also with a certain sex appeal. I couldn't think of many others who fit that description. This was confirmed once we were on set. He's excellent in the film.

He has a very precise way of looking at people, especially in the car scene with Ève, where he has a delicate conversation while paying close attention to the road.

That's because he was actually driving in real traffic. The cameras were mounted on the front of the vehicle. We specifically chose that car because it was the only model that allowed us to attach two professional cameras to the front, enabling continuous filming of both characters head-on. Most films today shoot these kinds of scenes from inside the car, with the camera placed in the back seat, framing the characters from behind, or they shoot from the side

Jean-Louis Trintignant in *Happy End.*

with the window open, as we did in *Funny Games*. Thanks to the latest small cameras, we were able to shoot the way we wanted, though we still had to find a car that was wide enough, with a windshield less sloped than most models, so the actors' faces wouldn't be distorted.

What about the fascinating scene where we follow Trintignant in his wheelchair, in a lateral tracking shot across a busy street. Was that filmed in real traffic?

It was. We waited for rush hour to make it feel realistic. Of course, we had to make absolutely sure it was safe. I tried the wheelchair out on the street myself and quickly realised how hard it was to control. The little front wheels veered off course at the slightest bump, so we cheated a bit by attaching two cords to the front and one to the back, which technicians used to guide it and keep it rolling straight. Then we digitally erased those cords frame by frame, as well as the reflections of the camera and crew in the shop windows. One person spent several days doing only that.

Watching Dominique Besnehard as the hairdresser was such a joy, and a surprise too. How did you think of casting him?

We held a huge casting call for that role, which isn't easy to play. The actor had to be able to cut hair while acting. After searching without success, my casting director, Kris de Bellair, suggested Dominique. I asked her why she hadn't mentioned him earlier, because I thought it was an excellent idea. I had loved him in Pialat's

Jean-Louis Trintignant and Dominique Besnehard in *Happy End.*

À nos amours. He's fantastic in *Happy End*—exactly what I was looking for, with the right mix of comedy and drama.

Was the hairdresser's homosexuality in the script from the start?

Yes, which made finding the right actor even more difficult. In addition to being able to cut hair, he had to be credible as a gay man, which isn't as easy as it sounds. Too often, actors portray homosexuality in a very caricatured way. Dominique had the perfect tone, but was terrified about cutting hair and trained for weeks with a real hairdresser. After filming, he was very relieved because he had been concerned that he wouldn't manage it, especially since it was a single long take, which we ended up doing about ten times, I think.

Did your experience working on Così *push you to dig deeper into sarcastic humour in* Happy End?

No. There was already a comedic element *Don Giovanni.* In fact, you could say that my staging of *Don Giovanni* and *Così* actually made those operas darker than normal. There are also elements of humour in *Lemminge* and almost all my other films. It's up to you to spot them. I'm not interested in saying, "I'm going to make a comedy" or "I'm going to make a drama." I want to tell a story with situations drawn from life. All I do is explore everyday experiences.

Tell us about the extraordinary young actress Fantine Harduin, who plays Ève.

Kris found her after auditioning dozens and dozens of teenage girls. We knew we couldn't afford to make a mistake with that role. If the audience didn't believe in the character, the whole film would collapse. It just wouldn't even be worth making the film. Fantine had already acted in films I hadn't seen, like Lola Doillon's *Le Voyage de Fanny*, but when Kris showed me her photo, I was immediately struck by her face. She's a child, but has the face of a woman, which I found quite unsettling. She was exactly who we needed for the part: a 13-year-old girl who, while appearing normal, could actually make you believe she had done what the character does. It was a very difficult role to cast. We had another very talented girl in mind, but after screen tests, I decided on Fantine. We worked with her a good deal on the set, especially the scene in Trintignant's office, where Kris and I took her aside to rehearse. She gives a remarkable performance.

Was she fully aware of all the psychological layers of her character?

I don't think so. In the car scene with Kassovitz, she couldn't manage to cry, and we ended up shooting all day before she reached the emotional state she needed. We asked her to think about something sad, but that wasn't enough. It was Kris who handled that side of things. She's also the one who got the tears from the other little girl, the one who gets bitten by the dog. I can't seem to get those kinds of results from children, mostly because my French isn't good enough.

Another inspired casting choice was Hille Perl as the musician-mistress.

She's a major star in Germany as a viola da gamba player and had appeared in concert videos and ads for her albums, but had never acted in a feature film before. I discovered her online while looking for a gambist for the role. I wanted someone older than Laura Verlinden, who plays Kassovitz's wife. I liked the idea that, while being married to a younger, more naive woman, his character would fall for someone more mature. When the production contacted Hille about the role, she said that all her online photos were over ten years old. That didn't bother us; she's still very beautiful. She was very disciplined in her work, and I think she's excellent on screen.

Did she have any concerns about playing a role like that?

We sent her the script in advance to get her approval and she had no objections. Before that, we actually approached an Italian musician who turned down the role after reading the script, citing concerns about her reputation.

Franz Rogowski, who plays Pierre, Huppert's son, has a fascinating mix of toughness and childlike vulnerability.

At first, I didn't want someone quite so appealing. Franz, like Joaquin Phoenix, has a natural sexual magnetism, with his cleft lip and athletic build. I originally wanted someone clumsy and heavyset, but couldn't find anyone suitable. Even when I looked at slimmer actors, I couldn't find a young man who seemed both cruel and, at the same time, so damaged. For me, the ideal choice would have been a young Philip Seymour Hoffman, truly a great actor, who, as I said, was also my first choice for the role of the father in the remake of *Funny Games*. Sadly, he's gone now. Eventually, I saw Franz in a film by one of my students and could feel his extraordinary presence. He's someone you immediately notice. Of course, casting him introduced the usual challenges of filming in two languages. Franz doesn't speak French, so we had to dub him, and finding the right French voice for him took a long time. The actor we chose had a slightly higher-pitched voice, but I'm happy with the result. We worked a lot in post-production to synchronise everything. The only scene where I kept Franz's original voice was the karaoke scene. He screams in English, so the difference isn't noticeable. And he's fantastic in that scene.

It is a remarkable moment, and would have been completely different with a heavier actor.

The whole point is just to show that he's failing. There are other ways we could have gotten that across; a bigger guy would have failed in his own way. When you're forced to change what you had originally imagined in the script, you just have to adapt.

This scene mirrors the moment when Ève watches a boy on her computer, laughing at how he used to look and how he dances.

That kid is great. We discovered him online.

You bought this scene and included it in the film exactly as it was, without any changes?

Yes. Everything you see and hear comes from the young man who created it. I could never have done something like that myself.

How did you come up with the idea of casting Toby Jones? He and Huppert make a striking couple.

He's such an extraordinary actor! He was suggested to me by my Austrian casting director, Markus Schleinzer. At first, Markus showed me photos of handsome men in their fifties and sixties, but I told him I was looking for the opposite: a short, bald man. That's when he mentioned Toby. I didn't recognise the name at first, but when I watched his demo reel, I immediately realised who he was. He played Truman Capote and, more importantly, Alfred Hitchcock. I remembered that when I had randomly caught *The Girl* on television, a rather mediocre film about Hitchcock's relationship with Tippi Hedren, I was amazed at how perfectly Toby reproduced Hitchcock's voice and mannerisms. I loved the idea of working with him. He has an incredible charm that works wonderfully alongside Isabelle. Their relationship remains open to interpretation. Do they truly love each other, or are they together for convenience?

Many other actors in Happy End *give remarkable performances.*

Starting with Laura Verlinden, who plays Anaïs. I first noticed her in Jaco Van Dormael's comedy *The Brand New Testament*, in which she wears a wooden prosthetic arm that a crazed shooter targets, and in which she has a completely endearing look of pure innocence. She's exactly like that in real life. In her final scene with Ève, where Ève, caught in her father's office, pretends to have computer trouble, Laura plays it as if she is completely oblivious to what is actually going on, which isn't easy to do. She's fantastic.

Did you write the role for her?

No. I only saw her once I got to France. During casting, I asked her to do the scene with Ève and she nailed it on the first go, so I hired her on the spot. The couple who play the house staff are great too. We spent ages looking for the husband; it isn't an easy part. He has to have a certain pride and dignity, and at the same time, feel a deep friendship for his longtime employer. I saw at least twenty actors and none of them were right. Kris saw around sixty. Apart from the hairdresser, he was the last role we cast. Philippe du Janerand, who plays Anne's lawyer, has the right mix of authority and elegance required for the role. Cinematically, the scene is quite risky because it's so long, with an uninterrupted monologue. I could have trimmed it, but I wanted to capture how notaries drown their clients in legal jargon. Philippe's delivery is so affected that by the end of his speech, you're really not sure what he's been saying, which was exactly the effect I was after.

Every character has their own way of speaking. Ève, for example, uses the language of her generation.

As usual, I wrote everything in German first before working with my translator, Bernard Mangiante. He does his own translation, and then we go over it. I'm very particular about specific words. With the smartphone texts, for example, it was important to use the kind of shorthand teenagers actually use. Bernard has children Ève's age, so he checked the dialogue with them. Not long ago, kids used to call their mom "reum," which is verlan slang, but that's outdated now. Today, they say "daronne." You can't make these things up. You have to ask people who know.

You must have put a lot of thought into naming your characters. We have the usual Anne and Georges for Huppert and Trintignant, but with so many characters, you had to find others.

Like Anaïs. Which I borrowed from Anaïs Demoustier, who is in *Time of the Wolf.* I even considered her for the role of Anaïs, but Laura Verlinden looks more naïve and vulnerable. She has more of a victim-like appearance than Demoustier.

Once again, you worked with Christian Berger.

He gives me exactly what I want, and on top of that, he always uses his own lighting system, which allows for very fast setup times. What frustrates me now — and it's been this way since *Amour* — is all the changes in digital technology. Initially, we agreed on a reference monitor with fixed settings, but those settings got changed multiple times, which caused us endless problems in colour grading. On one hand, digital has made everything easier; you can create any image you want, but on the other, it has become harder to control everything and get exactly what you envisioned.

Did you help choose the camera, as you did for Amour?

No, I left that to Berger because, unlike Darius Khondji, he doesn't insist on using the very latest equipment at any cost. He selected the gear and the technicians he wanted to work with, and everything went smoothly. As Steadicam operator, I would have liked to have had Jörg Widmer, who did wonders on *The White Ribbon*, but he was already committed to Terrence Malick's latest film. Instead, we had four different people—two French, two German—who took turns because of the many schedule changes brought on by bad weather. I wasn't too fond of those changes, but everyone did good work. Later, in postproduction, we digitally stabilised certain shots to smooth out the effect produced by the Steadicam.

Did you always have a camera operator on set?

Yes, Gerald Helf, Berger's former assistant, who works the same way. Before shooting, he visited all the locations and took photos. He was totally prepared.

Did you shoot with multiple cameras?

No, just one, except for the car scene we talked about. As for the shots of Ève's phone, they were filmed using a real smartphone. Likewise, the emails were genuinely displayed on the screens they appear on. This might be an issue for television broadcasts because the text might not be readable on a small screen, but reshooting closer shots would have felt artificial. What you see in the film is 100 percent real, although getting to that point was complicated. The production started negotiating with Apple for permission to use their interface without telling me. Since I didn't want to promote a specific brand, we gave Ève a Mac and Thomas and Claire a PC, and after shooting all their scenes, we realised we didn't have the rights to use Windows. It took weeks of negotiations to get resolved. Meanwhile, the tech team recreated Windows-style screens with legally altered details, following lawyers' advice. That was a big job. Eventually, we secured the rights, but we had to shoot those screen sequences frame by frame because typing at normal speed was too slow. We sped it up slightly, otherwise, the scene would have dragged.

The landslide at the construction site in *Happy End.*

One striking scene is the landslide at the large construction site, filmed in a wide shot with a very short focal length. How was it done?

Digitally, of course. It was a lot of work, and the technicians did an excellent job. We filmed the site with real workers and instructed them to react to a sound cue indicating the landslide. They had to react to something that wasn't actually happening. A few years ago, these kinds of effects would have been impossible.

What's fascinating about the landslide shot is that you don't know where to look. Then, suddenly, your eye is drawn to the collapsing earth. It's only on a second viewing that you notice everything the insurance inspector later describes: the truck reversing, the worker stepping out, the toilet cabin falling into the pit.

Because the audience has to be caught off guard, we show the site going about its usual business for a while. Later, we help them focus by having a second toilet cabin fall. That way, if they missed the first one, they'll catch the second.

In the landslide scene, one could say your sense of realism is sharpened by digital effects.

It's true. What we see is actually the screen of a surveillance monitor. Through sound design, we indicate the presence of a man working in his office, who is startled by the landslide. He rushes

Jean-Louis Trintignant in *Happy End.*

out, and a small beam of light on the right side of the frame signals the opening and closing of the door as he exits his cabin.

Your preference for screens is evident. In this film we see mobile phones, computers, surveillance cameras on the construction site.

It seems like a comment on how we increasingly experience reality through screens, and how hard it is to see what's right in front of us. But you don't push the point.

The phone and computer shots stand out because of their place and importance in the story, but there's no need to underline them. It's up to audiences to draw their own conclusions.

There is also Trintignant's story about the bird of prey tearing apart another bird, which he tells his granddaughter in his office. He says if it were shown on television, it would seem trivial, but witnessing it in real life, through his window, was much more powerful.

That's a story I actually lived, exactly as he tells it. I saw it happen from the window of our countryside home, and I had the same thought as he did. I wondered why it affected me so much, given that I had seen far worse things before.

As usual, you didn't have a score composed for the film.

The only pieces of music you hear are those integrated into the scenes, like the radio at the construction site, Pierre's karaoke, and Claire's concert. She plays *La Folia*, a famous Baroque piece from the 16th/17th centuries. I chose it because of the intense, almost mad love that ties her to Kassovitz's character.

How did you come up with the radio programme playing on the construction site?

I was given several options, since music rights are always an issue. I told them I wanted something completely unrelated to the story. It's not the first time I've made such a request. We often end up using traffic reports or weather updates, because as soon as you include any kind of news, audiences start looking for meaning and connections to the film.

Especially here, since the film takes place in Calais, where one might expect immigration to be mentioned.

That would have been a bit too obvious, although right after the construction site sequence I address the topic in a purely visual way, in the scene where Anne is driving and you can clearly see the infamous four-metre-high, kilometres-long barrier that was built to keep migrants out. It's up to the audience to recognise this and determine its significance based on what they know.

Did you think about The Burghers of Calais?

I mainly know Rodin's sculpture and Georg Kaiser's play, which tells the touching story, set during the Hundred Years' War, in which six prominent citizens of Calais offered their lives to the English in exchange for lifting the siege. The English commander, moved by their sacrifice, decided to spare them. It's a beautiful, near-mythical story, but it doesn't have a direct connection to the film.

You didn't shoot exclusively in Calais?

No. We couldn't find the family home there, so we went to Douai, which has lots of beautiful homes. Calais today is quite a depressing city. You see "For Rent/For Sale" signs on a lot of houses.

That isn't the impression we get from the film. It actually makes you think it would be nice to spend a weekend there.

The film doesn't have many outdoor scenes, but it does show the beach. We shot there on the only possible day, as the summer of 2016 was the coldest for years in Pas-de-Calais and the weather constantly forced us to adjust our shooting schedule. That day was the only warm one when the beach was full of people.

The 360 degree tracking shot you filmed there is impressive. How did you pull it off?

Hard work. We did more than twenty takes. It was complicated. The wind made things difficult for the Steadicam operator, plus there's a lot going on in the scene that had to unfold without a hitch, and there was always one thing that didn't work, so we had to keep starting over. All the people near the camera were extras, but in the background are real beachgoers who came to enjoy the sun.

You worked with a new production designer, Olivier Radot.

Christoph Kanter wasn't an option since we were filming in France. I thought of Jean-Vincent Puzos, who had worked on *Amour*, but he wasn't interested because there was nothing to build. His specialty is creating sets from scratch, and this film mainly involved adapting real locations. I met with several French production designers but didn't feel a real connection; not because of their skills, but just because we didn't click creatively. Then I thought of Olivier Radot, who had worked with Patrice Chéreau on *Gabrielle*. If he had managed to work with Patrice, I figured he could probably handle me too We met and immediately understood each other. He's very easygoing, a hard worker, and extremely competent. Plus, he has excellent taste.

Did you have to make many changes to the family house?

Yes. The only room we left untouched was the one where the concert takes place. All the others were repainted and transformed. Olivier did an enormous amount of work.

Where did the paintings in the house come from?

The house we used was large, but not big enough to accommodate three families, so we had to cheat with the space and turned what was originally a passageway into a living room. That's why we decorated it with paintings hung on the walls, like in some old châteaux. Initially, we planned to use 18th-century paintings, but then a collaborator of Margaret Menegoz, who is very knowledgeable about art, told us about a château with a bedroom decorated in a similar style. We went there, took photos, and then made full-scale reproductions, adjusting them to fit the architecture of our set.

Once the sets were finished, did you make many changes to your script?

Sometimes, when necessary. For *Amour*, I didn't change anything because the set was built exactly as needed, but in *Happy End*, where we used real locations, I had to rewrite some things that couldn't work as originally imagined. For example, in the script, the Arab domestic couple's apartment was located in a separate house at the back of the estate, but the real location had no estate, only a garden. Since the husband is the family's caretaker, we relocated their apartment inside the main house, in what was actually the caretakers' quarters. When he opens his door—which is covered with a mirror on the outside—it reflects the hall, which he then crosses to enter the Laurent family's home just opposite. This worked well in the final edit, but I could never have anticipated it during writing. These things happen naturally because I'm involved in every decision. As Olivier Radot progressed with the set design, he would show me models, colour samples, materials, chair styles... We decided on everything together. I did the same with the costumes, which are always closely tied to the characters' psychology. For Isabelle Huppert, I even picked pieces directly from her personal wardrobe.

Does the T-shirt Ève wears, which says "I Love Japan," have a particular meaning?

No. I asked Fantine to bring her own clothes so she would feel comfortable, and we chose it together. It's just a trendy item that someone her age would wear. The reference to Japan is purely coincidental. What mattered to me was that the inscription had no direct connection to the story. If someone finds one, they're reading too much into it.

One small detail we particularly liked is when Anaïs, before going to bed, turns off the kitchen light, then switches off four other lamps in the living room.

The idea came to me after working on the set design and deciding there should be multiple light sources in the room, not just one.

Naturally, when someone goes to bed, they have to turn them all off. I could have cut the shot earlier, and even while filming thought I might trim it in the editing, but I thought it was quite beautiful, like a fermata, a pause after the scene where Thomas returns from the hospital following the grandfather's suicide attempt. At that moment, the family seems settled after little Ève's arrival—or at least it appears that way. But that calm lasts only a moment, because the next scene is the erotic exchange between Thomas and Claire.

Can you tell us about your collaboration with the editor Monika Willi, with whom you have worked regularly since The Piano Teacher?

She took over from Andreas Prochaska, who had become a successful director at the time of *The Piano Teacher*. He was originally supposed to edit that film, and I was upset he dropped out. It was my producer, Michael Katz, who suggested Monika. I didn't know her, but I quickly realised she was brilliant. Working with her is always a pleasure.

How does your collaboration with her work, given that your scripts are practically written with the editing in mind?

I could manage with a less talented editor, but it would be ten times more work. I choose the takes and decide where to cut, but when you cut in the middle of a movement, you need real expertise to know exactly where to do it. It's not just a technical skill; it's about rhythm and musicality. Monika has the same sense of timing as I do. She is also incredibly dedicated, always searching for the best possible choices. I trust her completely and always consider her opinion when selecting takes.

Do you watch all the takes together?

Unlike most directors, I don't screen rushes. I don't want to watch them during filming. unless we're unsure if we got what we needed for a specific scene. In that case, I check right away, but in general, I don't want to dwell on what I shot yesterday. I prefer to focus on what I'm shooting tomorrow. Once filming is done, I take a break for a week or two before watching the whole film with fresh eyes, alongside Monika.

Does she make suggestions?

The final shot of *Happy End.*

Of course. She works with the script and my precise shot break-down, and sometimes suggests alternatives. If they're good, I use them. Most of the time, she agrees with me. It's the same with the cinematographer. It's rare that they suggest something different from what I had envisioned. This isn't because I think I'm a genius, but simply because I've been working on the project the longest, so I'm usually best positioned to make decisions. That said, having a talented collaborator with a fresh perspective can be invaluable. Sometimes, just by asking for clarification, they can point out a problem I hadn't considered. I have a lot of respect and gratitude for them because, without them, the work wouldn't be nearly as rich.

Is your editor present on set? Does she start working during filming?

Monika's assistant is on set taking notes, but no editing happens during the shoot. That only happened once, during *Lemminge.* The production edited an entire lake scene without telling me, and when I saw it, I was furious and made them redo everything. I can't accept editing without my involvement; it feels suffocating to watch something that I didn't shape myself. I need to see it all take shape with my own eyes in an almost organic way. That's why I feel less comfortable in theatre, where you have to react to what the actors are doing. In cinema, I start with a clear vision of what I want and work with actors and technicians to achieve it. If I can't get there, it's depressing. I'm not saying this is the only way to work; it's just my way, and I can't do it differently.

And what about sound?

Jean-Louis Trintignant, Michael Haneke and
Isabelle Huppert on the set of *Happy End*.

It's the same process. We refine everything in sound editing and post-synchronization. If a recorded line isn't perfect, I review all the takes to find a better one. When Ève asks, "What story?" in response to Jean-Louis Trintignant's "I told you my story, now tell me yours," her delivery wasn't bad, but it didn't really stand out, so we re-listened to all her takes and replaced it with one where she was more compelling. That's one of the great joys of editing, especially with sound. You can really enhance things.

What do you say to those who see Happy End *as a testament film, like people often said about Ingmar Bergman's last works?*

People kept calling every one of Bergman's last films a "testament film" because he never actually stopped making movies. We'll see if *Happy End* is my last film. Let's leave some room for surprises.

Photo credits and acknowledgements

© D. R. xiii, 3, 8, 10, 60, 253, 281, 283, 313, 320, 321, 344, 345, 356. Screenshots (courtesy of Les Films du Losange and Wega-Film): 39, 41, 42, 47, 50, 51, 54, 71, 76, 79, 83, 84, 98, 103, 105, 107, 119, 120, 136, 137, 141, 146, 154, 157, 167, 169, 175, 179, 208, 212, 215, 222, 227, 230, 240, 243, 246, 247, 249, 259, 260, 261, 263, 292, 295, 297, 300, 302, 304, 306, 307, 353, 355, 358, 359, 365, 366, 371 © Österreichisches Filmmuseum: 63, 67, 69, 72, 89, 91, 96, 100, 115, 117, 130, 134, 151, 159, 163, 182, 184, 187, 189, 195, 196, 197, 198, 199, 201, 210, 233, 264 © Yves Montmayeur: 311, 324, 327, 329, 333, 336, 337 © Reinhold Göhringer: 31 © C. Tschira: 27 © Stefan Haring: 126 © Österreichischer Rundfunk: 127, 128 © Sylvia v P: 219 © Christoph Kanter: 271, 273 © Éric Mahoudeau: 268, 277 © Reuters/Jean-Paul Pelissier: 316 © Javier del Real : 342, 348 © Schoemitz/Gavriel: 372.

Michel Cieutat and Philippe Rouyer would like to thank: Jean-Luc Douin, who gave this book its first push; Jean-Marc Roberts and Manuel Carcassonne, their publishers, and Debora Kahn-Sriber, their fairy godmother at Stock. At the Vienna Filmmuseum: Alexander Horwath and Roland Fischer-Briand, as well as Paolo Caneppele and Walter Moser. At the Paris Opera: Françoise Roussel and Gilles Pichon. At Les Films du Losange: Margaret Menegoz and Régine Vial. At Wega-Film: Veit Heiduschka; Monika Willi; Marin Karmitz; Matilde Incerti. Also Yves Montmayeur, for his invaluable making-of documentaries; Brigitte Cieutat, for her careful reading; N. T. Binh, Valérie Carré, Nicolas Guérin, Clara-Nour Chaponot, Arnaud Delcher, Susie Haneke, Christoph Kanter, Ida Rouyer, François Thomas and Jacques Zimmer for their invaluable help, and *Positif* magazine, where the encounter began. Above all, they wish to extend their warmest thanks to Michael Haneke, who gave himself unstintingly to bring this book into being and granted them access to numerous personal documents and photographs.

Index